POLITICS, RELIGION AND CLASSICAL POLITICAL ECONOMY IN BRITAIN

STUDIES IN THE HISTORY OF ECONOMICS

General Editor: D. E. Moggridge

Published in association with the History of Economics Society and with an international board of advisers, this series takes a broad definition of the history of economics. Titles will cover the major topics in the fields of economic theory, methodology and professional evolution, and will include both monographs and edited collections of essays.

Politics, Religion and Classical Political Economy in Britain

John Stuart Mill and his Followers

Jeff Lipkes

First published in Great Britain 1999 by
MACMILLAN PRESS LTD
Houndmills, Basingstoke, Hampshire RG21 6XS and London
Companies and representatives throughout the world

A catalogue record for this book is available from the British Library.

ISBN 0–333–73318–5

First published in the United States of America 1999 by
ST. MARTIN'S PRESS, INC.,
Scholarly and Reference Division,
175 Fifth Avenue, New York, N.Y. 10010

ISBN 0–312–21741–2

Library of Congress Cataloging-in-Publication Data
Lipkes, Jeff, 1950–
Politics, religion and classical political economy in Britain : John Stuart Mill and his followers / Jeff Lipkes.
p. cm. — (Studies in the history of economics)
Includes bibliographical references and index.
ISBN 0–312–21741–2 (cloth)
1. Mill, John Stuart, 1806–1873. 2. Economics—Great Britain–
–History—19th century. I. Title. II. Series.
HB103.M7L56 1998
330.15'3'094109034—dc21 98–23640
CIP

10 9 8 7 6 5 4 3 2 1
08 07 06 05 04 03 02 01 00 99

Printed and bound in Great Britain by
Antony Rowe Ltd, Chippenham, Wiltshire

For Rita, Celeste and Rita,
and in memory of Morey

Contents

Acknowledgements

It is a pleasure to be able to acknowledge at least some of the many debts I have incurred over a number of years in connection with this book. Among the individuals who offered encouragement and advice in the early stages of the project, I'd like to thank Sir Alec Cairncross, Alexander Shand, Neil de Marchi, Peter Mandler, Donald Walker (who told me point-blank that what I then had in mind would take at least ten years to complete), John Whitaker, and R. D. C. Black, who continued to provide valuable insights and assistance. I'd also like to thank Leonard Liggio and the Institute of Humane Studies for a grant during the initial stages of research. One of Professor Mandler's first suggestions was to read the past ten years of HOPE, and I was swept off my feet by the intelligence, acuity and charm of a great many of the articles I encountered. Not the least satisfaction of this project has been the opportunity to have read and, eventually, to have met some of that impressive cohort of economists interested in the history of economic thought. I'm very grateful to the History of Economics Society for the Joseph Dorfman Prize. I am especially indebted to Harold James, who directed the dissertation on which this book is based, and to additional readers Eugenio Biagini, Bruce Kinzer and Deborah Nord. Professor Biagini's suggestions were especially useful as the project evolved. An article incorporating some of the thesis benefited from the close readings of Drue Barker, Tom Ross and, in particular, Glenn Hueckle. Mark Donahue, Robert Ekelund, Gerard Koot, Rusty Martin and Ed Shapiro have generously shared information and insights about Mill's followers. Donald Winch's detailed comments on the manuscript have been a great help as I've revised it, as have Professor Kinzer's, whose expertise on Mill is unrivalled among historians. I'd like also to express my appreciation to Professor Winch and his sometime collaborators Stephan Collini and John Burrowes, and to Boyd Hilton and A. M. C. Waterman, whose books have long been an inspiration. All of the above must be absolved of responsibility for my conclusions naturally.

Anyone who works with John Stuart Mill owes an enormous debt to the late John Robson and his co-editors of the magnificent *Collected Works*. I would also like to thank librarians and archivists at the following institutions: Columbia, Seton Hall, Yale, Johns Hopkins, the Huntington Library, the British Library of Political and Economic

Science, University College London, Manchester College (Oxford), Dr Williams' Library, National Library of Ireland, Public Record Office (Belfast), and former Interlibrary Loan librarian Linda Beard at Hollins College. I appreciate the encouragement of colleagues in the History department of the University of South Florida, particularly Chair John Belohlavek and Kathleen Paul, who has kindly helped read proofs. Marianne Bell provided valuable word-processing assistance, and I've benefited greatly from Monica O'Connor's copy-editing and indexing skills.

Finally, I would like to thank family members for their forbearance and support. The generosity of my mother and father made possible much of the writing of this book. My wife Rita Ciresi has provided expert editorial assistance and my daughter Celeste has reminded me daily how much of life is not grist for the mill. My gratitude to all of them, and to my brother and sister-in-law, extends inexpressibly beyond their direct help on this project.

Part I
John Stuart Mill: The Final Years, 1860–73

1 Introduction

Until quite recently, John Stuart Mill's final dozen years and his association with the last classical economists have received comparatively little attention. The ambivalence of a son and the infatuation of a lover no doubt have more entertainment value than a series of high-minded and mutually instructive friendships. The comings and goings of a 'saint of rationalism' – even, or especially, a very busy and worldly one – are not likely to make a particularly beguiling saga. And although nearly everyone professes to admire the gallant defenders of a losing cause, the heroics of the final exponents of a superannuated system of economic thought, especially one widely perceived as doctrinaire and insensitive, do not promise to make a very inspiring epic.

This lack of interest begins with Mill himself. The seventh and final chapter of his *Autobiography*, 'A General View of the Remainder of My Life', compresses approximately 30 years into 61 pages (about 30 per cent of the volume). Mill devotes nearly a third of the chapter, moreover, to a spirited defence of his performance in Parliament during his three-year stint as Member for Westminster. The period following his defeat is polished off in a mere 120 words.[1]

This study examines Mill's relations with the group of younger economists who were in close contact with him from the early 1860s, when he emerged from seclusion after the death of his wife, until his own death in 1873. The circle included John Elliot Cairnes, Henry Fawcett, William Thornton, Thomas Edward Cliffe Leslie and John Morley. Though with some pretensions to being an economist (he solicited Mill's recommendation for Cairnes's chair when the latter was obliged to retire),[2] Morley was important to the group chiefly as editor of the *Fortnightly Review*, which served as something of a Millite organ from 1867 to 1875. The idea of a group of philosophical friends, with Mill as *primus inter pares* at the very least, meeting regularly and publishing in a party organ, recalls the Mill of the 1820s and 1830s. If the contacts among individuals were less frequent than among the Philosophic Radicals – owing in part to the positions and disabilities of Cairnes, Fawcett and Leslie – Mill cherished feelings for them which were appreciably warmer than for their earlier counterparts.[3]

There are three still more significant differences between the two groups:

1. While Mill retained during the 1860s – or, more properly speaking, reclaimed – the friendship of Bain, Chadwick, Grote and Spencer, among others,[4] most members of the Blackheath Park circle were considerably younger than himself. Differences ranged from seven years in the case of Thornton to the 32 years separating Mill from Morley. Fawcett was 27, Leslie 19 and Cairnes 16 years younger. The Philosophic Radicals were, of course, approximately Mill's own age.
2. As indicated, Mill's followers in the 1860s were almost entirely economists. While not entering into the question as to what constituted an 'economist' in the 1820s and 1830s, and acknowledging the fact that the Philosophic Radicals were young men at the outset of their careers, none went on to demonstrate any special interest in or aptitude for the science (though the son of economist William Tooke, Eyton Tooke, who committed suicide at 22, showed promise, as did William Ellis). The difference is revealing, and is made even more explicit in Helen Taylor's addendum to Mill's *Autobiography*. Mill regarded as his successor not the reverent Morley, not the philosopher and political ally Croom Robertson, but Cairnes, the most highly respected British economist after himself.[5] Mill may have revised the *Logic* one time more often than he did the *Principles*, but he knew full well with whom power and influence would lie. Politicians and editors did not seek the advice of moral philosophers.
3. Mill's designation of Cairnes as heir apparent instead of the seemingly more faithful Fawcett was not a hard call: Cairnes was an economist of impressive analytic power and rhetorical skill, while it is difficult to find evidence of originality in Fawcett. But Mill's mutually profitable association with Cairnes testifies to a third key difference: Mill learned considerably more from the Blackheath Park disciples than he did from the Philosophic Radicals. In one sense this is not surprising. Though they were his peers, James Mill's much-maligned experiment bequeathed his son a 25-year head start on his contemporaries, Mill himself estimated.[6] All the same, by the 1860s Mill was the 'Saint of Rationalism', with four editions of both the *Logic* and the *Principles* behind him (as of 1860), and despite his professed devotion to the continued testing of new ideas, one might be forgiven for suspecting that his views on most questions were fully formed and not likely to be amended. Nonetheless, and for various reasons,

Mill's followers, I will argue, inspired him to make small but significant changes in his economic and his religious thought.

What is particularly striking about the Mill circle is the degree of methodological diversity. One expects, naturally, that the last classical economists would be drawn to Mill, and so they were. Indeed, the degree to which the final representatives of the school were in fact devoted friends and political allies is sometimes not appreciated. But if Cairnes and the Fawcetts were 'loyalists', Thornton and Leslie were unmistakably 'heretics'. They were, in fact, the two most radical, and successful, critics of Ricardian economics during the 1860s.[7] That the Blackheath Park circle was divided into 'orthodox' and 'heterodox' wings is immediately intriguing. What, one wonders, did Mill make of the schism? To what extent was he aware of it?

Briefly, this study examines, and attempts to explain, the methodological diversity within the Mill circle and Mill's tolerance of some of his disciples' deviations from the *Principles*.

Restated more fully, this book has, in fact, five related objectives:

1. I propose to examine the economic thought of both 'loyalists' and 'dissidents', considering in particular to what extent and on what grounds members of each faction diverged from their mentor.
2. I will attempt to account for the range of perspectives. I will consider, in particular, whether or not differences in the religious beliefs and core values of the group's members do not help explain the methodological differences.[8]
3. Given the degree of methodological diversity, I will attempt to explain why the group remained a cohesive unit. What did the individuals derive from their association with each other and with Mill, personally and professionally? Conversely, what was in it for Mill himself? Why, in short, was he seemingly deaf to the dissonances? Was volume more important than pitch, or was Mill himself singing off-key?
4. This question raises the issue of the influence of Mill's younger associates on his own thinking during his final dozen years. To what extent did their criticisms induce him to modify his economic principles and religious beliefs? On what grounds did he do so, and with what success?
5. Finally, the last classical economists were the last classical economists because they rejected marginalism.[9] I will attempt to explain the hostility to a perspective that might superficially

seem congenial, and also account for the unsympathetic attitude of those in the circle who were already critical of Ricardian economics. In so doing, I hope to reveal the extent to which a theory of value in fact depends on core values – and thus rests on the answers individuals contrive to the weightiest questions they ask.

The book divides into two parts. Part I is devoted to Mill himself. Chapter 2 examines briefly the debate on Mill's debt to Ricardo and considers how his Ricardian principles furnished the basis for his political beliefs. (The beliefs are less derived from than buttressed by Mill's economic analysis; but he had, in consequence, no less a heavy investment in this analysis.) The supreme importance of politics for Mill is examined in Chapter 3, which considers his version of the Religion of Humanity, and its genesis. Chapter 4 treats Mill's actual forays into theology, documenting shifts in his religious thought during the 1860s and Morley's great chagrin at discovering these deviations. Mill's economic writing during his last six years, which occasioned a similar sense of dismay on the part of Cairnes, is the subject of Chapter 5. Both his economic and religious beliefs, I am arguing, deviated in tandem: as Mill became, hesitantly, more Christian, he became – also sporadically and inconsistently – less enamoured of the Ricardian assumptions he had done so much to revive.

Part II investigates the economic thought of the individual Millites, and the political and religious beliefs that influenced their methods and analyses. The experiences and propensities that shaped these beliefs are also considered. Chapters on Cairnes, Fawcett, Thornton and Leslie, respectively, follow Chapter 6, which discusses the group as a whole. It investigates what drew the members together, the tenor of their relationships, and the extent to which they sought, collectively, to influence the teaching of economics in Britain. A conclusion follows.

To argue that Mill's last dozen years, the years of the Mill Circle, constitute a distinctive episode in his intellectual history and that during this period he made small but significant emendations to his economic and religious thought is to engage in two debates – with those economists and philosophers who hold that Mill's thought comprises a coherent whole, and with those historians who, conceding that his ideas did indeed evolve, suggest alternative ways of periodizing Mill's life.[10]

> In this third period ... of my mental progress, which now went hand in hand with hers [Harriet Taylor's], my opinions gained equally in breadth and depth. I understood more things, and those which I had understood before, I now understood more thoroughly. I had now completely turned back from what there had been of excess in my reaction against Benthamism.[11]

Mill here casually combines three criteria for gauging his intellectual development: (1) significant increases in his 'understanding'; (2) shifts in his adherence to encompassing systems of thought; and (3) encounters with influential individuals. The relationship of the first two indices is straightforward: one would expect that either empirical evidence or new theoretical insights would lead to the reappraisal of a now inadequate paradigm, or, conversely to the acceptance of a modified version of a rejected paradigm. What is more problematic than is sometimes appreciated, however, is the impact of his personal relations on Mill's intellectual metamorphoses.

The conventional interpretation both of the intellectual changes themselves and the relationships responsible for them derives, naturally, from the *Autobiography*. Mill's mental growth assumes the pleasing form of a dialectic. He begins with the Utilitarianism of his father (that is, Hartleyean psychology, Benthamite ethics, and Ricardian political economy). Then, following his famous 'mental crisis', he becomes susceptible to new influences, chiefly German Romanticism (especially in English and Scottish – that is, Broad Church Anglican and Calvinist – guise, via Coleridge and Carlyle, respectively) and French social thought.[12] 'The influences of European, that is to say Continental, thought, and especially those of the reaction of the nineteenth century against the eighteenth, were now streaming in upon me', Mill wrote.[13] He denied, in retrospect, simply replacing one system of thought with another. 'If I am asked what system of political philosophy I substituted for that which, as a philosophy, I had abandoned, I answer, no system ...'[14] The denial, however, is belied by his next words: '... only a conviction that the true system was something much more complex and many sided than I had previously had any idea of ...'.[15] He still sought a 'true system', in short – not only a unified and coherent political philosophy, but one grounded in a systematic epistemology and metaphysics. When

> I found the fabric of my old and taught opinions giving way in many fresh places ... I never allowed it to fall to pieces, but was incessantly

occupied in weaving it anew. I never, in the course of my transition, was content to remain, for ever so short a time, confused and unsettled.[16]

While conceding the strength of the tailoring impulse, and the skill of the weaver, in the judgement of succeeding generations of critics (at least until the final quarter of the twentieth century) the result was not aesthetically appealing. 'Many-sidedness'[17] resulted, in their view, in a patchwork quilt, not a seamless sheet. Philosophical necessitarianism, utilitarian ethics, democratic politics and Ricardian economics were all refined and 'humanized' at a cost of logical rigour, and even intelligibility. Critics have often seized on an architectural metaphor: Mill built on an inappropriate site, erecting a 'half-way house' with Ricardian lumber where no one who valued intellectual consistency would choose to live, or else added so many rooms to the original edifice that its foundation was undermined.[18] At the heart of the problem is the failed attempt to reconcile the Romantic vision of a unique Self, the cultivation of which is the highest good, with Utilitarian assumptions about the uniformity of desires and the amenability of human behaviour to scientific laws, and of human beings to appeals to rational self-interest. In political thought, the consequent desire to elevate and purify is sometimes at odds with the campaign to liberate.[19]

Superficially, at least, there indeed appears to be much to be explained.[20] But my concern here, as indicated, is less with the continuing value of Mill's thought than with the way in which it was shaped. The influence of his father, his wife and others will be discussed in Chapters 3 and 6, but suffice it to say here that Mill perceived himself as serving under a succession of mentors. Though denying that he was ever (apart from a period of two or three years) 'a mere reasoning machine' fashioned by his father,[21] he acknowledged, in a passage deleted from the published *Autobiography*, that he 'acquired the habit of backwardness, of waiting to follow the lead of others, an absence of moral spontaneity, an inactivity of the moral sense and even to a large extent, of the intellect, unless roused by the appeal of some one else . . .'.[22]

His susceptibility to forceful personalities was not lost on others. Much of the initial interest in Mill was to see the results of his father's experiment; old friends were incredulous and embarrassed at the large claims Mill made for the influence of Harriet Taylor in dedications and prefaces;[23] acquaintances were nonplussed by his deference to the opinions of his step-daughter.[24] And his protracted and painful disengagement from his father's influence was facilitated by at least a couple of intellectual apprenticeships: both Carlyle and Comte, with some justification, mistook him for a disciple.

At the time of his wife's death Mill was 53 years old, the nation's premier philosopher, author of state-of-the-art treatises on logic and political economy. Nonetheless, he still claimed to be the pupil (if not the amanuensis) of a mentor more insightful and original than himself. It is of no little significance in assessing his intellectual drift during the 1860s that this individual was his step-daughter, who in fact had nothing to contribute to his intellectual development.[25]

As for the earlier apprenticeships, Mill's initial intellectual phase is obviously associated with the period in which he was dominated by his father. While he was capable of some principled acts of resistance – maintaining his friendship with Roebuck, for instance[26] – he largely accepted his father's direction. However, James Mill's emotional grip on his son clearly extended beyond the period of John's intellectual fealty. The whole poignancy – and enduring appeal – of Mill's account of his 'mental crisis' comes from the collision he depicts between *idées fixes* and emotional needs. But he did not rid himself of the incubus of his father at this juncture, even if he subconsciously recognized that his father would indeed die, and his fierce hold loosen.[27] James Mill disobligingly survived for another decade, and the spectre of his father's disapproval caused John much discomfort during the 1830s. Mill carefully concealed the full extent of his disagreements with James. And – such is the power and complexity of subconscious attachments – the latter's death in 1836, rather than immediately liberating the son, provoked a breakdown rather more severe than the original 'mental crisis' John experienced ten years earlier, at the age of 20. (The latter crisis had passed unnoticed by friends and associates at the time.)

Continuing the attempt to synchronize mentors and systems, it is still harder to reconcile the important personal influence Harriet Taylor wielded with the traditional version of Mill's intellectual chronology. Mill's friendships with Carlyle and Comte helped draw Mill further out of the utilitarian orbit. The relationship with Harriet Taylor, however, appears to bear no correlation to this phase of his development, though they met in 1830 and, despite Mill's contrary claim, became intimate almost immediately.[28] Nor can Taylor be associated with the 'synthesis' phase, the reaction to the excesses of Mill's romanticism. While her letters contain disparaging comments about Carlyle,[29] she was hostile to many of Mill's friends and former friends.[30]

(Her criticisms of Comte were largely *ex post facto*: Mill's repudiation of him was not sufficiently decisive.)[31] Mill's breaks with Comte and Carlyle were inevitable, and he continued to admire de Tocqueville despite Taylor's strictures. There is certainly nothing in the surviving letters to indicate that she lured him back to associationalist psychology, utilitarian ethics or Ricardian political economy.

This is not to suggest that Harriet Taylor was without influence. Her impact on Mill's support of socialism, feminism and 'libertarian' liberalism has been much discussed. The relationship has suggested to one scholar an alternative chronology. Himmelfarb sees a 'conservative-liberal' phase in the 1830s (the youthful utilitarian of the preceding decade being simply 'the aboriginal Mill').[32] During this period an admirable caution tempers radical enthusiasms about democracy, but it gives way, under Taylor's tutelage, to a shrill reductivism. Gradually detoxifying after his wife's death, Mill gives up expounding the kind of 'simple principles' and 'single truths' worthy of 'a young woman with romantic bohemian affectations'.[33] His work again becomes nuanced and sceptical, as he himself becomes more genial, patient and kind.[34] Particularly commendable in the post-Taylor recovery phase is the essay 'On Intervention' and *On Representative Government*.[35]

Unfortunately, the emergence of 'the other Mill' does not satisfactorily coincide with the period during which he was closely associated with Harriet Taylor. The 'conservative' phase, in fact, commences *after* he became enamoured of her.

The date that Mill offers for his second transformation provides a clue. 'From this time', Mill writes in the final chapter of the *Autobiography*, 'General View of the Remainder of My Life', 'what is worth relating of my life will come into a very small compass; for I have no further mental changes to tell of, but only, as I hope, a continued mental progress . . . '.[36] 'This time', it emerges, is spring of 1840. Clearly this date marks no new phase in Mill's relationship with Harriet Taylor. Nor is its significance clear in Mill's partial re-embracing of his father's positions.[37]

But what then happened in 1840 to distinguish it as an apt *terminus ad quem* for his 'second phase'? '[T]he last hope of the formation of a Radical party had disappeared . . . '[38] Durham, on whom the Radicals had long pinned their hopes, died in that year. Events dictated an end to a period of partisan political agitation. Mill sold the *London and Westminster Review* and buried himself in the *Logic*. In other words, a change in the political climate in England terminated one stage in his intellectual career and inaugurated another. This suggests an alternative and in some ways more illuminating scheme for periodizing Mill's life: observing the fluctuations between the study and the platform (or, more accurately, political journalism) – between, that is, the *vita activa* and the *vita contemplativa*.

The importance of securing a forum for advanced views cannot be overemphasized. Bentham and James Mill had long discussed the need for a Radical party organ. Bentham's choice of Bowring as editor, when the publication was finally launched in 1823, proved most unfortunate, in the Mills' view. After a promising first number, the *Westminster Review* bitterly disappointed the young Philosophic Radicals.[39] Eventually, the ardent – and wealthy – young Millite Sir William Molesworth came to the rescue, buying out the *Westminster* and merging it with his newly founded *London Review*. 'In the years between 1834 and 1840', Mill confesses, 'the conduct of this review occupied the greater part of my spare time.'[40] He produced, indeed, four times the number of articles subsequently republished in *Dissertations*: '...the Review engrossed...nearly all the time I could devote to authorship'.[41]

The early 1860s, it is generally agreed, marked another sea-change in public opinion – or, rather, the sense that a sea-change was imminent. With the impending death of Palmerston, the sceptre of the Liberal Party was likely to pass to Gladstone, and who knew where his intellectual peregrinations would take him? Once again Radicals of all persuasions hoped to move and shake the movers and shakers. And once again Mill became interested in founding, or at least dominating, a literary and political Review which would propagate 'sound' views. He initially focused his efforts on the *Reader*, after Spencer purchased it.[42] Mill tried assiduously to have more space allotted to discussions of political philosophy and contemporary politics, for which Cairnes was serving as sub-editor. Thwarted, Mill attempted to oust the editor, Frederick Pollock, and install the reluctant Cairnes in Pollock's place.[43]

Then, as sometimes happens, after he'd given up on the *Reader*, a greater prize fell into Mill's lap. John Morley, burning to serve the Radical cause, was offered the editorship of the *Fortnightly Review* when Lewes' poor health obliged him to retire.[44] Mill was soon taking an almost proprietary interest in the journal. By late 1870, he was hovering conspicuously at Morley's elbow.[45] At one point Mill even offered to take over the helm temporarily, in light of the apparent risk to Morley's health editing entailed.[46] After 1868, Mill published articles nowhere else.

If one considers Mill's life, then, in terms of fluctuations between political activism and scholarly endeavours (a somewhat artificial dichotomy, to be sure)[47] a more satisfying chronology emerges, and one that, at first sight at least, also appears to divide nicely into three segments. There was, initially, the very exacting apprenticeship to James Mill, which concluded in 1822, when John wrote his first argumentative essay (and commenced 'to carry on my own mental cultivation by writing still more than by reading')[48] and began associating with contemporaries – no longer 'a pupil under teachers, but a man among men'.[49] This active phase continued, with some strategic withdrawals, until his disengagement from politics in 1840.[50] (Mill implies, somewhat misleadingly, that his reservations about Philosophical Radical dogmas led to a sharp break and withdrawal of support.[51] Though his friends were certainly disturbed by some of his new opinions, especially those expressed in the 'Spirit of the Age' articles, Mill remained beside them in the trenches.) Selling his share of the *Westminster Review* enabled him to return to the *Logic* and 'to indulge the inclination, natural to thinking persons when the age of boyish vanity is once past, for limiting my own society to a very few persons' – chiefly Mrs Taylor.[52]

The scholarly retreat lasted until just after his wife's death (with, again, a few exceptions), during which time the *Logic* and *Principles* appeared. A partisan and polemical phase followed.

Periodizing Mill's life in terms of the degree of his involvement in day-to-day politics also has the merit of synchronizing these phases with the influence of his father and his wife. James Mill isolated his son from the contaminating influence of other children.[53] It comes as no surprise that once launched on his career as reformer, John Mill actively recruited every promising young man he ran across.[54] 'As a boy,' Packe dryly notes, 'John Mill had led no gangs, nor had he belonged to any team. And so his adolescent passion for founding societies was not easily quenched.'[55] Political activism gave Mill a social life.

Harriet Taylor then presided over a protracted retreat, although, as indicated, it began in response to political developments. The painful liaison with Taylor made Mill increasingly hypersensitive to slights. Ties with family and friends were severed, and the consumptive couple, in near seclusion and despairing of the present age, prepared to concentrate the pemmican of their thought for advanced thinkers of future generations. There appears to be, then, a loose correlation between Mill's discipleships and the periods of quiescence, and between sociability and activism.

Following his wife's death, Mill gradually renewed his old ties and began attending the Political Economy Club, where he soon encountered the younger admirers that are the subject of this study.

This reading contradicts the stereotypical image of Mill in his final years – the Saint of Rationalism, captured in Watts's famous portrait. The lips are firm, the chin resolute, but the eyelids are heavy and the gaze is downward, or even inward. There is something fragile and abstracted in the countenance. Three scholars, Carlisle, Collini and Kinzer, have recently done much to modify this image and my work on the Mill circle that formed in the 1860s is intended to complement and reinforce their readings.[56]

The important question for my purposes is the impact of Mill's re-politicization on his economic theory. I will suggest that it had the (superficially) curious effect of making him at once more rigid and more flexible. Very briefly, his political commitments, and their importance in his life, hardened his resistance to marginalism while it made him more receptive to historicist arguments. What the positions had in common, of course, was an increased scepticism about – or indifference to – economic laws. Mill was increasingly disinclined to see economic outcomes as determinate. On the issues that were most important to him, he frequently sanctioned behaviour that would appear to result in less than optimal consequences. In justifying these recommendations, he sometimes appealed to extra-economic criteria. More often he simply argued, with varying degrees of persuasiveness, that outcomes predicted by Ricardian political economy would not, in fact, come to pass – that, for example, economies of scale did not obtain in agriculture, that the short-run demand for labour was inelastic, and wage gains would not affect employment.

The drift of Mill's religious beliefs was no less dramatic, and equally distressing to his followers. From a position derisively critical of natural theology, Mill, albeit with much circumspection, conceded that nature offers some evidence of a Deity who is powerful and benevolent, if not omnipotent. And after arguing that Christianity was highly imperfect and in need of much emendation, near the end of his life Mill hailed its founder as 'the ideal representative and guide of humanity',[57] and suggested that Christ was divinely inspired.

Superficially, the simultaneous shift in Mill's economic and religious convictions appears paradoxical. A mellowing of hard-edged rationalism is not uncommon in old age. Depending on one's perspective, hope blossoms and a spirit of generosity and compromise prevails, or, alternatively, a new credulity clouds the mind and warps the critical faculties. In either case the efflorescence of spirituality in later life is a familiar phenomenon. On the other hand, political partisanship in modern Europe is generally associated with youth, with its characteristic mix of impatience, idealism and materialism. Radicalism implies a this-worldly perspective: an interest in collective and material salvation in the near future, not of individual spiritual salvation for eternity. Political radicalism rejects the status quo that religion traditionally accepts.

What Mill's growing religiosity would appear to have in common with his increased economic heterodoxy is simply a willingness to bend the rules. Increasingly, frustratingly, the true and the good diverge, and Mill's growing propensity is to back the good.[58] Such a position, baldly asserted, would have been anathema to Mill. Mill advocated the good surreptitiously, and his militant secularism and his no less militant (albeit updated) Ricardianism began to unravel in consequence.

2 The Politics of Mill's Political Economy

In November of 1844, Mill, feeling rather guilty for not having yet written to his friend Henry Chapman, who had sailed to New Zealand some 18 months earlier, took some time to update Chapman on certain arresting developments in English public opinion, and on his own plans.

> You will rather, I suppose, expect to hear from me about public matters; but even these I have scarcely anything prominent . . . to relate, in the way of events. It is rather the state of the public mind which is curious and interesting. There is a prodigious current setting in every day more strongly, of superficial philanthropy. English benevolence can no longer be accused of confining itself to niggers and other distant folks; on the contrary everybody is all agog to do something for the poor. A great many things have conduced to this, some good, some bad. The anti-poor-law cry; the state of the houses of the poor, and their sanitary condition, as made known by Chadwick's official investigations, the conditions of large masses of people as shown by the enquiries of Commissions about factories, mines, etc., then in another way the speculations of Carlyle, the Puseyites, and others, about the impossibility of any social stability or security if there is not a habitual bond of good offices and sympathy between the ruling classes and the ruled, especially the poor – which speculations would have had no effect whatever if there were no chartism and socialism to frighten the rich. One sees plainly that while the noise is made up by a few sincere people, the bulk of the following has for its motive the desire of preventing revolution, and perhaps still more, the desire of taking the *popularis aura* out of the sails of the Anti-Corn-law league. In both these things they will fail. The Corn Law *must* go, and very soon, and as for revolution, there has been nothing in our day so calculated to produce it as the talk now in vogue, none of which is lost upon the working class, who do not thank them for it one jot, but whom it greatly strengthens in the faith that it is other people's business to take care of them, that all the rich have more than they is a wrong to

> them, and that the rich themselves are partly ashamed of this wrong, and partly afraid of its consequences and desiring to buy them off at the expense of those who are better off...; and I never remember a time when any suggestion of anti-population doctrine or of forethought and self-command on the part of the poor was so contemptuously scouted as it is now... . Things never seemed to tend so rapidly to a complete bouleversement of our social system, though whether peaceably or violently, none can tell.

All of the foregoing prefaces the announcement that 'I am thinking of saying out my say on all these things in a treatise on political economy, not in the abstract manner of Ricardo and my father, but in the practical and popular manner of Adam Smith'.[1] Mill was motivated to write the *Principles*, in short, to oppose a 'superficial philanthropy'. What was objectionable about it, first, was its insincerity: it was motivated, at bottom, by fear of revolution. But the attempt to beguile the poor, and to soothe the conscience of the rich, was still more objectionable because it was based on a false analysis: that the gains of the rich come at the expense of the poor and it is therefore the duty of the former to care for the latter.

What was especially pernicious about this idea was that it froze in place the existing social order: the rich man in his mansion, the poor man at his gate, though now better clothed and fed, thanks to the former's benevolence. Only by becoming responsible – by developing 'forethought and self-command' – could the working class and poor truly improve their material well-being. 'Forethought and self-command' meant, above all, controlling the sexual appetite. Moral development thus preceded, and would facilitate, the redistribution of wealth and, ultimately, the intellectual development and, finally, the political emancipation of the working class. But moral behaviour itself was to be inspired not by exhortation but by rational argument. And the first principle to be mastered was the distinction between the wealth of aristocratic landlords and that of middle-class bankers, merchants or manufacturers.

I

All radicals were anti-aristocratic. Such sentiments were at the heart of radicalism until the final quarter of the century, and, arguably, well beyond (thanks partly to Lloyd George, partly to Lord Curzon). British aristocrats were not accused of oppression, unlike their counterparts on the continent. Rather, the principal charge, repeated *ad infinitum*, was 'corruption': the aristocracy was using special legal privileges to enrich themselves and their church. Nonconformists, Chartists, Manchester School supporters (among which Grampp discusses no fewer than six discrete groups),[2] philosophical and unaligned radicals all shared this animus, which can be traced to eighteenth-century classical republicans, themselves resurrecting (and revising) the civic humanism of Harrington and Machiavelli.[3]

Mill himself differentiated the Philosophic Radicals from four other types of Radicals.

> There are the historical radicals, who demand popular institutions as the inheritance of Englishmen, transmitted to us from the Saxons or the barons of Runnymede. There are the metaphysical radicals, who hold the principles of democracy, not as means to good government, but as corollaries from some unreal abstraction, – from 'natural liberty' or 'natural rights'. There are the radicals of occasion and circumstance, who are radicals because they disapprove the measure of the government for the time being. There are, lastly, the Radicals of position, who are radicals, as somebody said, because they are not lords. Those whom, in contradistinction to all these, we call philosophical radicals are those who in politics observe the common manner of philosophers; that is, who, when they are discussing means, begin by considering the end, and, when they desire to produce effects, think of causes. These persons became Radicals because they saw immense practical evils existing in the government and social condition of this country, and because the same examination which showed them the evils showed also that the cause of these evils was the aristocratic principle in our government, – the subjection of the many to the control of a comparatively few . . . [T]he motto of their radicalism was, enmity to the Aristocratical principle.[4]

To focus on the first principles of government is to assure that one's goals are to be more encompassing – the object is to uproot the plant, not to trim it: Mill and his friends took the etymology of 'radical' seriously. As Hamburger notes, their goal was 'to achieve total political victory, i.e., to destroy aristocratic power',[5] not to restore a balanced Constitution.

Hamburger makes the case that the Philosophic Radicals were the first true ideologues in modern Britain: they regarded themselves as disinterested intellectuals *pur et simple*, not the representatives of a particular class or interest. (They were, indeed, of diverse social backgrounds.)[6] And they acted, as Mill notes, not out of a belief in natural or constitutional rights, but simply to secure efficient and equitable government. In their analyses as in their objectives, they were good utilitarians. Indeed, the name 'Philosophic Radicals' was deliberately chosen by John Mill in the early 1830s to replace the latter label because of the opprobrium associated with it.[7]

Mill's analysis of the pernicious effects of an aristocracy shifted somewhat – he was increasingly concerned with their corruption of public morals – and he came to have significant reservations about the alternatives – but the privileged class remained for him the chief source of evil in Britain.[8] Characteristically, his maiden speech in the House, where, late in life, he sat for Westminster, concluded with the memorable injunction:

> An aristocracy should have the feelings of an aristocracy; and, inasmuch as they enjoy the highest honours and advantages, they ought to be willing to bear the first brunt of the inconveniences and evils which fall on the country generally. This is the ideal character of an aristocracy: it is the character with which all privileged classes are accustomed to credit themselves; though I am not aware of any aristocracy in history that has fulfilled those requirements.[9]

Clearly, the philosophy which dictated the sustained attack on the aristocracy was something more than the dispassionate empiricism Mill claims for it – the commitment to trace effects to causes. The profound animus toward the aristocracy was both rationalized and intensified by Ricardian economics.[10] The analytic insight that distinguishes Philosophic Radical grievances from those of rival radicals was Ricardian rent, the chief consequence of the law of diminishing returns. Rent – 'that portion of the produce of the earth, which is paid to the landlord for the use of the original and indestructible powers of the soil', as Ricardo defines it[11] – is determined by two things: the demand for food and the quantity and quality of arable land. As the former increases, the latter decreases, and rents rise. This is simply because a less fertile (or marginal) acre requires greater 'doses', in James Mill's phrase,[12] of labour and capital (itself largely the embodiment of previous labour),[13] compared to a more richly endowed acre, to produce an equivalent amount of corn; equal values are produced at unequal costs. As increasingly worse land is cultivated, rents rise. Rent thus does not contribute to price. 'Corn is not high', Ricardo observes,

> because a rent is paid, but a rent is paid because corn is high; and it has been justly observed, that no reduction would take place in the price of corn, although landlords should forego the whole of their rent. Such a measure would only enable some farmers to live like gentlemen, but would not diminish the quantity of labour necessary to raise raw produce on the least productive land in cultivation.[14]

Historically, 'the rise of rent is always the effect of the increasing wealth of the country, and of the difficulty of providing food for its augmented population. It is a symptom, but it is never a cause of wealth ...'.[15] More specifically, rising rents, a result of accumulated capital having increased employment, necessitate a continued rise in the rate of wages, with a consequent decline in the rate of profit (employers being unable to transfer costs to consumers).[16] Eventually, productive investment will cease.[17] 'It follows, then, that the interest of the landlord is always opposed to the interest of every other class in the community. His situation is never so prosperous, as when food is scarce and dear.'[18]

The final quotation is from 'Essay on the Influence of a Low Price of Corn on the Profits of Stock' (1815); Ricardo is never quite as explicit in the *Principles*. John Stuart Mill had no such compunctions: the most caustic passages in *his Principles* concern rent. The law of diminishing returns, 'the most important proposition in political economy',[19] eventuates in rank injustice: rent remunerates theft and sloth. It rewards the former because 'no man made the land. It is the original inheritance of the whole species. Its appropriation is wholly a question of general expediency. When private property in land is not expedient, it is unjust.'[20] It rewards indolence because 'landed proprietors are the only class ... who have a claim to a share in the distribution of the produce, through their ownership of something which neither they nor anyone else have produced'. Land is 'the gift of nature, and requires no labour or outlay as the condition of its existence ...'.[21] Rent is cost-free, in short. There is no self-sacrifice; hence, no virtue. Landlords 'grow rich, as it were in their sleep, without working, risking, or economizing. What claim have they, on the general principle of social justice, to this accession of riches?'[22] Mill's sense of the immorality of aristocratic income lay behind his vexing fourth 'proposition respecting capital': 'Demand for commodities is not demand for labour'.[23] Of the two (related) Malthusian heresies – the possibility of over-production and the beneficent effect of 'non-productive' expenditure – the latter, an obvious rationale for the existence of a parasitic aristocracy, was deeply offensive to Ricardian economists. Thrift was a virtue, profligacy a vice. '[A] person does good to labourers, not by what he consumes on himself, but solely by what he does not so consume.'[24]

The morality of a people came to be more important for Mill than its prosperity. Thus he eventually decided that the chief evil of the aristocracy was its role 'as a great demoralizing agency in the country'.[25] Both in its use of legislation to serve class rather than public ends, and in its crass materialism (legitimized by its power), the aristocracy offered negative examples to the uneducated and disenfranchised – with, Mill predicted, grave future consequences. But the doctrine of rent was a still more lethal – and durable – weapon than the latter charges. Particularly as those aristocratic preserves, the Church, army and universities, began to be breached, and the Irish Question had come to the fore, it was necessary and desirable to shift anti-aristocratic arguments from the actions of its representatives in Parliament to the *raison d'être* of the class itself – from rent-seeking to rent. For this purpose, Ricardian analysis was indispensable. The sword, naturally, was double-edged. In the hands of Henry George, the notion of an 'unearned increment'[26] proved a sufficiently potent rallying cry to galvanize tens of thousands of English and Irish workers in the early 1880s on behalf of land nationalization.[27] Mill, his letters reveal, was far more sympathetic to that cause than he led his middle-class audience to believe. And in *England and Ireland* (1868) he went on record as advocating immediate state intervention to set rents in Ireland.[28] Still, he would undoubtedly have considered George's objective premature – for Britain.[29] Worse still, naturally, were those popular theorists who declined to observe Ricardo's (and George's) distinctions between landed and moveable property.

Conceiving of the problem posed by the aristocracy in terms of the inequity of differential rent rather than the use of legislation to serve class interests suggested different solutions to the problem. For all radicals, including the Philosophic Radicals, extending the franchise was the *sine qua non* of political reform. For the Chartists it was a matter of right, for the Philosophic Radicals of expediency. The People, for James Mill, have no partial ('sinister') interests. Representative government will enable them to check the tendency of any administration to subordinate public to private good. Democracy means the identity of interests between rulers and ruled. From the late 1820s on, his son was far less sanguine about the capacities of 'the People', based on a more subtle and refined understanding of happiness. Good government is desirable precisely as it conduces to the moral and intellectual development of its citizens. The exercise of political power by the majority, in short, though a necessary condition, did not itself guarantee the mental progress he envisioned.

Still less could representative government, by itself, secure their economic well-being – a mischievous fallacy for Mill. True, there remained clear legal barriers to a more desirable distribution of property – primogeniture, entail – which had to be addressed through Acts of Parliament. However, the chief solution to the problem of rent – itself, I've argued, the core grievance against the aristocracy – was the creation of peasant proprietorships. These would enable agricultural workers to receive both economic rent and profits, rather than wages. The distributive gains, as well as the moral gains, would outweigh any losses in productivity that economies of scale would have afforded.[30]

The subject was of supreme importance to Mill throughout the 1860s. One of the few organizations in which he was active was the Land Tenure Reform Association: he frequently addressed its meetings, drafted its manifesto, and left it £500 in his will. His last two articles were written in the organization's behalf, as well as two important *Fortnightly* articles.[31] Mill's views on the subject are discussed further in Chapter 5.

To summarize and simplify, at the heart of the problem posed by the aristocracy was economic rent rather than political corruption, and the solution, rather than democracy, was the encouragement of numerous small holdings.

Similarly, in Mill's discussions of the working class, their social and economic amelioration soon took precedence over their political emancipation.

II

The plight of the working classes was understood in terms of the law of population and its corollary, the natural rate of wages. Again, the doctrine was taken from Ricardo (who, of course, appropriated it from Malthus):[32] population increases in a geometric ratio, food in an arithmetic ratio. The natural price of labour was pegged to the price of food 'and necessaries'.[33] Given diminishing returns in agriculture and the powerful drive to procreate, the tendency of wages in the long run was downward.[34] The only solution was to regulate the birthrate of the poor: this could be accomplished voluntarily, through a growing 'taste for comforts and enjoyments',[35] or through legislative intervention.[36] (Malthus was, notoriously, more pessimistic than his friend and rival.)

Mill more than reiterated these claims. It is difficult to overemphasize his commitment to Malthus.[37] Among the Philosophic Radicals, Mill later recalled,

> Malthus's population principle was quite as much a banner, and point of union among us, as any opinion specially belonging to Bentham. This great doctrine, originally brought forward as an argument against the indefinite improvability of human affairs, we took up with ardent zeal in the contrary sense, as indicating the sole means of realizing that improvability by securing full employment at high wages to the whole labouring population through a voluntary restriction of the increase of their numbers.[38]

The wages fund controversy and the import of Mill's 'recantation' will be treated in Chapter 5. But the implications of the Law of Population are clear-cut: if the average rate of wages is determined by that part of the circulating capital 'expended in the direct purchase of labour', divided by the number of 'those who work for hire', the only recourse for workers is to reduce the denominator – to lower the number of those competing for a share of the 'wages fund'.[39]

Somewhat problematically, the amelioration of working-class poverty depended on changes in behaviour which elsewhere were assumed to *flow from* changes in economic well-being: self-reliance, responsibility and prudence.[40] The working classes needed to reduce their numbers if they wanted to improve their standard of living; but conversely, an improved standard of living, Mill argued, would itself inspire the capacity to delay gratification that was necessary to maintain that standard.

A significant episode that Mill failed to mention in his autobiography, naturally enough, was his arrest at age 17 or 18 for distributing Francis Place's 'diabolical handbills' explaining contraception 'to the married of both sexes of the working people'. (The device was a damp sponge withdrawn by means of a twisted thread.) The incident surfaced only after Mill's death, and resulted in Gladstone's withdrawing from a committee charged with erecting a memorial to Mill.[41]

Needless to say, after his brush with the law, Mill never again explicitly advocated artificial birth control, stressing instead the need for prudence and self-control – Malthus's negative check, delayed marriage.

Nonetheless, his zeal for birth-control never waned. Indeed, the feminism of his later years reinforced it, for he believed it essential to women's full self-realization.

> It is seldom by the choice of the wife that families are too numerous; on her devolves (along with all the physical suffering and at least a full share of the privations) the whole of the intolerable domestic drudgery resulting from the excess. To be relieved from it would be hailed as a blessing by multitudes of women.[42]

Emancipation, then, in addition to benefiting women and men directly, would have the beneficent additional effect of diminishing 'the evil of over-population', while, simultaneously, moralizing society.

> It is by devoting one-half of the human species to that exclusive function, by making it fill the entire life of one sex, and interweave itself with almost all the objects of the other, that the animal instinct in question is nursed into the disproportionate preponderance which it has hitherto exercised in human life.[43]

But, apart from reproducing less, a second solution for the condition of the working classes increasingly recommended itself: co-operation. What peasant proprietorships were to agricultural labourers, co-operative enterprises were for the urban working class. Revealingly, as his feminism grew, he shifted allegiance from the former to the latter. His glowing account of continental peasant holdings in Book II – not the least recommendation for which was their tendency to reduce population growth[44] – is overshadowed by a somewhat censorious attitude in Chapter 7 of Book IV.[45] Mill openly concedes, first of all, that 'labour is unquestionably more productive on the system of large industrial enterprises'. 'And', he continues, 'in the moral aspect of the question, which is still more important than the economical, something better should be aimed at as the goal of industrial improvement, than to disperse mankind over the earth in single families, each ruled internally, as families now are, by a patriarchal despot, and having scarcely any community of interest, or necessary mental communion, with other human beings.' While family responsibilities can convert 'brute instincts into prudential foresight and self-government,... if public spirit, generous sentiments, or true justice and equality are desired, association, not isolation of interests, is the school in which these excellences are nurtured'.[46]

The economic argument is straightforward: just as peasant proprietorships divert rent directly to the farmer (as well as allowing returns on, and thus fostering, capital improvements), so co-operative enterprises enable workers to receive profits as well as wages. But once again the moral benefits are paramount:

> It is scarcely possible to rate too highly this material benefit, which yet is as nothing compared with the moral revolution in society that would accompany it: the healing of the standing feud between capital and labour; the transformation of human life, from a conflict of classes struggling for opposite interests, to a friendly rivalry in pursuit of a good common to all; the elevation of the dignity of labour; a new sense of security and independence in the labouring class; and the conversion of each human being's daily occupation into a school of the social sympathies and the practical intelligence.[47]

A final benefit: if co-operation, true socialism, were to establish itself, it would discredit that socialism requiring the confiscation of existing capital.[48] Mill's chief disagreement with socialist writers is over their desire to abolish competition: 'They forget that wherever competition is not, monopoly is; and that monopoly, in all its forms, is the taxation of the industrious for the support of indolence, if not of plunder.'[49] Co-operation combines the benefits of voluntary association with those of a market economy, encouraging empathy while simultaneously stimulating energy and imagination.[50]

Co-operation, Mill believes, will evolve from profit-sharing. Mill appeals not only to workers, for whom he feels the rewards of co-ownership answer a deep yearning, but to employers: profit-sharing is in their own best interest, for workers will be more efficient if they have a direct interest in the sale of their product.[51]

3 The Religion of Humanity

The previous chapter considered the political conclusions that Mill derived from his economic thought. This chapter attempts to explain the force of Mill's attachment to those conclusions – and to the economic analyses that supported them – by emphasizing the supreme importance for Mill of the project of improving mankind. As he himself acknowledged, the pursuit of this objective was a religion; and Mill, I hope to show, proved a devout communicant.

'If to labor fearlessly and ceaselessly for the good of society, and with the completest self-abnegation that is consistent with healthy individuality, be the true form of religion, Mr Mill exhibited such genuine and profound religion – so permeating his whole life, and so engrossing his every action – as can hardly be looked for in any other man of his generation', wrote H. R. Fox Bourne, editor of *The Examiner*. 'Great as were his intellectual qualities they were dwarfed by his moral excellences.'[1]

This is a recurrent theme in a number of descriptions of Mill by contemporaries. One might expect such invidious comparisons from intellectual adversaries. And indeed, such writers repeatedly praised the man as they condemned his work. 'One who knew Mill only through his writings knew but half of him, and that not the best half', wrote Fitzjames Stephen.[2] T. H. Green described Mill as 'an extraordinarily good man'.[3] Even W. S. Jevons acknowledged his 'respect for Mill's straightforward & zealous character'.[4] And Alfred Marshall, attempting to convince Jevons that 'the plausible sophistries' of Mill's *Principles* are actually 'only incomplete truths', admitted that 'Mill was not a constructive genius of the first order, and that, generally the most important benefits he has conferred on the science are due rather to his character than his intellect'.[5] Leslie Stephen, too, had his doubts about the durability of Mill's *oeuvre*. However, 'no human being', he concluded, 'ever devoted himself more unreservedly to a worthy end from his earliest to his latest years; the end was the propagation of truths of the highest importance to mankind, and the devotion implied entire freedom from all meaner or subsidiary ambitions'.[6]

But surprisingly, even loyal disciples, perhaps in imitation of their master's diffidence, declined to pass judgement on Mill's intellectual contributions, while praising the man himself. Thus Morley, in his fulsome *Fortnightly Review* obituary, made no great claims for Mill's opus: 'Much will one day have to be said as to the precise value of Mr Mill's philosophical principles . . . '. Unwilling to predict the outcome of this evaluation, Morley was content to conclude only that 'we shall at any rate be sure that with his reputation will stand or fall the intellectual repute of a whole generation of his countrymen'. Instead, he celebrates Mill's character. Morley emphasizes its luminousness over its sweetness: 'Its force lies not in single elements, but in that combination of an ardent interest in human improvement with a reasoned attention to the law of its conditions, which alone deserves to be honoured with the high name of wisdom.' It unites 'intellectual gravity with a passionate love of improvement in all the aims and instruments of life'.[7] Similarly, Fox Bourne, while wishing to 'abstain as far as possible from any estimate of either the value or extent of his work in philosophy, in economics, in politics . . . ', finds it impossible 'to lay down the pen without some slight reference, however inadequate . . . , to the nobility of his character, and the peculiar grace with which he exhibited it in all his dealings with his friends and with the whole community among whom he lived, and for whom he worked with the self sacrificing zeal of an apostle'.[8]

Mill, in fact, appears to have been that rare philanthropist who actually loved men, the Friend of Humanity who was also a friend of individuals. For it was not just his crusading zeal that attracted admirers, but his selflessness in daily intercourse. The Saint of Rationalism (the epithet is deployed with varying degrees of irony)[9] was, according to the testimony of his friends, if not his family, truly saintly.

Memoirs abound with examples of his generosity. Herbert Spencer recounted with gratitude Mill's offer to subsidize the publication of his *System of Philosophy*.[10] W. T. Thornton recalled that during his year-long nervous breakdown, Mill discharged all of Thornton's duties in the Public Works Department of the East India Company, in addition to his own.[11] Mill lent money freely to working-class leaders like George Odger, and his contribution to Charles Bradlaugh's election campaign in 1868 probably did more than anything (apart from the Eyre prosecution) to ensure his own defeat.[12]

But not only was Mill generous, he was kind. 'Nothing', Henry Fawcett recalled, ' . . . was so remarkable in his character as his tenderness to the feelings of others, and the deference with which he listened to those in every respect inferior to himself. . . . The most humble youth would have found in Mr Mill the warmest and most kindly sympathy.'[13] His courtesy and consideration were always remarked upon. 'The Tender Feeling must in him have been very considerable. He was, throughout, affectionate, genial, kindly,' Alexander Bain reported.[14] Spencer, regarded by contemporaries as the nation's other leading psychologist, also noted 'an unusual predominance of the higher sentiments – a predominance which tended to subordinate the lower nature unduly'.[15] American visitors seem to have been especially struck by what they regarded as his femininity. Norton commented on Mill's 'sensitiveness of... expression', 'his refined face' and 'acute and delicate sensibilities'. Mill's manner has 'a tender grace and sweetness about it rarely met with', and a 'fine feminine susceptibility'.[16] Moncure Conway describes Mill as 'a man of delicate sentiment, elegant manners, and affectionate nature'. The 'personal care he had given to the culture of his stepdaughter' was 'maternal as well as paternal'.[17] The most sustained analysis of Mill's 'femininity' is Leslie Stephen's; however, in his case the label is hardly intended as a compliment.[18]

Mill's religiosity, in short, was sufficiently profound to infuse his daily activities. Selflessness was more than an article of faith.

Mill's commitment to the task of improving mankind can also be approached through his accounts of his relations with Benthamism, his first credo. Far from subjecting his son to dogmatic indoctrination, the common understanding of his educational experiment, James Mill provided a wide range of readings.[19] While John had learned to apply the Benthamic standard of 'the greatest happiness', it was not until late 1821 that he first read Bentham, in Dumont's more palatable translation. He describes the experience in the language of a religious conversion:

> in the first pages of Bentham, it [the felicific calculus] burst upon me with all the force of novelty... . The feeling rushed upon me, that all previous moralists were superseded, and that here indeed was the commencement of a new era in thought... . I felt taken up to an eminence from which I could survey a vast mental domain, and see stretching out into the distance intellectual results beyond all computation. As I proceeded farther, there seemed to be added to this intellectual clearness, the most inspiring prospects of practical improvement in human affairs.... When I laid down the last volume of the *Traite* I had become a different being. The 'principle of utility', understood as Bentham understood it... fell exactly into its place as

> the keystone which held together the detached and fragmentary component parts of my knowledge and beliefs. It gave unity to my conceptions of things. I now had opinions; a creed, a doctrine, a philosophy; in one among the best senses of the word, a religion; the inculcation and diffusion of which could be made the principal outward purpose of a life.[20]

Just as the impact of Bentham is undervalued, casual late twentieth-century readers tend to assume that Mill's 'mental crisis' in 1826 culminated in his recognition that he had to 'fulfil his own needs' (though, owing to the regrettable constraints of the time and place, he had to be content with reading poetry and walking in the woods). In fact, Mill's list of the activities which now gave him pleasure is revealing:

> Relieved from my ever present sense of irremediably wretchedness, I gradually found... that I could again find enjoyment, not intense, but sufficient for cheerfulness, in sunshine and sky, in books, in conversation, in public affairs; and that there was, once more, excitement, though of a moderate kind, in exerting myself for my opinions, and for the public good.[21]

The pleasures of nature are quickly superseded by the pleasures of reforming mankind. The lesson, then, is not that a little bit of innocent fun is a necessary concomitant to the virtuous life, or that sensuous experiences, if not sensuality, ought to accompany sustained intellectuality, but, quite the contrary, that,

> Those only are happy (I thought) who have their minds fixed on some object other than their own happiness; on the happiness of others, on the improvement of mankind, even on some art or pursuit, followed not as a means, but as itself an ideal end. Aiming thus at something else, they find happiness by the way.[22]

This paradox he calls 'the anti-self-consciousness theory of Carlyle'.[23] Clearly, it confirmed Mill in the role to which he was reared.

Admittedly, following his crisis, Mill tells us, he began to acknowledge the importance of 'internal culture'.[24] By this he appears to mean listening to music and reading poetry. Melody, unfortunately, suffers from diminishing returns, and the possible combination of tones is finite[25] – a contingency that caused him much distress. Poetry, however, proved to be a salve. Nonetheless, what made Wordsworth's poetry 'a medicine for my state of mind', Mill says, are the 'states of feeling' it expresses, not merely 'beautiful pictures of natural scenery'. Significantly, these feelings – 'a source of inward joy' – 'would be made richer by every improvement in the physical or social condition of mankind'.[26] Thus, Wordsworth refreshed him 'not only without turning me away from, but with greatly increased interest in, the common feelings and common destiny of human beings'.[27] Poetry is thus not a diversion from but a summons to political activity.

Mill thereafter – at least while he continued to write about the subject during the 1830s – held poetry in great esteem. '[T]he noblest end of poetry is as an intellectual pursuit, that of acting upon the desires and characters of mankind through their emotions, to raise them towards the perfection of their nature.'[28] The poet is not, in the end, merely blessed with a nervous sensibility and a gift for language, but is a visionary – seeing and communicating truths inaccessible to prosaic logicians.[29] When Mill gropes for praise of Harriet Taylor to convey her extraordinary, but oddly elusive, virtues, he describes her, in a well-known passage, as a poet: '. . . I have often compared her, as she was at this time, to Shelley: but in thought and intellect, Shelley, so far as his powers were developed in his short life, was but a child compared with what she ultimately became'.[30] And Shelley performed the office of poet with near perfection. 'After dinner Mr Mill read us Shelley's Ode to Liberty & he got quite excited & moved over it rocking backwards & forwards & nearly choking with emotion; he said himself: "it is almost too much for one".'[31]

This is to preface one of Mill's more revealing comments about politics, in a review of the writings of de Vigny:

> Worldly advancement, or religion, are an Englishman's real interests: for Politics, except in connexion with one of those two objects, and for Art, he keeps only bye-corners of his mind, which naturally are far apart from each other: and it is but a small minority among Englishmen who can comprehend, that there are nations among whom Politics, or the pursuit of social well-being, and Poetry, or the love of beauty and of imaginative emotion, are passions as intense, as absorbing – influencing as much the whole tendencies of the character, and constituting as large a part of the objects in life of a considerable portion of the cultivated classes, as either the religious feelings, or those of worldly interest. Where both politics and poetry, instead of being either a trade or a pastime, are taken

completely *au serieux*, each will be more or less coloured by the other; and that close relation between an author's politics and his poetry, which with us is only seen in the great poetic figures of their age . . . is broadly conspicuous in France . . . through the whole range of her literature.[32]

The implication is clear: for cultivated minds, poetry and politics are exalted – and related – pursuits, and analogous to religion.[33]

In the end, Mill decided to call a grail a grail. The feelings he entertained about reforming mankind did indeed constitute a religion. But leery, obviously, of the response to Comte's *Systeme de Politique Positive* and *Catechisme Positiviste*, he withheld publication of his views until after his death.

To call these sentiments [the desire to act on one's 'highest feelings and convictions'] by the name morality, exclusively of any other title, is claiming too little for them. They are a real religion; of which, as of other religions, outward good works (the utmost meaning usually suggested by the word morality) are only a part, and are indeed rather the fruits of the religion than the religion itself. The essence of religion is the strong and earnest direction of the emotions and desires towards an ideal object, recognized as of the highest excellence, and as rightfully paramount over all selfish objects of desire. This condition is fulfilled by the Religion of Humanity in as eminent a degree, and in as high a sense, as by the supernatural religions even in their best manifestations, and far more so than in any of their others.[34]

Not only can 'the sense of unity with mankind, and a deep feeling for the general good . . . be cultivated into a sentiment and a principle capable of fulfilling every important function of religion', but, insofar as 'it is disinterested', the Religion of Humanity is superior to religions holding 'out the direct promise of reward from heaven as a primary inducement to . . . beneficence towards our fellow-creatures'.[35] Thus politics, correctly understood and selflessly pursued, is a religious sacrament.

All this is simply to say the Mill took his utilitarianism seriously: it did not provide merely legislative objectives but a spiritual calling. Such a conversion of the doctrine – from a dictum to a credo – would have been difficult had not Mill altered Benthamism. The 'mental crisis' that ultimately reconfirmed him in the service of the greatest happiness of the greatest number also enabled him to broaden and deepen his definition of happiness. Though it has been discussed by a number of commentators, the process is worth taking a very brief look at.[36] I am ultimately trying to explain Mill's attachment to Ricardian postulates. They supported a politics – again, broadly construed – that exercised the force of a religion.

Briefly, and familiarly, under the influence of Carlyle and Coleridge – and, hence, German poets and philosophers – and French engineers and social theorists, Mill, during the late 1820s and early 1830s, revised utilitarianism in two ways:

1. No longer was 'happiness' its object (that is, the happiness uninstructed individuals intuitively sought), but self-cultivation: as a *desideratum*, the exercise of freedom, was superseded by the development of intelligence (discrimination, essentially) and virtue.[37]
2. A different role for political institutions followed. No longer was it sufficient to check the rapacity of rulers by identifying the interests of the governed with the governors. Rather, active encouragement of the moral and intellectual progress of the citizenry was the *summum bonum*, implying a master–disciple or teacher–student relationship between governor and governed.[38]

More specifically, Mill sought to overcome two tendencies in individuals and societies. He repeatedly attacked the reliance on custom, habit and convention, on traditions unquestioningly obeyed or verified intuitively. This was the kind of behaviour encouraged by aristocratic, hierarchical societies.[39] But Mill also disapproved of a middle-class culture that encouraged restless activity in pursuit of shallow, materialistic goals, a culture valuing sensual over moral, intellectual and aesthetic pleasure, and comfort over wisdom.[40]

It followed for Mill that while much remained to be done to eliminate aristocratic prerogatives, legislation itself was insufficient. While representative government afforded its citizens an admirable political education,[41] its institutions ought, Mill felt, to be supplemented by a learned class – distinguished intellectuals acting in concert to help mould public opinion.[42]

Thus we are led to Mill's awkward half-embrace of a national clerisy. Space does not permit a discussion of the controversy over this and related issues that enlivened Mill scholarship during the 1960s and

1970s. It centred on the seriousness of Mill's flirtation with the Coleridgian notion of a clerisy and with St Simonian beliefs that similarly exalted intellectuals. It was a debate also about the tasks envisioned for this elite and about the true objective of Mill's greatest polemic, *On Liberty*.[43]

As to the first issue, even in the 1820s Mill opposed the actual organization of a *pouvoir spirituel*. Its instruments ought to be 'private communication, the pulpit, and the press'.[44] (As Mill later argued, with cool logic, if there was disagreement among spiritual leaders, a formal organization would be harmful; if agreement existed, an organization would be superfluous.[45]) Nonetheless, Mill did hope for something like a trade union of superior intellects:

> It has often struck me that one of the many causes which prevent those who cultivate moral and political truth from occupying the place and possessing the influence which properly belong to them as the instructors and leaders of mankind, is that they never consider themselves as other labourers do, to constitute a guild or fraternity, combining their exertions for certain common ends.[46]

By the end of the 1830s, Mill despaired of ever achieving anything like this.[47] But such a group coalesced in the 1860s, and Mill doubtless welcomed it all the more eagerly for his not having had to take pains to organize it; members gravitated to him out of respect and remained loyal out of affection.

As for the ultimate goal of Mill and his acolytes, the other hotly debated issue, I've come to believe a close reading of *On Liberty* (such as Hamburger provides)[48] leaves little question that it was intended to further the great Enlightenment task of replacing revelation with reason, and thereby reconstitute the social order. The tolerance Mill preached was instrumental: his great rhetorical strategy consisted in substituting 'truth' for subversive ideas (especially atheism), and equating the pursuit of truth with 'experiments of living',[49] engaging in what today would be called alternative lifestyles. Thus, *On Liberty* envisions the discoverer of truth as a lonely heretic ranged against public opinion; truth emerges dialectically, through confrontation and synthesis, following public debate. Truth is iconoclastic; truth is controversial. The Mill who wrote the *Logic* and *Principles* in salubrious solitude knew otherwise – and said as much.[50] Claims of political philosophers about the priority of 'the liberty principle' over 'the utility principle' (paradoxically, on utilitarian grounds) or that 'self-determination is a *necessary component* of self-perfection and non-interference is a *necessary condition* of self-determination' (emphasis in original) are not persuasive.[51] A chief object of the Religion of Humanity was to supplant the Religion of Christ.

The deconversion of the West was not going to be accomplished overnight, and certainly not by a direct assault on its core institutions and beliefs. Public opinion was shaped incrementally, over issues as unpromising as the Cattle Diseases Bill, the Extradition Treaties Act, and an Act to Amend the Law Relating to Railways, authorizing smoking compartments.[52] Just as the Church was anathema because it supported the existing class structure and encouraged early marriage and large families, so, Mill seems to have thought, would its own authority be undermined by the political and social changes he agitated for.

Mill had two primary political objectives during his final years, following the two crusades to mobilize opinion on behalf of the rights of Africans in the Western Hemisphere – campaigns in opposition to the South during the Civil War and Governor Eyre shortly thereafter:[53] 'The emancipation of women, and co-operative production, are, I fully believe, the two great changes that will regenerate society'.[54] Co-operative production, however, was rather difficult to achieve by the fiat of committees of middle-class intellectuals. Land reform, which could be achieved by legislation, was more promising.[55]

Then as now, a fairly reliable measure of one's commitment to a cause is a willingness to serve on a committee on its behalf, long the sacrament of penance for secular intellectuals. Mill, naturally, was besieged by invitations to join or address a great number of groups, to which he generally gave careful attention.[56] But only two organizations commanded his active support throughout his last half-decade: the London National Society for Women's Suffrage[57] and the Land Tenure Reform Committee.[58] Mill saw the two causes neatly dovetailing to serve a project especially close to his heart, the preserving of commons: 'Women's suffrage will help us in this as in so many other things, for women will be much more unwilling than men to submit to the expulsion of all beauty from common life.'[59] Differences over more peripheral issues could be tolerated, however disappointing – Thornton's support of the South, Leslie's support of the Contagious Diseases Acts. But transferring political power to women and workers were core objectives.[60] And their pursuit was the practice of the Religion of Humanity.

4 Mystifying Morley: Developments in Mill's Religious Beliefs

At intervals between 1850 and 1870 Mill addressed himself directly to theological questions, asking what was true and what was useful in traditional Christianity. I want to examine these essays from the point of view of John Morley. I will be arguing that, paradoxically, a deepening commitment to the *practice* of the Religion of Humanity led Mill to alter his view of religious orthodoxy – a shift that alarmed and distressed Morley.

Helen Taylor, in her introduction to her step-father's posthumous *Three Essays on Religion*, recognized that she had to address two concerns. First was Mill's failure to make his views on religion known during his lifetime, for the essays 'Nature' and 'Utility of Religion' were completed between 1850 and 1858. She wished to absolve Mill of moral cowardice, naturally, and offered two excuses: (a) that Mill in fact intended to publish 'Nature' in 1873, and (b) that he was habitually cautious and methodical, took a long time to make up his mind, and was never provoked by the curiosity of others into publishing prematurely.[1] Taylor did not mention what was clearly a more compelling motive: Mill's estimate not of the correctness of his own views, but of the public's receptivity to them.

The second and more pressing problem Taylor recognized was the apparent inconsistency between the earlier two essays and 'Theism'. Here again she made two points: (a) In the careful revisions to which he subjected all his work before publication, Mill would have eliminated these discrepancies – more apparent than real, in any case.[2] (b) Shifting tack, Taylor implicitly acknowledged inconsistencies, but attributed them to Mill's 'taking a wider view' of the subject in the final essay.[3] This resulted in a difference both 'in tone' and in 'the relative weight' accorded 'different considerations'.[4]

Despite the appearance of special pleading, Taylor's claim is accurate: strictly speaking, there are no logical inconsistencies between the first two essays and 'Theism'. But the shifts in emphasis, and in tone, are striking, and revealing.

The *Essays* certainly disturbed Mill's closest friends and disciples. 'They do not correspond', Alexander Bain observed tartly, 'with what we should have expected from him on that subject.'[5] As for 'Theism' in particular, Mill's defence of the argument from Design is 'not only short, but extremely unsatisfactory'.[6] John Morley was still more severe: the final essay represented 'an aberration not less grave than the aberration with which he rightly charged Comte'.[7] Even 'Utility of Religion' is 'fatally well-fitted – though assuredly without any such design in the mind of the author – to justify all those conformities, compliances, economies, and accommodations, that men are naturally so ready to practise'.[8] In 'Theism', Mill's wholly uncritical depiction of Christ is 'one of the puzzles and perplexities of the book'.[9] Morley, as we shall see, was no less disturbed by Mill's arguments for the existence of an intelligent and probably benevolent Mind[10] and for the immortality of the soul.[11]

> [W]e are hardly to be blamed for having expected that the last word of the great positive thinker of our day would have been a warning to people to remember how arbitrary all such hypotheses must be, and a clear-voiced counsel to abandon them.[12]

Half a century later, Mill's betrayal still rankled. The final essay, Morley recalled, 'dismayed his disciples not merely as an infelicitous compromise with orthodoxy, but, what was far more formidable, as actually involving a fatal relaxation of his own rules and methods of reasoning. It made a sort of intellectual scandal.' 'Theism', in sum, was 'a laboured evasion of plain answers to plain questions'.[13] Some rationalists and freethinkers were less disappointed. Though acknowledging 'Theism's 'philosophical infirmities', W. M. W. Call, writing in the *Westminster Review*, was confident that the essay would not be of service to 'the despairing champions of Orthodoxy'.[14] And if W. G. Ward's bemused reaction was typical of Mill's orthodox opponents, Call was correct. But this was not to Mill's credit. 'Theism', for Ward, was,

> by far the weakest thing he has ever published. ... [H]is passionate attempts to construct some kind of religious edifice do more credit

> (if we may use the common antithesis) to his heart than to his head. Such attempts, we think, are due to that passionate emotionism [*sic*], which was so very prominent and so very singular a part of his character.[15]

Henry Reeve, the quintessential Whig, was no less contemptuous, and on the same ground:

> To substitute a dream of imagination, or a thrill of emotion, for that which is, if it exist at all, the foundation of all Being and all Knowledge, appears to us to be but a feeble attempt to dispel the gloom of this philosophy of despair.[16]

The most important of the shifts between the earlier and final essay concern Mill's conception of the Deity. Mill, it is true, does not abandon the belief that informs all his writings on religion: God cannot be at once omnipotent and benevolent. But while the first two essays are content to let the matter rest, and to argue, respectively, against natural theology and for an alternative to orthodox Christianity which preserves its best features while improving on its shortcomings, in the final essay Mill gamely attempts to demonstrate that God nonetheless exercises *some* power and displays *some* kindliness toward mankind. Hence, one may be simultaneously an advanced thinker and at least a lukewarm Christian, a possibility the earlier essays do not entertain.

The tone, correspondingly, differs considerably. The voice in 'Nature' is boisterous, sometimes exultant, in its derision. Its spirit is actually best exemplified in Mill's famous passage from *An Examination of the Philosophy of Sir William Hamilton*, 'I will call no being good, who is not what I mean when I apply that epithet to my fellow creatures; and if such a being can sentence me to hell for so calling him, to hell I will go.'[17] What is perhaps the most memorable paragraph in 'Nature', Mill's chronicle of Nature's wickedness, displays a similar exuberance.[18]

The tone of 'Theism' is quite different. The prose of the final essay – though, we are assured, it would have been subjected to at least two more revisions[19] – is, for the most part, studied, cautious and reserved. There are few exclamation points; a logician, not a pamphleteer, addresses us. Throughout – but especially in Part V – there is also a notable scrupulousness, an earnest effort to make every concession possible to believers, that is entirely absent from the earlier essays. This is especially obvious in Mill's characterization of Christ.[20] And toward God the Father there is almost an elegiac note, a sigh of regret, that 'those who take a rational view of the nature and amount of the evidence for the existence and attributes of the Creator' cannot 'have their aspirations towards goodness stimulated and encouraged' by 'the undoubting belief of the real existence of a Being who realizes our own best ideas of perfection'.[21]

I would like to take up the three essays in somewhat greater detail, and, in viewing them through the eyes of Morley, gauge the extent of their departure from what his closest followers believed, with good reason, were Mill's long-standing views.

Mill's disciples' enjoyment of 'Nature' was least diminished by reservations and regrets. 'Nature', Mill argues, has two meanings. Either the term denotes 'everything that happens'[22] or else it means simply that which happens without human agency. To enjoin anyone to follow nature in the first sense is meaningless, for no one can do otherwise. In the second sense, worse yet, it is immoral, for 'natural phenomena [are] replete with everything which when committed by human beings is most worthy of abhorrence'.[23] Anyone following nature in the second sense would be committing vicious crimes every waking moment.

The essay broaches a theme close to Mill's heart. Using 'nature' as a guide is ultimately to abandon reason – to be bound by custom and superstition. The result is moral, as well as intellectual, stagnation. If mankind is to be improved, what is useful, that is, what promotes happiness, must be the standard, not what is 'natural'. 'You look upon nature as something we should do well to follow', Mill reportedly told Spencer. 'I look upon nature as a horrible old harridan.'[24]

Mill is in fact aware that in urging someone to follow nature most people intend nothing more than to counsel prudence. To follow nature means to appreciate more fully the possible remote consequences of one's actions. Mill therefore insists that *naturam sequi* is an ethical, not a prudential, maxim; that not merely the intelligent adaptation of means to ends is intended, but the ends themselves are to be derived from nature.[25]

Without belabouring the issue, the understanding of nature expressed in this essay is at the core of Mill's 'Calvinism'. '[T]he duty of man is the same in respect to his own nature as in respect to the nature of all other things, namely not to follow but to amend it.'[26]

What good Nature brings humans 'is mostly the result of their own exertions'.[27] An appeal to duty recurs in the essay's final sentence: duty consists in 'striving to amend the course of nature – and bringing that part of it over which we can exercise control, more nearly into conformity with a high standard of justice and goodness'.[28]

At least one contemporary professed to hear echoes of the Kirk: 'No Calvinist', wrote Henry Reeve, in his review of the book in the *Edinburgh*, 'ever took a darker view than Mr Mill of this eternal conflict of Nature and Grace, only he calls it by another name: and we are not sure that something of the hereditary theology of Scotland does not lurk under all his philosophy.'[29] The deepest abyss separates Millean from Rousseauean romanticism: man is not naturally good; natural man lies, cheats, robs and murders. He is also cowardly and dirty.[30] Romanticism is cultivating the feelings and imagination, as unnatural an enterprise as cultivating a garden in a desert.

Ultimately, 'naturalness' cannot be an ethical standard because there is, for Mill, no human nature. The belief informs all his writings on social questions, and is perhaps stated no more explicitly than in another work written at this time, and also withheld from publication, *On the Subjection of Women*.

While Mill's essay spoke deeply to those who shared his belief that human character must evolve, he failed, naturally enough, to engage the question of the evolution of the species. What if Nature, and Nature's God, were indifferent to the fate of individuals precisely because their objective was the perfection of the race? Intent on flaying 'the Nature of theology', in Morley's phrase, Mill was unaware that 'the Nature of science' had usurped the throne of the former.[31]

Nonetheless, Mill's conclusions in 'Nature' are reconcilable with Darwinism, Morley believes, and he goes on to attempt to integrate them. What concerns Morley is the possibility that a belief in Darwinism would lead to fatalism and passivity. Morley assures himself that it does not. 'Human effort is the channel through which the transforming forces are poured. Human forethought, contrivance, energy, sociability, are the indispensable conditions of the continuance of the long process of development.'[32] Nonetheless,

> it can never be sufficiently deplored that the author did not find time to give us the result of his meditations as to the effect upon his own long-settled line of thought of the theory of Evolution and its moral and sociological applications.[33]

The deficiencies of Mill's second essay are somewhat more disturbing for Morley, though nothing as compared to the third. Morley feels that his erstwhile mentor has once again defined his subject too narrowly. If Mill's conception of 'nature' in the first essay ignored the theory of evolution, his understanding of 'religion' in the second neglects 'holiness', a no less significant omission.[34]

Mill's objective in the second essay is clearly to appeal to those who may privately doubt the truth of Christianity, but feel strongly that it nonetheless promotes both individual virtue and social stability – that it 'may be morally useful without being intellectually sustainable'.[35] He is addressing, in short, the *Edinburgh Review* crowd.

Predictably, Mill attempts to show that the benefits of religion are not intrinsic to it. This he does very cursorily;[36] he is mainly concerned with analysing *how* religion has effected what work it has done, for good or evil. He claims that in fact it derives its power from its being inculcated in childhood and enforced by public opinion – testimony to 'the influence of authority on the human mind'.[37] When public opinion supports behaviour religion forbids, such behaviour flourishes. Oaths, duelling and 'illicit sexual intercourse' are examples of such nominally proscribed conduct.[38] The threat of hell, Mill argues, is ineffective; God is understood to be either too venal or too merciful.

When Mill turns from the social utility of religion to explain its appeal to cultivated minds, his strategy is to demonstrate that poetry and the idealization of unborn men and women are sufficient to offer the consolations religion supplies. He begins with a (no doubt unintentional) sleight of hand. Poetry and religion both offer 'idealized conceptions grander and more beautiful than we see realized in the prose of human life'. However, 'religion, as distinguished from poetry, is the product of the craving to know whether these imaginative conceptions have realities answering to them in some other world than ours'.[39] This distinction is then jettisoned. As the argument proceeds, religion comes to consist in the 'elevated feelings' themselves. 'The essence of religion' is now simply 'the strong and earnest direction of the emotions and desires towards an ideal object, recognized as of the highest excellence, and as rightfully paramount over all selfish objects of desire'.[40] Mill is then able to ask if these elevated feelings cannot be induced by the contemplation of this-worldly possibilities. The answer, of course, is yes – given 'favourable circumstances', that is, indoctrination.

> If, then, persons could be trained... not only to believe in theory that the good of their country was an object to which all others ought

> to yield, but to feel this practically as the grand duty of life, so also may they be made to feel the same absolute obligation towards the universal good.[41]

Morality, in other words, may suffice.

Mill goes on to enumerate the advantages of what he now openly calls 'the Religion of Humanity': (1) it is disinterested – there are no promises or threats; (2) it does not demand the intellectual gyrations required of someone believing that God is at one and the same time omnipotent and benevolent. (Thornton's 'Manichaeism' is warmly recommended for its intellectual consistency.) The one advantage of supernatural religions – the promise of life after death – will be less significant as life on earth becomes happier.

Morley duly notes Mill's shifting definition of religion, but he finds that the essay suffers most not from lapses of logic, but from Mill's inexperience. Morality cannot be elevated into a religion because, quite simply, 'morality is not the essence of religion; is not its vital or constitutive element; does not give us the secret of its deep attachments in the human heart'.[42] In a lengthy and rather passionate excursus, Morley, the uncompromising rationalist, celebrates the 'religious emotions' of 'the *Imitatio*', Thomas à Kempis's *Imitation of Christ*. To read it merely as 'a guide to conscience' is 'to lose the whole soul of those divine musings, that ethereal meditation, those soft-glowing ecstasies, that passion of contemplation by the inmost eye'.[43] Morley never quite gets around to providing his own definition of religion. He implies, though, that religion consists in a more exalted emotional state than Mill conveys, and that such a state cannot be achieved by appeals to a code of conduct. One must presumably have either experienced God directly or have unshakeable faith in those claiming to be his intermediaries.

If Mill's 'Religion of Humanity' is a pale and attenuated thing, lacking the rich spirituality of Christian monasticism, his final essay, 'Theism', concedes altogether too much to the enemy, Morley argues.

'The Utility of Religion', to be sure, credited Christianity with exemplary moral teachings. Unfortunately, these had been contaminated with 'Paulism', which was responsible for beliefs in original sin and eternal damnation, in atonement and redemption, and in the acceptance of Christ's divinity as essential for salvation.[44] The moral teachings of Christianity were also undermined, as indicated, by the selfishness it inspired and the intellectual contortions it demanded. The injunctions of Christ, moreover, had been very nearly equalled by those of Marcus Aurelius and anticipated by the New Testament.

Some ten years later Christianity, and Christ in particular, were treated far more reverently. Even Nature was painted in softer, more flattering colours. Morley, who had been disinherited for his renunciation of orthodox Christianity, felt deeply betrayed. There is every reason to expect that in conversation, as in private letters, Mill had characterized Christianity quite differently.[45]

Mill's representation of Christ perhaps most irritated him. He commences with that, and then moves on to attack Mill's claims about God the Creator or *primum mobile*. With perfunctory apologies for seeming to 'disparage a lovely and noble character', Morley denies that Christ was as unique as Mill depicts him. He is particularly shocked by Mill's willingness to accept, however tentatively, that Christ was 'a man charged with a special, express and unique commission from God to lead mankind to truth and virtue'.[46] If the phrase would apply equally to Socrates, Confucius and others, then Mill 'for the first time in ... his whole life is doing nothing less than trifling with words'.[47] But if Mill does mean what he says, 'what becomes of sociology and the science of history?'[48] There is no point in attempting to discover laws of ethnological development if they can be arbitrarily violated by a Supreme Being. As Morley notes, Mill is more sceptical elsewhere even within 'Theism', claiming that Christianity arose 'by natural development' and that 'in pre-scientific times men always supposed that unusual faculties ... were an inspiration from God'.[49] Morley also strenuously resists Mill's attempt to distinguish Christ from his predecessors and followers. This is unhistoric[50] and does the disciples an injustice.[51] Once again Morley's chagrin may be intensified by his sense of personal betrayal.

Morley then goes on to question the value of Christ's teachings. Again he quotes Mill against himself. 'Many essential elements of the highest morality' are missing from Christianity. 'Other ethics ... must exist side by side with Christian ethics to produce the moral regeneration of mankind.'[52] In fact, to hold up Christ as the 'ideal representative and guide', one must read the New Testament very selectively. 'For any enlightened person of our day' many of Christ's sayings are 'morally objectionable and superstitious in the highest degree'.[53] Mill has unhistorically projected back a far more evolved morality on Jesus.

Turning to Mill's characterization of God, Morley objects, first, to the notion of a disembodied Mind, devoid of personality. This is to make of an unintelligible abstraction the superhuman agency of causation.

Morley objects still more vehemently to Mill's imputing a degree of benevolence to this supernatural Mind. Mill's modified Manicheism is merely a ploy to preserve God's goodness by sacrificing his omnipotence. Morley quotes the Mill of 'Nature' against that of 'Theism', and concludes that pretending to distinguish in the phenomenal world the work of a beneficent Mind and a neutral or ill-disposed Nature is to indulge in pure anthropomorphism.

Once again Morley has occasion to regret that Mill had not grappled with Darwinism, which, of course, supplies an alternative to the idea of an Intelligent Mind. Morley, nothing if not *au courant* in natural science, appeals additionally to the conservation principle, as adumbrated by Spencer – what Morley calls 'the persistence of Force and the Transformation and Equivalence of Forces'.[54] This postulate still further reduces the probability that a Divine Contriver tinkers with phenomena of which he is not a part.

Finally, Morley attacks Mill's vague hopes that 'the relation of thought to a material brain' is merely 'a constant co-existence within the limits of observation' and that it is therefore possible the soul is immortal.[55] Morley accuses Mill of espousing an antiquated and discredited Idealism, and concludes by warning those defenders of orthodoxy who might wish to use Mill against materialists that his argument leads equally to the doctrine of Metempsychosis as to the Immortality of the Soul.

After some 45 pages, Morley had not exhausted his objections to the *Essays*, and promised to return to the subject. He apparently never did, and refrained from republishing his two-part response to Mill. Even a couple of years after the article appeared, when he was actively contemplating reprinting it, he had begun to lose touch with the whole question. 'I am reprinting some of my essays from the Fortnightly, and among them one on Mill's essay on Theism', he wrote to James Scully. 'The line of objection to his views on the immortality of the soul has gone rather dead in my mind and I cannot now feel sure that my criticism is just or effective.' He asks Scully to 'just tell me plainly... whether you advise me to throw it away or print it'.[56]

The personal reasons for Morley's disengagement with the issue are beyond our purview, as are, indeed, the personal reasons contributing to his distress at Mill's essays. Hirst attributes Morley's subsequent lack of passion on metaphysical questions to (1) the change in the Zeitgeist during the 1880s (the shift in interest from religious to social questions), and (2) the fact that in important public policy debates – particularly in foreign affairs – Morley found himself allied with 'God-fearing Nonconformists' and opposed to agnostics.[57] While these reasons were no doubt significant (and the letter to Scully seems to testify to the first), Morley's political ambitions and his close association with the pious Gladstone may have provided more immediate motives.

As for Morley's sense of betrayal upon reading *Three Essays* (apart from their intellectual deficiencies), I have mentioned (1) the feeling of abandonment by one who had broken with his father at great personal cost, on account largely of ideas introduced to him by Mill, with whom he had subsequently enjoyed a warm, filial relationship, and (2) of less significance, Mill's reference to Christ's superiority to his disciples, after Mill had pointedly endowed Jesus with his own values. Whatever elements of subjectivity coloured Morley's response, it registers, I am arguing, a genuine drift on Mill's part from principles the two men shared. It is Mill's waywardness that needs explaining, not Morley's pained response.

5 Confounding Cairnes: Developments in Mill's Economic Thought

It is necessary to state at the outset that Mill does not experience a 'conversion' late in life to the historicism of Leslie or the relativism of Thornton.[1] There is no blinding light, no plunge from the Ricardian steed on the road to Damascus. Mill no more becomes an historicist than he becomes a Christian.

Rather, what one sees in his essays on economics during his final half dozen years is what one sees in 'Theism': confusion, equivocation, contradictions and arguments that sometimes lead him to conclusions he does not seem to have intended.

The case is different from that of 'Theism' in two important respects. Mill is not, at this stage of his life, attempting to make new contributions to economic theory, or even to reassess his own chief doctrines. His primary objective is to change the minds of readers about key political issues. Specifically, he seeks to gain their approval for policies and activities the opposition to which had been sanctioned, he believes, by appeals to the principles of political economy – viz., strikes and government regulation of rent. It is precisely because Mill's polemical objectives so overshadow his concern with theoretical niceties that the inconsistencies occur. In advancing on his enemies, he sometimes retreats from the *Principles*. Or more accurately, he feels obliged to sever his supply lines and resort to intermittent pillaging.

A second difference is that there is no systematic analysis of Mill's departures by a betrayed disciple. Nonetheless, the degree to which Cairnes was disturbed by some of Mill's analyses is clearly evident in a number of passages in *Leading Principles* and in his correspondence. Indeed, an unwary reader, picking up Cairnes's 1874 treatise, might be pardoned for assuming that one of its primary objectives was to expose Mill's false and mischievous reasoning. Mill's conception of cost – not a trivial issue – is

> radically unsound, confounding things in their own nature distinct and even antithetical, and setting in an essentially false light the

> incidents of production and exchange; further, I think it will appear that it leads to practical errors of a serious kind, not merely with regard to value, but also with regard to some other important doctrines of the science.[2]

Mill fares no better in the short run: 'Mr Mill's theory fails to explain the phenomenon of market price... Mr Mill's doctrine not merely fails to solve the problem of market price, but pointedly excludes from consideration conditions which are essential to the solution of that problem.'[3] The sarcasm continues: '[I]t cannot be denied that Mr Mill's position is logically impregnable. Unfortunately, however, the same limitations which render it logically impregnable make it also not worth defending; for... the doctrine becomes a mere identical proposition.'[4] Mill's recantation of the wages fund doctrine leaves Cairnes incredulous:

> I should have confidently asserted, I will not say that no economist, but that no reasonable being had ever advanced the theory of a Wages-fund in this sense [as Thornton represents it], if it had not been that Mr Mill had accepted the reasoning I have quoted as a refutation of that theory.[5]

Cairnes, furthermore, was clearly distressed by the passage in Mill's *Autobiography* in which his mentor labelled himself a Socialist. 'If to look forward to such a state of things [in which "society will no longer be divided into the idle and the industrious", etc.] as an ideal to be striven for is Socialism, I at once acknowledge myself a Socialist.'[6] The depth of Cairnes's irony would be fully apparent to *Fortnightly Review* readers (or readers of Cairnes's *Essays in Political Economy*) who recalled the brass-knuckled conclusion to his essay attacking (paradoxically) *laissez-faire*, where socialism is denounced as 'that rank growth of economic ignorance' which 'breeds despotism, and... issues in war, misery, and ruin'.[7]

To his friend and former student Leonard Courtney, Cairnes expressed his chagrin at Mill's *England and Ireland*: 'I have been much mortified by this last pamphlet of Mill.... [I]t will neither add to his influence nor help the settlement of Ireland. In fact the crudity of the scheme is, after all, that which most impresses one.'[8] (To Mill himself Cairnes was naturally more gracious, 'As I anticipated, I was not able to concur in your practical suggestions, though sympathizing in your views.'[9])

The political objectives that helped move Mill's economic doctrines in directions that disturbed Cairnes were straightforward – and largely shared by Cairnes: Mill hoped to assist workers and thwart landlords, to increase wages and reduce rents. These desires resulted in two collaborations with his 'heterodox' disciples: he supported (with reservations) Thornton's attack on the wages fund and Leslie's attack on private property in land (and, more important, the theoretic route to the latter's conclusions). Again, in neither case (despite what Mill himself would have readers believe in the first instance) was he breaking decisively with the *Principles*. Indeed one could hardly hope to come up with a more thoroughgoing rejection of landlords' claims than in some passages in Book II, Chapter 2, already cited.[10] And even in the renunciation of the wages fund, Mill travesties his own earlier views. Nonetheless, in both instances, as he pursues his analysis of the consequences of the applications he advocates, he runs into theoretical difficulties.

It is perhaps unnecessary to add that to criticize the way in which political concerns dictated *ad hoc* and sometimes problematic revisions in theory is not to criticize either those concerns themselves or the solutions Mill proposed. Clearly, relations between the working and the middle classes and between the Irish and the English would have improved had he been heeded.

I will first discuss Mill's articles on the wages fund and then on the land question. But perhaps no less telling is what Mill didn't write: in letters to and articles on Leslie and Thornton, he does not allude to clear-cut theoretical differences in the manner one would expect.[11] Granted, Mill was unfailingly polite; granted that he practised as well as advocated toleration. Still, he gives Leslie in particular the impression that he acquiesces in large measure in the latter's profound distrust of Ricardo.[12] Mill spends a considerable part of another letter criticizing Thornton for rejecting utility in his prefatory discussion of justice in the first of the *Fortnightly Review* articles that were to become *On Labour*.[13] But in no surviving correspondence does he take issue with, for instance, Thornton's jejune dismissal of the significance of supply and demand analysis, on which Thornton's attack on the wages fund is partly based, or any of his other claims.

I

The wages fund controversy is the subject of a large literature, and of continuing debate, Mill's recantation representing 'one of the most difficult problems in the history of economics'.[14] After being vilified for decades, the doctrine has been stoutly defended more recently by some of the most eminent historians of economic thought.[15] Whatever its merits, the ability of the theory to explain the wage rate is ultimately limited by its failure to recognize the role of worker productivity and of consumer demand in determining that rate, and the role of the price of labour in determining the real 'fund', wage capital.

The formulation of the doctrine differed from economist to economist, naturally. As in many controversies, at one extreme was a general definition which was true, but of very limited usefulness, and at another was a definition that was admirably specific, but thereby problematic. Forget has usefully characterized the first version as the 'wage fund identity' and the second as the 'wage fund theory'.[16]

The *identity* is the tautological macroeconomic proposition that the average wage depends on the amount of capital expended on labour divided by the number of labourers employed – the doctrine Jevons dismissed as 'simply a truism ... wholly illusory as a real solution of the problem'.[17] The *theory*, on the other hand, I believe can be summarized in the seven points below.

1. It assumes that industries operate in cycles of production analogous to harvest cycles. Workers are paid throughout the cycle, while capitalists are rewarded only at the end, at which time the whole of the wages fund has been exhausted. In other words, capital is allocated only at the start of the cycle, wages distributed regularly during its course, and profits received only at its termination. The demand for labour is therefore determined solely by the amount in the fund at the start of the cycle.
2. The supply of labour is determined simply by the number of workers; 'labour' is uniform and homogeneous. (There is even confusion, in some instances, between working and total population.) If the wage fund is the numerator, the denominator is the number of workers multiplied by the annual cost of subsistence (albeit determined as much by culture as physiology). In other words, a short-run production cycle – of about a year – is linked to a long-run reproductive cycle of, presumably, something like ten to fifteen years, the time between the conception of a child and his or her entering the labour market.
3. The theory assumes that wages and profits are inversely proportional, the former determining the latter, and being determined in turn, in the long run, by the cost of producing food on the most

marginal acreage. Average wages, therefore, can't be raised at the expense of rent, nor can the aggregate increases be passed along to consumers. A general rise in prices is impossible. Wage gains always come at the expense of profits.

4. Furthermore, the ratio of profits to wages, though varying somewhat from industry to industry, remains constant. Capitalists cannot, in the long run, divert less to themselves, thus increasing the fund. This is sometimes a consequence of regarding wages in terms of wage goods – grain – rather than money wages, but it more generally reflects the belief that only one rate of profit can prevail in the country, in the long run, and capital will flee investments generating below-market returns.
5. As one would also expect, one wage rate prevails throughout the country, other than differences attributable to the varying risks or disutilities of different jobs. Thus, 'artificial' fluctuations are speedily redressed through competition: just as capital flows to industries with relatively high profits, labour migrates to those with relatively high wages, restoring equilibrium. Short-term wage gains brought about by union activity – if wages were already at their 'natural' level – mean unemployment or falling wages in the long term.
6. Like the ratio of profit and wages, the ratio of fixed to circulating capital is similarly constant. (Or, alternatively, capital inputs apart from wage goods are ignored.)
7. The usual Ricardian *ceteris paribus* assumptions apply: throughout the production cycle, costs of production and worker productivity are constant, as is the money supply, consumer demand, etc.[18]

The controversy is easiest to untangle if we approach it from the standpoint of what Mill hoped to accomplish. What was objectionable in the doctrine, from his perspective, was what led to cynicism or despair about the efficacy of strikes – and hence to the discrediting of political economy in the eyes of labourers. Two postulates were responsible.

The first was the proposition that the wages fund was not merely determinate but predetermined: that there was a fixed amount of capital that could not be exceeded. Apologists for employers routinely, and illegitimately, moved from a macro to a micro context, arguing that because the wages fund had already been arrived at, they themselves, representing an individual firm or industry, could not afford to raise wages and risk violating an economic law. Thornton simply turned the argument on its head. The wages fund was indeed composed of discrete individual funds. But employers, he argued, clearly have discretion over these – they can take more or less for themselves and their family, as they choose. Since the wage fund is merely the aggregate of such arbitrary sums, it could not be said to be predetermined.[19] Thornton thus expressed the fund in monetary rather than real terms; actual wages are confused with capital.

Mill, despite explicit caveats in the *Principles*, follows Thornton's logic here.[20] He even improves on the latter's caricature of the doctrine, arguing that the wages fund in fact implied unitary elasticity – that employers dutifully exhausted the entire fund whatever the cost of labour.[21] Of course in most versions it stipulated no such thing.

If, then, there is no pre-ordained amount, what actually determines the workers' share? 'Competition', says Thornton.[22] But the competition among employers is very imperfect: workers are at a distinct disadvantage for three reasons: (a) 'labour won't keep' – workers, because they are unable to save and, being human, have pressing physiological needs, can't hold out the way wealthy employers can.[23] (b) The labour market is anomalous in a second way: sellers normally set prices, not buyers, who are generally unorganized and more needy than dealers. In the labour market, however, this is reversed – and the sellers, moreover, vastly outnumber the buyers.[24] (c) Shrewd employers avail themselves of these natural advantages. They do not, as a rule, compete, but enter into formal and informal combinations. This is really the strongest argument (albeit hardly a novel one) against simple-minded applications of the wages fund doctrine, and Mill endorses it: as the conditions of a free market do not obtain for labour, workers are obliged to form combinations of their own.[25]

Thornton, however, presents the case summarized above as an afterthought, preferring to parade at great length his specious refutations of the law of supply and demand. These consist of a series of examples positing small markets with idiosyncratic (inflexible or congruent) demand schedules on the part of buyers.[26] Alternatively, in a couple of examples, Thornton stipulates that to clear a market, everything offered for sale must be sold – that no price is extramarginal and that equilibrium is achieved instantly. Mill patiently demolishes Thornton's proofs.[27]

The reason the wages fund was determinate, its defenders argued, had to do ultimately with the liquidity of capital. If the profit rate dropped too low as the wage rate increased, capital would flow out of the industry affected to more lucrative employments. Wages, perforce, would decline. The reasoning followed from the zero-sum game Ricardian political economy posited: profits were determined by the wage rate.

If Thornton didn't recognize this problem, Mill did, and attempted to tiptoe around it. In order to claim that raising wages would not lower profits – the only conclusion, given his principles – Mill reverts from the long term to the short term, logically following his switch from a real to a monetary conception of the fund, from capital to individual wage bills. The legerdemain consists of representing what is a short-term possibility as a long-term probability: that wages could conceivably consume all of the employer's capital.[28] Mill must ignore not only the dictum that capital seeks the highest rate of return, but the so-called Ricardo effect as well – that wage increases tend to result in the substitution of fixed for wage capital. There is an additional problem: an increase in the fund at the employer's discretion would simply raise prices of wage goods (their supply being fixed) while it lowered the price of capitalists' goods – 'luxuries'. The real wage rate would thus stay the same.[29]

First, Mill seeks to represent the wages fund as 'co-extensive with the whole proceeds of his business, after keeping up his machinery, buildings and materials, and feeding his family' – a crude conflation of profits, circulating capital and fixed capital. He then claims, in typically qualified language, that

> there is no law of nature making it inherently impossible for wages to rise to the point of absorbing not only the funds which he had intended to devote to carrying on his business, but the whole of what he allows for his private expenses, beyond the necessaries of life.[30]

The 'real limit' he dismisses as a 'practical consideration' and 'not the inexorable limits of the wages-fund'.[31] But of course the wages fund did not purport to speculate about the whims of individual employers or investors. It only assumed that, at the macro level, fresh capital will tend not to flow to firms failing to return the average rate of profit.

The second grim consequence of the wages fund doctrine that Mill feels obliged to deny is a no less important classical axiom. Just as wage gains will inevitably affect profits, the two being inversely correlated, so gains will similarly affect future employment within a given firm. If the price of labour goes up, less will be demanded.

This reality (for a believer in classical or neo-classical political economy) inspires a particularly bold ploy – or serious lapse – on Mill's part: he denies the elasticity of the demand for labour. Where he earlier stigmatized the wages fund doctrine for assuming unitary elasticity, he now himself suggests there is zero elasticity.[32] He again couches his claim in very qualified language: 'A fall of wages does not necessarily make him expect a larger sale for his commodity, nor, therefore, does it necessarily increase his demand for labour.'[33] Mill is again suggesting that a short-run possibility can be sustained over the long run.[34]

Inevitably, Mill is obliged to retract this dubious claim, and this involves him in some moral discomfort in the second of his two articles on Thornton. If there were a possibility of a general strike, all wages would go up. Prices, however, would not do so, absent an increase in the money supply. The rise would come solely at the expense of profits – to which Mill would, of course, have no objection.[35] The wage gains cannot be passed along to consumers. But in reality, as Mill grudgingly admits, strikes affect specific firms and industries. In consequence, consumers and other workers can indeed suffer. (Characteristically, Mill has nothing to say about consumers, and never acknowledges that labourers are, in fact, also consumers.) Mill is thus forced to confront a dilemma he was never able to resolve in the *Principles*.

Trade unions, he acknowledged in Book II, Chapter 14, can enable skilled workers to isolate themselves from their class and enjoy a higher standard of living (by exercising sexual restraint, naturally).[36] But Mill could not decide how he felt about this. As Hafer and West point out, and Robson's footnotes document, in the first and second editions, Mill endorsed the trade union movement: '...I should rejoice if by trade regulations, or even by trades unions, the employments thus specially protected could be multiplied to a much greater extent than experience has shown to be practicable.'[37] But in the 1852 and 1857 editions (the third and fourth), Mill deleted the sentences and unequivocally condemned the monopolistic practices of unions.

> The time, however, is past when the friends of human improvement can look with complacency on the attempts of small sections of the community, whether belonging to the labouring or any other class, to organize a separate class interest in antagonism to the general body of labourers, and to protect that interest by shutting out... all competitors from their more highly paid departments.[38]

Sometime between 1857 and 1862, however, probably after his wife's death, Mill decided once again that trades unions weren't so bad after all, despite the external costs:

> What at first seems the injustice of excluding the more numerous body from sharing the gains of a comparatively few, disappears when we consider that by being admitted they would not be made better off, for more than a short time; the only permanent effect which their admission would produce, would be to lower the other to their own level.[39]

This appraisal was retained in all subsequent editions.

At this point, however, the innocent reader is referred to Mill's discussion of the Combination Laws. These are taken up in Book V. Readers of the first two editions were assured that 'combinations to keep up wages are therefore not only permissible, but useful, whenever really calculated to have that effect' – a fairly warm endorsement, whatever the last phrase may mean.[40] When Mill decided in the early 1850s that such practices were anti-social, probably influenced by his wife, he excised the passage and substituted a lengthy paragraph. The grounds for his disapproval are essentially that (1) the elevation of *all* workers is now becoming feasible, and class solidarity will assist this development, and (2) thinking exclusively in terms of one's own wages has a bad effect on one's character. 'Success,' he concludes, 'even if attainable, in raising up a protected class of working people, would now be a hindrance, instead of a help, to the emancipation of the working classes at large.'[41] Unfortunately, this objection to strikes was retained *even after* 1857, so that in all remaining editions, he strongly recommends a practice in Book II that he condemns in Book V.

Things get more muddled still. After defending the right of trades unions to strike, though efforts are 'seldom effectual, and when effectual... seldom desirable',[42] Mill compounds the confusion by then noting that supply and demand do not 'thrust a given amount of wages into a labourer's hand without the participation of his own will and actions'. After several rhetorical questions, he works himself up to the declaration that 'trades unions, far from being a hindrance to a free market for labour, are the necessary instrumentality of that free market'.[43] Censured in one paragraph as 'a hindrance... to the emancipation of the working class' and 'seldom desirable', unions are hailed a paragraph later as 'a valuable part of the existing machinery of society'.[44] But then, a paragraph later, when he gets around to examining the demands of the Amalgamated Society of Engineers, the most powerful and influential trade union at the time, he is horrified: its objectives

> are pernicious. Their success, even when only partial, is a public mischief; and were it complete, would be equal in magnitude to almost any of the evils arising from bad economical legislation. Hardly anything worse can be said of the worst laws on the subject of industry.[45]

Mill was obliged to have one more go at the problem in the second article on Thornton.

In Part I, Mill's discussion of the wages fund is preceded by a detailed and highly critical analysis of Thornton's attempt to refute the law of supply and demand. Similarly, in the opening section of Part II, Mill takes issue with an even more provocative position Thornton adopts: his recourse, in Mill's eyes, to arguments derived from 'intuitive' assumptions about natural rights.[46] Never one to resist such bait, Mill makes the case for utilitarianism once again.[47]

When Mill once more turns to the wages fund, he offers the familiar proposition that within upper and lower limits, the wage level is indeterminate, depending on 'the higgling of the market'.[48] Then, after discussing the impact of a general increase in wages, he acknowledges that, in the case of specific industries, a rise in the price of one commodity – if a 'necessity' – will inevitably diminish demand for others, and that the producers of commodities now suddenly extra-marginal will suffer, particularly those workers not in a position to force up their wages. The impact of unions on would-be workers *within* the unionized trade is still more dire and immediate: 'there is no keeping up wages without limiting the number of competitors for employment'.[49] Thus, Mill quietly drops the notion that the demand for labour is inelastic. Indeed he concedes that if the increased price of an article results in reduced consumption, and if the wages in that industry don't correspondingly decline, 'employers, weary of having less profit than other people, [may] withdraw part of their capital'.[50]

Of the 'two considerations, either of which, in the mind of an upright and public spirited working man, may fairly legitimate his adhesion to Unionism', one, he concedes on further reflection – building a national union piecemeal – may be 'too remote, and even visionary to be an actuating motive'.[51] The second, while plausible, is sufficiently cynical that Mill promptly distances himself from it by attributing it to 'an intelligent Unionist':[52]

> The ignorant and untrained part of the poorer classes (such Unionist may say) will people up to the point which will keep their wages at that miserable rate which the low scale of their ideas and habits makes endurable to them. As long as their minds remain in their present state, our preventing them from competing with us for employment does them no real injury; it only saves ourselves from being brought down to their level. Those whom we exclude are a morally inferior class of labourers to us.[53]

However uncomfortable with this bit of Social Darwinism *avant la lettre*, Mill nonetheless defends the 'less elevated but not fallacious point of view' by arguing that the pursuit of narrow self-interest among unionists is 'not more culpable in them than is the same indifference in classes far more powerful and more privileged by society'.[54] He then hastily cites the support of unionists for universal and compulsory education as evidence that 'the brutish ignorance of the lowest order of unskilled labourers has no more determined enemies... than the comparatively educated workmen who direct the Unions'.[55] But no sooner has he gallantly defended unionism, than Mill finds himself vigorously censuring the numerous union practices which impair efficiency. Mill then appears to perform another *volte face*, justifying such measures as 'weapons of war, like the devastation of a country and the slaughter of its innocent inhabitants – things abominable in themselves, but which may unhappily be the only means of forcing a powerful adversary to consent to just terms of accommodation'.[56] He eventually grasps on to that favourite flotation device, co-operation, which carries him safely to the end of the review. Seemingly unsure as to whether he has not done more harm than benefit to the unionist cause, Mill concludes with a long, soaring quotation from Thornton to re-establish the latter's – and Mill's own – warm feelings for unions.

To summarize, Mill wants to make the case that strikes and combinations can actually raise wages, without decreasing employment and raising the price of consumer goods in the long run. In order to do this, he asserts the following: (1) that there is no fixed fund at the start of the production cycle determining how much can be spent on labour;

(2) rather, there is a continuous flow of income (he abandons the notion that the fund consists of real wage goods), and the way this income is proportioned between profits and wages is indeterminate, a function of 'higgling'; (3) the demand for labour is inelastic in the short run – insensitive to price: higher wages will not result in fewer workers being hired or increased investment in fixed capital; (4) wage increases cannot be passed along to the consumer, but must come out of profits – even, apparently, for individual firms and sectors in the short run; (5) but employers and investors, happily, are not as sensitive to profit rates as is generally assumed, though they want enough to feed and clothe their families.

Mill encounters two obvious problems. (a) He doesn't really believe in the third claim, and winds up covertly abandoning it in Part II. The demand curve is not inelastic – employers don't hire labourers irrespective of their cost. Higher wages will result in unemployment. He justifies this outcome by a pejorative representation of the character of the workers likely to be affected, 'a morally inferior class'. (b) The fifth claim obliges Mill to deny the long-run impact of wage increases on the accumulation of capital (and hence, on the long-run demand for labour) – without completely convincing himself.

Thus, as West and Hafer argue, Mill's chief objective – to repudiate the idea that it is impossible for unions to raise wages in the long run – was accomplished with an insidious twist. Unions can indeed raise wages, but for a shrunken population in which unfit and improvident workers don't survive; unionists limit family size, so wage rates remain high. 'Unions', West and Hafer cynically conclude, 'were a means of population control'.[57]

Marshall's objection seems warranted: Mill conceded too much that was valid in the doctrine.[58] As Schwartz complains, instead of trying to determine why the demand for labour might fluctuate in a firm or industry – and thus arrive at the concept of the marginal value product of labour, or at least integrate into his explanation the price and productivity of labour, and anticipated consumer demand for the augmented product – Mill retreats to the aggregate level, where he invokes the Ricardian principle that 'profits depend upon wages'.[59]

In the opinion of most historians of economic thought, any emendation of the wages fund doctrine which did not point toward a marginal productivity theory of distribution was a net loss.[60] Mill's recantation did nothing to enhance his reputation as a theorist.

Two distinct questions have been asked about Mill's motives: first, why did he do it, and second, why did he see fit to travesty his own previous representation of the relation of wages and capital?

The first of these questions has long been satisfactorily accounted for. Most commentators agree that, in Marshall's words, Mill 'allowed his zeal for giving a more human tone to economics to get the better of his judgment'[61] – a 'human tone' presumably meaning a humane outlook, one sympathetic, in particular, to trade unions.[62] Mill was influenced, in short, by political considerations.[63]

The second question, why Mill should misrepresent his own position, is trickier to answer. What makes the problem particularly puzzling is that neither Mill, nor his father, nor Ricardo, nor McCulloch originally used the doctrine to attack trades unionism. Senior, who rejected the classical definition of the fund, was considerably more hostile to unions.[64] Rather, as many historians have observed, the formula was invariably employed to urge workers to limit the size of their families. What seems to have been on Mill's mind in particular when he wrote about wages in the *Principles*, some twenty years before the recantation, was to exculpate his father and Ricardo for having egregiously confused 'productive' labour with the whole of the population.[65]

Cairnes described it as 'perplexing' that Mill should have accepted Thornton's caricature of the wages fund, in lieu of Book II, Chapter 11. Critics have generally attributed Mill's acquiescence to forgetfulness and confusion.[66]

Forget has broken new ground in implicitly linking the two questions – why Mill not only attacked common representations of the wages fund, but issued his unwarranted *mea culpa*. A formal recantation was simply the best strategy to legitimate trades union claims: it would attract the most attention. In other words, not absent-mindedness, but cool logic, and commitment, dictated Mill's decision.[67] Forget's interpretation is supported by the fact that Mill, in the final edition of the *Principles*, did not alter anything that he had written on wages. But if her analysis is convincing, one might go even further.

'There is in the doctrine I maintain [utilitarianism] nothing inconsistent with the loftiest estimation of the heroism of martyrs. There are times when ... martyrdom may be a duty.'[68] What was attractive about Christ to the sexagenarian Mill was that his 'pre-eminent genius is combined with the qualities of probably the greatest moral reformer, and martyr to that mission, who ever existed upon earth'.[69] It would be ludicrous to push the analogy too far. Nonetheless, the strong strain of altruism in Mill's character (the word, of course, was coined by Comte) is likely to have contributed to the decision to recant. It was a trait, as we have seen, that opponents as well as allies observed and commented on. Attributing to Mill 'a generosity that might almost be called romantic', Herbert Spencer concluded that the 'extreme desire to further human welfare was that to which he sacrificed himself'.[70]

Of course Mill would have assumed that he was not permanently endangering his great reputation in claiming that his theory of wages had been inaccurate. He could not have guessed, however, that the recantation itself would inflict greater damage on that reputation, and would go some way to confirm the familiar image of him (not necessarily an entirely pejorative one) that will likely survive all attempts to discover coherence and consistency in his thought: that of a man whose heart periodically over-ruled his head.

II

In the case of unions, it was the *efficacy* of their actions that needed to be defended. The Combination Act of 1800 had been repealed in 1824, though the scope of union activities was again restricted the following year. The Molestation of Workmen Act in 1859 reinstated picketing, and the Master and Servant Act of 1867 expanded the protection of strikers. By the time Mill responded to Thornton, despite the Hornby vs Close decision of 1866, which jeopardized union funding, middle-class writers did not question the right to strike as much as its value.[71] While briefly defending this right in the *Principles*, Mill did not bother to do so in his articles on Thornton.

Land reform in Ireland, however, turned in part on a question of right. Could the abrogation of contracts by the government be justified? Mill was more than happy to join this issue, armed with Leslie's and Maine's accounts of the origins of private property. But the case against land reform also rested on questions of utility, and appealed to well-known principles of classical political economy. Writers opposing peasant proprietorships invoked the doctrine of economies of scale and, inevitably, the population principle: small holdings were both inefficient and liable to become 'rabbit-warrens'. They offered incentives neither to scientific farming nor to prudence. Mill's strategy was to reject both of these arguments on empirical grounds, with the help of Leslie, Thornton and other witnesses.

Thus, when Mill late in life addressed the wage question, his discussion was almost wholly theoretical: what did sound economic doctrines about capital, he asked, really imply about union activities? The strategy to justify land reform, however, was rather different. The questions Mill appears to be asking here are, how must we revise, or limit the applications of, theory in light of (1) empirical evidence, and two things more important than maximizing wealth and optimizing distribution, (2) considerations of justice and (3) the improvement of mankind through the elevation of morals? The third goal is never far from Mill's mind, of course, and enters briefly into his case for unions: union activities help inform workers about commerce and industry, and in enlarging their perspectives, pave the way for co-operation.[72] And when arguing *against* unions in specific trades or industries, he also invokes an extra-economic criterion – the selfish focusing on one's own wages retards the progress of mankind.[73] Nonetheless, the progress of mankind is much more to the front and centre in Mill's discussions of peasant proprietorship. Similarly, Mill's occasional writings, insofar as they are informed by utilitarian ethics, are always animated by the quest for justice. What is distinctive about the arguments Mill makes on the land question is the appeal to non-utilitarian standards: rights based on customs, on antecedent practices, are freely invoked.

Departures from prior arguments do not necessarily represent mental lapses or disingenuousness. What is missing from Mill's late polemical writing on land is a clear recognition of the implications of his arguments, and how they refine, or contravene, earlier claims.

Apart from any new difficulties Mill introduces in his work on land reform, he had an opportunity, when he addressed the issue, to resolve earlier inconsistencies. Just as Mill in his essays on Thornton might have cleared up the contradiction between Book II, Chapter 14, and Book V, Chapter 10, so, in his reviews of Leslie and Maine, he had a chance to make up his mind on a no less glaring inconsistency between Book II, Chapters 6 and 7, and Book IV, Chapter 7. The former chapters sing the praises of peasant proprietorship:

> no other existing state of agricultural economy has so beneficial an effect on the industry, the intelligence, the frugality, and the prudence of the population, nor tends on the whole so much to discourage an improvident increase of their numbers; and that no existing state, therefore is on the whole so favourable both to their moral and their physical welfare.[74]

Some 450 pages later, the judgement is quite reversed. Proprietorships are a reactionary vestige standing squarely in the way of the elevation of mankind:

> But a people who have once adopted the large system of production, either in manufactures or in agriculture, are not likely to recede from it; and . . . it is not desirable that they should. Labour is unquestionably more productive on the system of large industrial enterprises; the produce if not great absolutely, is greater in proportion to the labour employed . . . . And in the moral aspect of the question, which is still more important than the economical, something better should be aimed at as the goal of industrial improvement, than to disperse mankind over the earth in single families, each ruled internally, as families now are, by a patriarchal despot, and having scarcely any community of interest, or necessary mental communion, with other human beings.[75]

It does not take a particularly practiced ear to detect in this passage the voice of Harriet Taylor; and indeed, the quotation is from the chapter 'On the Probable Futurity of the Labouring Classes' that is 'entirely due to her'.[76] It is quite likely that Mill's earlier sentiments on peasant proprietorship were partially indebted to, and reinforced by Thornton, with whom Mill conversed daily while at India House. In the essays, as in the *Principles*, Mill freely acknowledges his debt to his friend's *Overpopulation and its Remedy* (1846) and its sequel, *A Plea for Peasant Proprietors* (1848). Mill's initial conversion to the cause of the peasant proprietor was also influenced, as Dewey notes, by the work of Richard Jones.[77] So in moving closer to his 'heterodox' followers during his sixties, he was also, on this issue (as with trade unions), parting company with his wife, who would probably have endorsed Marx's famous sentiments about 'the idiocy of rural life'.

Thus, prior to the changes beginning in the mid–1860s, Mill's thought on the subject had already evolved twice. After believing in economies of scale, he becomes convinced in the mid–1840s that small holdings – owing to the way ownership energizes the faculties, and improves morals, if not manners – might be nearly as efficient as larger farms, and more beneficial. But by 1848 Mill had moved some way back toward his earlier position, having perceived reactionary qualities in the independent yeoman-farmer he had previously celebrated.

Converting tenants to owners would take decades. In the meantime, what was to be done with rents? Mill had addressed the issue of fixing rents in the *Principles*, but in a typically equivocal way. Indeed, Mill's hedging on the issue of fixing rents, in Book II, Chapter 10, is almost comic. After conceding, in the conditional past tense, that 'there would not have been any injustice' in fixity of tenure 'provided the landlords were compensated', Mill draws up short: 'This, however, would have been . . . a complete expropriation of the higher classes of Ireland' – he pauses to reconsider – 'which, if there is any truth in the principles we have laid down, would be perfectly warrantable' – the momentary indignation subsiding, he reconsiders again – 'but only if it were the sole means of effecting a great public good'. He goes on to give other reasons militating against the proposals of the Repeal Association.[78]

In 1867 Mill's position shifted dramatically – though in this case without a formal recantation.[79] In no uncertain terms, *England and Ireland* endorses the fixing of tenure.[80] A commission would immediately determine rents throughout the country, which would be paid to and received from 'the national treasury': 'There must be compulsory powers.'[81] The essay's fervent tone may have given nearly as much offence as its contents.

In rationalizing the legislation he advocates, Mill effortlessly couples Ricardian with historicist arguments. After trundling out the distinction between landed and moveable capital once again,[82] he goes on to consider the conditions on which private property in land depend: these are cultural, 'rooted in the traditions and oldest recollections of the people'.[83] In a lengthy passage, he appeals to pre-Conquest conceptions of land, tribe and chief as the warrant for land tenure legislation. At the end of the peroration, he acknowledges that he has been arguing 'according to the received doctrines of our historical Conservatives',[84] but this appears to faze him not in the least.

Cairnes, regrettably, did not enlarge on his disparaging comments on the essay either to Courtney or to Mill. Naturally, Mill stopped well short of urging Irish independence; he argues at some length against it, in fact.[85] So Mill's innocent belief that he could 'see nothing that Ireland could gain by separation which might not be obtained by union, except the satisfaction, which she is thought to prize, of being governed solely by Irishmen' could not have been the 'crudity' Cairnes responded to, as he fully shared the sentiments.[86]

The pamphlet's tone may have been too overwrought for Cairnes's taste. But the sketchiness of the proposal to fix rents is likely to have been the chief objection, as well as Mill's failure to express any reservations about – or to suggest checks upon, or oversight of – the commission's work. It is Mill's 'scheme', after all, that Cairnes criticizes in his letter to Courtney, and, he tells Mill, the 'practical suggestions', with which he is 'not able to concur'.[87] More than likely, Cairnes continued to share the reservations to wholesale expropriation that Mill had carefully expressed in the *Principles* – especially to the degree that these reflected, in the 1865 edition, his own painstaking notes on Ireland.[88] And Cairnes may have been troubled by so heavy a reliance on historicist arguments, arguments that made as little appeal to utility or to economic principles as they did to the evidence he had amassed for Mill.

In 1870 Mill, now happily (in his view) retired by the Westminster electors, chose to reconsider the implications of the Irish Land Question for economic theory in a review of Cliffe Leslie's *Land Systems and Industrial Economy of Ireland, England, and Continental Countries* that was the lead article in the June *Fortnightly Review*.

The essay purports to discuss methodology at the outset, opening with an invidious comparison between 'those who have carried on the work of the masters, and those who think that the masters have left them no work to do'.[89] The difference appears to lie in the way in which assumptions are conceived as well as applied. Mill's opponents use 'catch-words' or 'formulae'; his allies deploy 'principles'. But the chief difference is in the way these generalizations are used: for Mill's opponents they have great explanatory power. The claims don't need to be validated. For the legitimate students of political economy, however, principles are 'helps to thought'.[90] Their validity is not assumed; they are tested by an analysis of the 'circumstances'.

The problems with this pleasing formula are obvious. Principles are not hypotheses. The a priori method Mill recommended (which in fact combines induction and deduction – 'the Inverse Deductive Method')[91] culminates in laws – predictions of outcomes, given certain conditions – and not a series of open questions.[92] Though he seems poised to do so, Mill is not about to follow Leslie in denying the validity of Ricardian generalizations about the correlation of wages, profit and prices, and their respective movements.

The burden of Mill's charges is that his opponents have derived universal maxims from 'English customs': the product of particular historical conditions has been deemed applicable in all times and places. The 'customs' indiscriminately applied are, naturally, those legitimating private property: the recognition of the right of individuals to freely dispose of land and goods they have come to possess. Mill is interested in rebutting the utilitarian justification for this: that the self-interest thus stimulated coincides with 'the general interest of the community'.[93] His second argument, after criticizing his opponents' methodology, thus consists of a demonstration that small holdings secured by legislation are likely to be more productive. First, though, he makes several familiar appeals to his audience's conception of justice, concluding that land is a monopoly showering wealth 'down upon landlords without any exertion or sacrifice of their own' and thus the state has both a right and duty to regulate ownership for the public good.[94]

The main line of argument, however, is that private ownership of land does not maximize productivity, for which claim he cites Leslie:

> It is as contrary to political economy as to common sense to assume that a rich sinecure makes its possessor industrious and improving; and the landholders of this country are the holders, not only of rich sinecures, but of sinecures the value of which tends steadily, and often rapidly, to increase without any exertion on their part.[95]

Thus, 'the self-interest of the landlords frequently operates to frustrate, instead of promoting, the interest which the community has in the most effective use of the productive powers of the soil'. Luckily, 'there is another party concerned whose self-interest does work in that useful direction; and that is, the actual cultivator of the soil'.[96] But 'security of tenure is indispensable to enlist the self-interest of the occupier of land on the side of good cultivation'. And in Ireland this cannot 'be trusted to the operation of contract'.[97]

Mill recognizes that an argument on utilitarian grounds calls for empirical evidence that peasant proprietorship can indeed be more productive than large holdings, particularly in light of the presumption (vigorously asserted by McCulloch) that economies of scale suggest otherwise. The evidence he culls from Leslie, however, is less than convincing. It consists of the observations of two individuals, one anonymous, who testify that (1) the consolidation of farms has led to an extension of grazing and the exhaustion of the soil (this is supplemented by a reference to an essay by Lyon Playfair), and (2) that, in at least one instance, Irish peasants in a southern county – an English landlord's 'good example being followed by his tenants' – now farm efficiently, using £25,000 worth of manure a year.[98]

Mill next feels compelled to take on a rival prescription for Ireland's misfortune – emigration. Again citing Leslie, Mill contradicts the suggestion he made the previous year, in his first essay on Thornton, that the short-run demand for labour is inelastic, and, hence, wage gains don't affect employment. Here he argues 'as a matter of science' that even a small rise in the price of labour may have a significant impact on its demand, thus offsetting the gains to workers that a decrease in their numbers might be expected to bring.[99] Workers' wages have, in fact, increased recently, but the rise is nominal, not real: the price of consumer goods has risen in tandem, owing to (1) inflation caused by recent gold discoveries and, in a rather breathtaking repudiation of the case for free trade, to (2) 'the railways, which have everywhere so greatly increased the price of agricultural produce in what were once, from the inaccessibility of markets, the cheap regions of the world'.[100]

The final line of argument Mill pursues, no less problematically, is a straightforward historicist case. There are two land questions, Mill notes: 'in Ireland it is a tenant's question ... in England it is mainly a labourer's question'.[101] But in turning to England, the attempt to compile data demonstrating the comparative efficiency of small over large holdings – limited as it was – is abandoned. Instead, drawing on Thornton's *Overpopulation and Its Remedy* as well as Leslie's book, Mill concentrates on disputing the *right* of great landowners to maintain their estates, retreating from the claims of utility to equity. His argument is historical: sturdy yeomen were dispossessed, commons seized and local markets obliterated once the landed gentry and nobility consolidated their power.

The shift in rationales reflects, in part, a change in political objectives. In England, unlike in Ireland, a goal close to Mill's heart was the preservation of common land. Indeed, through his lobbying on behalf of the Commons Preservation Society, he is credited with preserving Epping Forest.[102]

Mill concludes his argument based on historic injustices with a rather dubious assessment of English agriculture. Writing in 1870, he condemns its 'complete ... failure' to improve 'the condition of the mass of population'.[103] He offers no empirical evidence to support this claim.

Mill then returns to the agricultural labourer question. After surveying Leslie's solutions, Mill admonishes his friend for his caution: free trade in land is not sufficient. More land put up for sale means more land for the rich.

> If the greater marketableness of land is to be made a benefit to the labouring class, it must be in another manner entirely; as, for example, by buying from time to time on account of the public, as much of the land that comes into the market as may be sufficient to give a full trial to such modes of leasing it, either to small farmers with due security of tenure, or to co-operative associations of labourers.[104]

To return to the methodological question he raises at the outset, Mill appears to be substituting one set of axioms for another: viz., when cultivators own the land, it is more productive. Nor does he abjure from the practice of advocating specific policy prescriptions in the name of political economy: 'The absolute power of landlords over the soil is what political economy really condemns'.[105] Moreover, his argument that the success of small-scale farming in Belgium is relevant to the situation in Ireland necessitates the same kind of mechanistic reasoning he deplores in his opening paragraphs. He must dismiss appeals to 'climate and other causes' that differentiate the two regions.[106] Yet these 'other causes' are precisely the customs, habits and values that historicists like Leslie inevitably appealed to. Again, Mill's political predispositions, and his cast of mind, enabled him to embrace the conclusions while only incompletely appropriating the methodology of his anti-Ricardian allies.

The extent to which Mill was willing to go to sacrifice theoretical consistency to advocacy is also revealed in his review of Maine's *Village Communities in the East and West*.[107] Mill announces at the outset that although *Ancient Law* was not written 'for any such purpose', it 'is a most powerful solvent of a large class of conservative prejudices'.[108] Whereas, for Mill, *Ancient Law* demonstrated that 'institutions and ideas belonging to past times have been unduly prolonged into an age to which they are unsuitable', *Village Communities* reveals, conversely, that 'old institutions and ideas have been set aside in favour of others of comparatively modern origin'. Both insights undermine the tendency 'to accept the existing order of things as final'.[109]

There follows a summary of the way the Marks of the Teutonic village, the three categories of communal land, were transformed into manorial holdings by feudal lords. Mill dismisses in a sentence the beneficent effects of the 'conversion of collective to individual property', while, oddly, conveying the impression that this was something freely chosen after lengthy debate.[110] After detailing the 'disgraceful' (as opposed to the 'honourable') 'side of the movement', Mill arrives at the unimpeachable conclusion that because the present property system 'is not the oldest form', therefore 'there is no natural necessity for its being preferred to all other forms'.[111] 'The nation' would thus be justified in suspending, or even reversing, the transformation of collective to individual ownership.[112]

Mill's admirable objective is the preservation of commons, points 8 and 9 of the Land Tenure Reform Association's programme and the *raison d'être* of the Commons Preservation Society. But he moves with disquieting speed and stealth from the descriptive to the prescriptive, first deriving a right based solely on the antiquity of a practice, and then stipulating that the State 'should absolutely suspend all further proceedings in the old direction – all further conversion into the absolute property of individuals'.[113] Needless to say, Mill's argument contravenes bedrock utilitarian assumptions and practices. He does not attempt to compare the costs and benefits of either past or subsequent conversions, nor does he even allude to the desirability of so doing. He simply inverts the oldest conservative argument, primly concluding that 'this is the moral which we deduce from that part of Mr Maine's researches which relates to the ancient landed institutions of England'.[114]

The strongest argument Mill could have made on behalf of Irish land reform was the same one he might have offered on behalf of trade unions – that the market in land, as in labour, was radically imperfect. (In the case of land reform, he might also have candidly confessed that equity and efficiency were sometimes at odds, and there might be valid political reasons for adopting policies that did not maximize output.) The problematic *ad hoc* arguments he adopted instead were more damaging to Ricardian economics than would have been a straightforward avowal of the limits of its principles.

'By the time Mill died, the campaign for peasant proprietorships came to absorb almost his whole intellectual and political life', Dewey claims.[115] This is something of an exaggeration. Mill was certainly no less devoted to the cause of the emancipation of women.

A year before he reviewed Leslie's book, Mill decided to publish a manuscript he had commenced working on in 1860.[116] The contrast between *The Subjection of Women* and 'Leslie on the Land Question' or 'Maine's Village Communities' is instructive. One of the principal arguments in the former book is, in effect, a sustained plea not to confuse 'is' and 'ought': what exists, what has existed from time immemorial, has no prescriptive value. After all, Mill notes, 'the authority of men over women' was not 'the result of a conscientious comparison between different modes of constituting the government of society'.[117] Custom carries no weight because it is not determined rationally; its decrees may seem 'natural', but that is only because they have become habitual.[118] The improvement of the species is, as always, the chief objective. Today, 'young men of the greatest promise generally cease to improve as soon as they marry, and, not improving, inevitably degenerate'.[119] The marriage of the future, however, will unite,

> two persons of cultivated faculties, identical in opinions and purposes, between whom there exists the best kind of equality ... so that each can enjoy the luxury of looking up to the other, and can have alternately the pleasure of leading and of being led in the path of development ... [T]his, and this only, is the ideal of marriage; and ... all opinions, customs, and institutions which favour any other notion of it ... are relics of primitive barbarism.[120]

The contrast with the whole thrust of Mill's arguments on the land question is too obvious to belabour. The gravamen of Mill's charges against Lowe could be levelled against himself – and was: that he wished to impose English customs on humanity and his own idiosyncratic conception of conjugal happiness on England – in the teeth of customs still more ancient and tenacious than those governing land tenure.[121]

It would be a mistake to assign too much credit for the positions Mill adopted on trades unionism and the land question to the influence of his followers. We have emphasized throughout that the over-riding objective of most of Mill's late work was to influence public policy by transforming public opinion. When Mill turned to Leslie and when he turned to Thornton, he was responding to headline news. In his writings on land reform in particular, he sought, after 1867, to dramatize the injustice which lay behind a well-publicized 'outrage', and to avert a middle-class backlash.

'Fenian violence would move Mill to re-examine his position on the Irish land question', Kinzer concludes.[122] This consisted of two incidents, the murder of a policeman in Manchester in September 1867, and the explosion at Clerkenwell prison in London in December of that year, which killed 12 people. The conclusion Mill drew was 'that England is bound either to govern Ireland so that Ireland shall be satisfied with her government, or to set Ireland free to govern herself'.[123]

Unfortunately, there is no such direct evidence of Mill's response to trade union violence in the mid–1860s.[124] Thornton himself, who can be maddeningly diffuse, does not indicate what moved *him* to consider trades union questions. Nonetheless, one can infer that the book grew out of what Thornton considered recent retrograde tendencies in a movement that had shown great promise during the previous half-dozen years, and continued to do so. The formation of the London Trades Council in 1860 and the emergence of a group of articulate and intelligent spokesmen in its 'junta', no doubt encouraged Thornton's and Mill's hope that trades unionism would metamorphose into co-operation.[125]

Thus, rather than a specific event, it is probably accurate to conclude that a mix of hope and anxiety in the wake of the Sheffield strike violence and the notorious Hyde Park demonstration in July 1866 convinced Mill that it was an appropriate moment to make political economy a more effective tool of moderate union leaders. That this assumption was warranted is demonstrated by Biagini, who charts the interest in and use made of economic theory by the working-class press.[126]

The large and thorny question of the influence of Mill's economic writing surveyed in this chapter is one into which we cannot enter in any detail. Black has characterized *England and Ireland* as 'probably the most influential single contribution to the extended debate on Irish land problems which was carried on in England between 1865 and 1870',[127] and Kinzer has noted its impact on Gladstone.[128] It is likely that the pamphlet contributed indirectly to the passage of the Irish Land Act of 1870, if only by holding out a far more radical option, and thus shifting the *via media* leftward.

As for his recantation, while Biagini documents Mill's influence on working-class writers, his influence on middle-class readers – his target audience, according to Forget – is less clear. He is likely to have contributed in a small way, and for a few years, to the growing acceptance of trades unions, but this kind of impact is notoriously difficult to document.

The effect of the recantation on political economists is more evident. In pulling down one of the pillars of classical political economy, Mill clearly accelerated the collapse of that system.[129]

Over the longer run, it was Mill's fate, in common with so many public intellectuals, to be misinterpreted. Collini describes how Mill was assigned by 'Collectivists' to the 'Individualist' side of the debate on state intervention during the final two decades of the century.[130] Though true 'Individualists' would have none of it, the view prevailed – based on an unwarranted reading of *On Liberty* as an essay on the role of government.[131] W. L. Courtney's assessment of that book in his 1889 biography of Mill sums up a judgement of the entire *oeuvre* that may be said to have persisted into the 1950s. It 'is out of harmony with the tendencies and ideas of the modern age. We have advanced fast and far in the last thirty years, and organisation and synthesis are our mottoes rather than atomism and individuality.'[132] *On Liberty* is obviously far more accessible and unequivocal than the *Principles*, and intellectuals like to think of themselves as nothing if not critical – advancing beyond myopic predecessors. So the typecasting was inevitable. Nonetheless, the leading English 'Collectivists' – the early Fabians – did, in actuality, absorb much from Mill. The Webbs were Mill's intellectual godchildren.[133]

Part II
Mill's Followers

6 The Mill Circle

Until his liaison with Harriet Taylor – 'the most valuable friendship of my life' – John Stuart Mill had been an eager organizer of and participant in a number of small groups debating discomforting truths and, in due course, agitating for political reforms.[1] Not the least painful consequence of Mill's break with the Philosophic Radicals was the loss of the *esprit de corps* that association provided.

Writing to Sterling, Mill regretted the waning of

> that feeling which has accompanied me through the greater part of my life, that which one fellow-traveller, or one fellow soldier has towards another – the feeling of being engaged in the pursuit of a common object, and of mutually cheering one another on, and helping one another in an arduous undertaking.[2]

The following year he met Mrs Taylor. As 'she possessed in combination, the qualities which in all other persons whom I had known I had been only too happy to find singly',[3] Mill found that he had need of no one else. The most innocuous overtures by family members following the eventual marriage were coldly spurned, and even old friends like the Grotes, Roebuck and Bain were dropped. Mill's extreme sensitivity, not to say paranoia, in perceiving slights to his wife make this period in his life the least attractive for his biographers.[4] And his hyperboles and the couple's conceit in diary and letters still make for painful reading.[5]

Even during his most reclusive years, Mill occasionally attended meetings of the Political Economy Club when in London. It is not surprising that when he eventually emerged from seclusion following his wife's death, Mill first resurfaced at the Club. One of the new members he encountered there was John Elliot Cairnes (1823–75), Whately Professor of Political Economy at Trinity and the author of a state-of-the-art methodological treatise. Cairnes effusively recorded the first meeting in a letter to his best friend William Nesbitt.

> There was a discussion after dinner led off by J. S. Mill in which most of the persons, your humble servant amongst the number (don't damn my impudence) took part.... I never knew a question

> better discussed. Mill spoke like a leaf from the *Principles*.... But my greatest triumph has to be recorded yet. On leaving, J. S. Mill happened to be going the same way, and actually took my arm and walked along Pall Mall with me! You would suppose from his manner that *I* was conferring a compliment upon *him*.[6]

The other friendship commencing around this time of consequence for classical political economy was that with Henry Fawcett (1833–84). The forthright Fawcett initiated contact by inviting Mill to Christmas festivities at Cambridge in 1859, holding out as bait Mill's opportunity to meet with Hare. Mill declined.[7] Nonetheless, he responded warmly to Fawcett's proposal to write a pamphlet with the Fawcettian title 'Mr Hare's Reform Bill, Simplified and Explained', eventually published in March 1860.[8] Hare, who had called Fawcett to Mill's attention in the autumn of 1859, effected the introduction.[9] Mill knew that it was not as the explicator of Hare that Fawcett hoped to make his mark, for when Mill turned down the Christmas invitation, Fawcett responded with a confession and a vow:

> For the last three years your books have been the chief education of my mind. I consequently entertain towards you such a sense of gratitude as I can only hope at all adequately to repay by doing what lies in my power to propagate the invaluable truths contained in every page of your writings.[10]

Mill's friendship with T. E. Cliffe Leslie (1827–82) also began with correspondence about a prospective publication, in this case an article attacking Buckle that was due to appear in Macmillan's. Mill generously commented at some length on the draft or proof, and Leslie incorporated some suggestions.[11] Though the first exchange of letters took place not long after Mill had met Cairnes and Fawcett, the friendship was slower to ripen. Until 1869, there are few notes of intimacy in the detailed letters discussing economic issues, largely the gold question. Mill's tone shifts markedly in a gossipy letter consoling Leslie about the arbitrariness of editors, reminding him that they 'are not half such good judges' of the public good as Leslie himself was. They are like children; there is no point in being 'on your dignity with them'. Instead, Mill advised Leslie to write more travel articles and to conceal 'good doctrine in this form'.[12]

Though Leslie lived in London from 1853, despite serving as professor of jurisprudence and political economy at Queen's College,

Belfast, he appears not to have been as frequent a guest at Blackheath Park as Cairnes and Fawcett. Perhaps the letter cited provides a clue: Leslie may have appeared somewhat importunate and, certainly compared to Cairnes and Fawcett, hypochondriacal. Nevertheless – or on account of this – Mill did what he could to advance Leslie's career, at the expense, in one instance, as noted, of Morley's and Cairnes's claims.

The other friend who did most to further Mill's interest in and knowledge of peasant proprietorships was W. T. Thornton (1813–80), the second 'heretic' within the Blackheath circle. Mill's friendship with Thornton was of much longer standing than with the younger men. The two were colleagues at East India House, where Thornton, coincidentally, was selected to fill the vacancy created by James Mill's death. Owing to 'mutual shyness', according to Thornton, they barely acknowledged each other for a decade. Then, in 1846, Thornton ventured to send Mill a copy of *Overpopulation*. The subject was, of course, close to Mill's heart, and when he stopped by to thank the younger man 'during the half-hour's conversation that thereupon ensued, sprang up, full grown at its birth, an intimate friendship, of which I feel that I am not unduly boasting in declaring it to have been equally sincere and fervent on both sides'. They conversed nearly every day thereafter. 'And what talks we had on such occasions, and on what various subjects!'[13] When Mill was appointed Chief Examiner in 1856, he insisted as a condition of acceptance that Thornton accompany him as his assistant. Mill may soon have regretted this, for when Thornton suffered a protracted nervous breakdown shortly thereafter, Mill felt obliged to undertake all of his friend's work for a full year, in addition to his own.[14] (The episode says much about Mill's generosity, but also something about the work load of an East India Company official.)

Thornton was one of a very select few who were welcomed at Avignon. Indeed, Mill pointedly referred to the guest room as '*your* room' when it was being refurbished by Helen Taylor.[15] Thornton was able to provide the most detailed extant account of the life Mill and his step-daughter led in Provence.[16]

Mill was pleased when his new friends of the early 1860s hit it off with Thornton. Glad to learn of Cairnes's warm feelings for his former colleague, Mill described Thornton as 'a person I singularly respect and like. In perfect candour, sincerity, and singleness of mind, few men come near him.'[17] Leslie Stephen recalled seeing 'the excellent W. T. Thornton' often at Cambridge, when the older man visited Fawcett.[18]

Not an economist, despite brief pretensions, John Morley (1838–1926) was the final member of the Blackheath circle of importance for this study. Morley, too, came to Mill's attention through an article, though Morley himself did not submit it to the master and it was not derived from the *Principles*, but from *On Liberty*, of which it was a précis – 'the pure milk of the Millite word', as Morley wrote later.[19] Revealingly, Mill's brief note to Morley in response praises the author for exhibiting 'an unusual amount of qualities which go towards making the most valuable kind of writer for the general public'.[20] Morley, in other words, was to be a conduit to the world, not an investigator of what was to be disseminated – a medium, in short. His appointment as *Fortnightly Review* editor in 1867 proved to be a great coup for the Millites.[21]

What was in it for Mill?

On one level, the importance of the group for Mill requires little explanation. To find oneself at the centre of a small party of intelligent and devoted followers cannot have been anything other than satisfying. The fact that these individuals were sufficiently bright and independent to stimulate Mill's own thoughts, even forcing additional clarity through opposition, was obviously crucial to someone who believed truth advanced dialectically.[22] As his letters to Cairnes make clear, Mill solicited and profited from criticisms of his views.[23]

Furthermore, the causes Mill worked for demanded small platoons. Serving as public moralist was more than a full-time job: there were articles and letters to write (and Mill, like so many nineteenth-century men of letters, wrote copiously to total strangers); there were committees to organize and to sit on, worthy projects to subscribe to, and lectures to deliver, including, for three years, lectures to the curious and respectful, if sometimes bemused, members of Parliament. Mill's comrades-in-arms would further disseminate his teaching, in different, perhaps more effective, language, and, especially, in novel applications. More reassuring still, they would carry on Mill's mission after his death. Cairnes had been specifically singled out for this task.[24]

His devotion to the cause was, in part, what made Mill so attractive, particularly the union of crusading zeal with 'tenderness', with deference and compassion.[25] Precisely because of the way his father had deployed him in his own campaigns, Mill was incapable of commanding his troops in a peremptory and manipulative manner.[26]

Why was this so? Bruce Mazlish, the author of the most sustained and ambitious psychological portrait, claims that James Mill was the very first of that great scourge, the 'intrusive parent'.[27] The seemingly idiosyncratic relationship of Mill senior and junior in fact illuminates a fundamental and pervasive change in the way the generations interacted in Western Europe – a consequence, no less, of the 'industrial and scientific revolutions, along with the political ones', and itself constituting a revolution of equal magnitude. The conflict of fathers and sons, Mazlish argues, became as important as the conflict of classes.[28]

As for James Mill's impact on John's friendships, Mazlish sees evidence of a pattern on the son's part of breaking off intimate relations in disillusionment after pursuing them eagerly, and even prostrating himself, disciple-like, before the would-be mentor.[29] This tendency is connected by Mazlish, not very persuasively, to Mill's 'bisexuality' – a consequence, like his other pathologies, of his father's remarkable, loveless domination.[30] The strongest evidence for Mill's 'bisexuality' comes from a letter he wrote to Carlyle in 1833.[31] 'Asexuality' may be a more appropriate term. Bain's judgement was widely shared: 'in the so-called sensual feelings, he was below average ... he was not a good representative specimen of humanity in respect of these; and scarcely did justice to them in his theories'.[32]

Moreover, the only two cases in which Mill played anything like the 'supine pupil'[33] were in his friendships with Carlyle and Comte, both prodigiously original – and supremely self-confident – writers who were also forceful and charismatic personalities, and his senior by 11 and 8 years, respectively.

Nevertheless, there does appear to be something submissive in Mill's nature, which obviously owes much to his feeling himself a 'made man', 'a mere reasoning machine'.[34] 'My father was the extreme opposite ... his senses and his mental faculties were always on the alert; he carried decision and energy of character ... into every action of life .... The education he gave me was more fitted to *know* than to *do* ... I was so much accustomed to expect to be told what to do ... that I acquired a habit of leaving my responsibility as a moral agent to rest on my father, my conscience never speaking to me except by his voice.'[35] (Clearly, the confession sheds some light on the great emphasis Mill placed on the necessity of developing independence.) By his own abundant testimony, Mill subsequently looked to Harriet Taylor (and, after her death, to her daughter Helen) for guidance and assistance both in the little conundra of daily life (where Mill was hopelessly incompetent), and for inspiration and approbation of his intellectual endeavours. If he was not the mere mouthpiece for Harriet Taylor that he repeatedly represents himself as being,[36] he certainly depended on her approval, dutifully making, as noted, the deletions and emendations she demanded in the *Principles of Political Economy*.

From this perspective, his extravagant praise of Harriet Taylor was clearly at one level an attempt to rationalize this intellectual prostration. She was James Mill, returned – and improved. For she combined, her husband claimed, the keen mind and determined will of his father with the warm, spontaneous, affectionate heart he had lacked.[37] It was no small merit to be a Taylor-made man.

Love, for Mill, seems to have been inseparable from worship. Only individuals with superior intellects and wills were capable of being loved – and of loving. The 'Rejected Leaves' contain this revealing comment about his mother (who is, of course, never mentioned in the published *Autobiography*):

> That rarity in England, a really warm hearted mother, would in the first place have made my father a totally different being, and in the second would have made the children grow up loving and being loved. But my mother, with the very best intentions, only knew how to pass her life in drudging for them. Whatever she could do for them she did, and they liked her, because she was kind to them, but to make herself loved, looked up to, or even obeyed, required qualities which she unfortunately did not possess.[38]

Clearly, Mill conflated the final three attributes. Warm-heartedness apparently required intellectual parity with the recipient; otherwise it was mere kindness. And, as Mazlish notes, apart from Harriet, Mill seems to have been drawn to women who were vivacious and authoritative, not to say manipulative – women who made themselves obeyed.[39]

Perhaps the most astonishing evidence of this tendency is the way he regarded his step-daughter Helen. This opinionated would-be actress, 25 years his junior and without formal education, he regarded not merely as his intellectual peer, but as senior partner in their collaboration:

> of what I owe in the way of instruction to her great powers of original thought and soundness of practical judgement, it would be a vain attempt to give an adequate idea. Surely no one ever before was so fortunate, as, after such a loss as mine, to draw another such prize in the lottery of life – another...instructor of rarest quality. Whoever...may think of me and of the work I have done, must never forget that it is the product not of one intellect and conscience but of three, the least considerable of whom, and above all the least original, is the one whose name is attached to it.[40]

The last sentence may provide a key to the way Mill might have rationalized his appraisal of Helen, and that of her mother. He allowed himself to equate conscience with intellect, political soundness with knowledge and wisdom. Mill cannot acknowledge his step-daughter's large contributions to his emotional life (which included, of course, sharing her opinions on politics, religion and society) without prostrating himself before her mind. 'Her words have an oracular value to him', Norton complained.[41] And Helen wielded her great influence freely, owning that she was 'a *very* severe critic on [*sic*] Mr Mill'.[42]

During his final dozen years, James and Harriet now departed if not forgotten, Mill was able to juggle in a fairly satisfying way the not unproblematic roles of master and disciple. In tutelage to his step-daughter, Mill was not likely to have unpalatable ideas thrust upon him. His 'mastership', in turn, rested on admiration for his work, not on the force of his will, or his father's sanction. His 'feminine' traits – sympathy and compassion – rather than undermining his authority, enhanced it: unlike his own father, he was loved rather than feared.[43] He could be both father and brother – the kind of brother he could have been were he not his father's instrument.[44] And, arguably, he could be mother as well: throughout the 1860s, Mill's correspondence reveals a certain predisposition to nurture and nurse. More than perfunctory enquiries and expressions of concern about his friends' health pervade his letters.[45] And he hovered around Helen, dutifully attending to her symptoms and obeying her commands with alacrity, providing 'a care maternal as well as paternal'.[46]

What was in it for Mill's followers?

To be the beneficiary of the attention and kindness of a brilliant and original thinker was deeply gratifying, needless to say. And one had the pleasure of his company.

There are a number of accounts of the 5 o'clock Sunday dinners that the Mill circle enjoyed at Blackheath, beginning in the early 1860s. 'In later days', Hirst relates, 'Morley never tired of talking about the afternoon dinner parties at Blackheath.'[47] There are some descriptions of the house and garden (though few of the food served),[48] but everyone unfailingly lingers over the beauty of Mill's character, some accounts of which were cited in Chapter 3. Mill did not hold forth. 'In manner he was quiet and unassuming', Spencer remarked, and Cairnes confessed himself 'quite fascinated by . . . his modesty'. Mill seemed 'equally anxious to open his own & an interlocutor's mind upon every question'.[49] 'Though Mill was more eager to listen than to talk, we managed to throw the burden of conversation upon him, and never failed to go away enriched by his ample knowledge and ideas', the expatriate American Unitarian minister Moncure Conway recalled.[50] If there were no conspicuous displays of eloquence or badinage, Mill nonetheless possessed 'remarkable conversational powers', Cliffe Leslie reminisced, and, quoting Steele, concluded that 'the perspicuity of his discourse gave the same pleasure that wit would in another man'.[51] Similarly, Charles Eliot Norton, found 'nothing epigrammatic, or strained in Mill's talk . . . . His manner is entirely that of a gentleman and man of the world, with a tender grace and sweetness about it rarely met with . . . . He is entirely simple, and modest, and makes no claim to the position of superiority and authority which most men would readily grant him.' Norton concludes with the comparison so frequently made by guests between the man and his *oeuvre*: 'His expression and manner reveal a very large and important part of his character which is but indirectly and imperfectly indicated by his writings'.[52] Bain provides perhaps the most detailed account of Mill's conversational style, but the Amberley papers offer the most vivid picture of the man *chez lui* during his last years. Regrettably, Cairnes never acted on the desire he expressed at the height of his infatuation with Mill to become 'a sort of Boswell to him'.[53]

Apart from the stimulating table-talk, Mill's followers had the immense satisfaction of working for a great and urgent cause – of championing the principles and policies that would improve mankind.[54] Yet despite their common political goals, they were acutely aware of the division within their ranks, even if Mill chose to ignore it.

The rivalry of Cairnes and Leslie was especially bitter. At one time the two had respected each other. When he applied for a position at Queen's College Galway, Cairnes received from Leslie a recommendation 'which, from its overpraise of me I am somewhat ashamed to insert'.[55] But within four years, the relationship had deteriorated; methodological disagreements led to keen animosity. Leslie 'continues to plague me as usual', Cairnes complained. 'I never knew of such a man.' They exchanged angry letters.[56] Cairnes clearly resented Mill's aggressively lobbying for the young historicist to replace him during a leave necessitated by his deteriorating health. 'For some years', he protested to Mill, 'my relations with him have not been of a cordial kind and I should be unwilling to accept from him a favour'.[57] He will agree to Leslie's appointment, he stiffly informed Mill, if it is understood that the arrangement is only a matter of 'mutual convenience'.[58] Soon after, Cairnes ventured to disagree with Mill for the first time in their correspondence, though he continued to conceal his deep aversion to Leslie.[59]

Leslie amply reciprocated Cairnes's dislike. 'I look upon him', he told his good friend J. K. Ingram, 'as the man who has done most to obstruct the progress of philosophy in relation to society, by bolstering a false method of investigation as well as false Doctrines'.[60] Cairnes was unscrupulous as well as doctrinaire: Leslie hinted to Mill that Cairnes had plagiarized his own work on the military systems of Europe.[61] There was naturally some envy in Leslie's reproaches: Cairnes seemed to be monopolizing the limelight, while he received scant notice – particularly from Cairnes himself. Cairnes failed to mention him even when listing British economists, 'hoping to suppress me and all opposition to his dogmatism'.[62] In defence of their 'wretched old system of economics', Cairnes and Fawcett were unscrupulous, Fawcett acting as kingmaker, Cairnes as his willing tool.[63]

The two orthodox Millites, however, did not begin as co-conspirators. Cairnes was hardly less contemptuous of Fawcett than of Leslie. He dismissed Fawcett's 'pretensions' to the Cambridge professorship; Fawcett's 'speculations on gold', in particular, he found 'exceedingly flimsy'.[64] Cairnes was derisive toward the *Manual*, doubted that Fawcett was capable of advancing the science, and ridiculed his sail-trimming while campaigning for a seat in Parliament.[65] Nonetheless, by the late 1860s their relationship had warmed considerably, in part as a result of their alliance over the vitally important (for Cairnes) Irish University question. Equally important, orthodoxy was increasingly under siege as the decade advanced, and this doubtless drew the two together. Both, moreover, were affable men, and Fawcett's touching tribute, after Cairnes's death, to the 'charm, vivacity, and humour' of his 'dear and valued friend' rings true.[66]

Thornton was no less likeable, but, as with Fawcett, Cairnes's regard for the man, ten years his senior, clearly exceeded his admiration for his work. While Cairnes urged Courtney to review *On Labour* in *The Times*, he conceded he thought little of its 'theoretical expositions'.[67] By the time he published *Leading Principles*, Cairnes was quite dismissive.[68] Nor did he think much of Thornton's attack on utilitarianism.[69]

Only Morley does Cairnes seem to have liked unreservedly, perhaps because he published nothing on economics. Cairnes recognized a loyalist when he saw one, though, and lobbied brazenly for Morley's candidacy as his successor at University College. He was obliged to argue the professorship would be just the thing to induce Morley to think about political economy: 'I should be glad of Morley's appointment, as it would probably lead him to make a conscientious study of the subject'.[70] Morley, even more than Thornton, had 'a genius for friendship',[71] but Cairnes was no doubt also moved by the need to circle the wagons. By the end of the 1860s, he was beginning to suspect that Mill was occasionally riding with the Indians.

With such cleavages within the group, it should not come as a surprise that the circle did not function as a well-oiled political action committee lobbying for economic orthodoxy, as it has sometimes been depicted. De Marchi, in an examination of five contested elections for professorships of political economy, finds no monolithic Mill faction supporting orthodox Ricardians; members were arrayed against each other or aligned themselves with Jevons.[72] It should not be inferred, naturally, that the group had no wish to influence public policy – quite the opposite, as we've seen. Still, members of the circle could hardly apply tests of doctrinal purity to other political economists when they themselves disagreed so fundamentally. The anarchy of which Cairnes complained vociferously in public and private emanated from Mill's dining room at Blackheath Park.[73]

How can one explain the diverging perspectives? Much must remain mysterious about an individual economist's methodological predilections. Most scholarship arguing for exogenous influences on the development of economic thought stresses the economic or professional self-interest of the individual practitioner, or, more familiarly, the interests of his or her class.[74] There is, nonetheless, a small but impressive body of work emphasizing the role of religious beliefs in shaping economic theory in early nineteenth-century England.[75] I believe that it is not entirely coincidental that Mill's religious beliefs and allegiance to economic principles shifted in tandem, and inversely. Evidence for the Mill circle also appears to support the conclusion of scholars focusing on early nineteenth-century Britain that the two are indeed connected, that core beliefs influenced approaches to economics. Among the Millites, religious orthodoxy seems to have eventuated in economic unorthodoxy. A belief in God made less attractive Mill's version of the Religion of Humanity, with its deep commitment to enacting a political agenda validated by Ricardian economics.

Any brief discussion of this claim is necessarily at a high level of abstraction, with liberal recourse to Weberian ideal types, in this case the Theist and the Secular Humanist (practitioner of the Religion of Humanity).[76] A belief in God cooled the ardour for the improvement of mankind primarily because credulity led to doubt about the ability to interpret and predict. Individuals were too complex – too free, too irrational – to be captured by the generalizations of a social science. Human nature (for Theists believed in such a thing) was therefore more impervious to perfectability than their optimistic secular colleagues believed. For the latter, naturally, human nature was malleable; political reform could improve character (which did duty for an immortal, unchanging soul). Improvement consisted of an increase in the exercise of reason. Reason meant the ability to make choices based on reliable evidence (i.e. derived from the senses) that would maximize utility. And the reforms that would inculcate reason depended themselves on reason – on a scientific understanding of the laws of behaviour on the part of legislators and their newly important advisers. Political changes might be urgently advocated by Theists, but the scope of these was more limited and they were intended primarily to arrest a degeneration that had resulted from new and disturbing economic forces. Theistic liberalism, in short, was more conservative.

The radicalism of the Humanists was a consequence of their faith in reason, which owed something to a familiar paradox: like the return of the repressed, the Religion of Humanity resembled the Calvinism that was often a feature of its adherents' childhoods.[77] Without a direct knowledge of God, a greater urgency was attached to works. The concepts of sin and salvation, albeit radically redefined, surfaced with renewed force: man was in a fallen state, and in urgent need of redemption, and this was to be effected by the selfless labours of an elect. Something of the millenarian spirit was abroad – heaven would be realized on earth.

Space does not permit a more detailed discussion of this argument,[78] but subsequent chapters will consider the religious beliefs and core values of the individual members of the circle, in the expectation that these beliefs will provide some clues about the economic analyses each found congenial. While the likelihood that there are contemporary applications is remote, I believe that one can venture certain predictions about mid- and late-Victorian economists based on how they spent their Sunday mornings.

7 John Elliot Cairnes

The first part of this chapter attempts to account for Cairnes's attraction to the Ricardian economics of John Stuart Mill. In Part 2 I will examine some of the ways in which Cairnes modified his mentor's doctrines.

Cairnes, as we've seen, rejected Mill's tinkering with Ricardian premises. His loyalty was to the values to which political economy gave its imprimatur – self-control, hard work. Land reform and trade unionism, while excellent means of moralizing, and enriching, the lower classes, were certainly not of such paramount importance as to warrant anything like a recantation – especially as, in his view, there was nothing to recant.

There *was* a political controversy that engaged Cairnes passionately – but it was the Irish university education question, and political economy contributed nothing to his arguments opposing Church involvement in higher education.

That Ricardian political economy so ably supported his core values inspired Cairnes to heroic defences of its scientific claims. These rested on logic rather than empirical evidence, and, ironically, Cairnes's analytic prowess led him to conclusions that undermined Ricardian assumptions even more devastatingly than Mill's politically-inspired equivocations.

I

In January of 1866, Cairnes was asked by H. D. McCleod to submit an autobiographical sketch for the latter's *Dictionary of Political Economy*. The canny Cairnes suspected this was merely a ploy by McCleod to sell more copies and didn't respond. Nonetheless, he wrote for his friend William Nesbitt a jaunty, tongue-in-cheek account of his 'interesting and edifying career'. 'My talent', he lamented, 'was unrecognized at school and not noted even at college, and when placed at the mash tub, I broke away from the paternal thralldom, guided by nobler instincts.'[1] Cairnes, like Morley, arrived at Mill's doorstep after breaking with a domineering father of Evangelical persuasion. Mill's philosophy formed the basis of something like a calling that sanctioned this rupture, providing Cairnes with a much-needed sense of purpose and direction, while permitting him to exploit brilliantly his talents as a logician and rhetorician.

Cairnes was born in 1823, at Castlebellingham, County Louth, to a family of Scottish descent distinguished by 'a long tradition of religious fervor and military exploits'.[2] His 'background' Weinberg characterizes as 'earnest if not severe. Cairnes's father was an unusually able man of high moral qualities. Both his parents were profoundly religious.'[3] Cairnes's mother was a clergyman's daughter. His father rejected a military career to become a partner in a brewery. Two years after Cairnes was born, his father set up his own establishment at Drogheda.

Named after his grandfather, Cairnes grew up in a household of women; he was the sixth child, but the oldest surviving son in a family of eight children.[4] Weinberg surmises that 'his religious feelings' as a young boy 'appear to have inclined him towards Calvinism'.[5] Leslie Stephen attributes Cairnes's early Calvinism to 'a young man named La Bart', who conducted prayer meetings.[6] Cairnes had been educated at a boarding school at Kingstown and then in the home of a clergyman in Chester, who thought him 'a dull boy... unfit for college'.[7] But Cairnes resisted the idea of a career in his father's firm, reading late into the night, to the detriment of his health. After a period of coolness, his father was won over to the extent of offering his son a small allowance that enabled him to matriculate at Trinity College. The estrangement between father and eldest son appears to have continued through college. Cairnes, however, was apparently in no hurry to launch himself into a profession. After graduating in 1845 with a first in 'Logics and Metaphysics', he continued his studies, receiving a gold medal in 'Ethics and Logics' two years later, and, eventually, an MA in 1854. 'He led a desultory life for some time', Stephen writes, studying chemistry and engineering.[8] Something or someone (perhaps Archbishop Whately or William Nesbitt, Professor of Greek at Queen's College Galway) drew him to political economy, for the same year he received his MA he published a pamphlet on the Bank Charter Act of 1844, which attracted the attention of Tooke and George Pryme, the Cambridge professor of political economy. Encouraged by Nesbitt, now his best friend and mentor (and future brother-in-law), Cairnes applied for the Whately Chair, and was elected in 1856. His first course of lectures on methodology was published by Whately himself as *The Character and Logical Method of Political Economy*.

Cairnes sent Mill a copy of the book. Early the following year, he requested from Mill a testimonial for a position as Examiner in Political Economy in the India Civil Service. (The Chair was worth only £100 a year.) About a year after receiving Mill's imprimatur (his book having been judged 'thoroughly sound and philosophical'),[9] Cairnes wrote back to praise Mill's *Thoughts on Parliamentary Reform* and suggest an alternative to plural voting. In his response, Mill warmly recommended Hare's book, confessing that he had 'not been so delighted with any political treatise for many years'.[10] In his first surviving letter to Mill, Cairnes reciprocated in kind: 'I have just finished a careful study of it with feelings of admiration and pleasure greater than I can describe'.[11] The pleasure was exceeded when Cairnes picked up *On Representative Government*.

> I have never read a book with greater admiration for the ability of the writer, with more thorough sympathy in its aims, or with more general concurrence in its conclusions. I have endeavoured to avoid reading it in the spirit of servile acquiescence: and yet . . . I am unable to fix on a single position which I would deliberately decline to adopt.

Perhaps sensing Mill's priorities even at this date, Cairnes continued: 'That one which conflicts most with my traditional ideas is your view respecting the position of women; yet on this point I feel I have nothing but prejudices to oppose to your arguments.'[12] Even Mill was impressed by the intensity of the encomia. 'No expression of opinion which I have received respecting my book', he responded, 'has given me so much pleasure as yours; your adhesion being so much more complete than any knowledge I had of you entitled me to hope for.'[13]

The next exchange with Mill, in August of 1861, concerned a manuscript Cairnes submitted, the basis for *The Slave Power*, the book that established Cairnes's reputation. Mill's praise at first is somewhat modest: it is 'a most valuable paper and one particularly wanted at the present time'. As he contemplates the way the subject has been treated in the English press, and reviews Cairnes's thesis, he grows more enthusiastic. 'English organs of opinion cry out for . . . letting slavery alone; but slavery will not let freedom alone.' Soon the Northern cause becomes 'a crusade of all civilized humanity'. Mill quickly passes on to strategic considerations: 'I think it very important . . . that in recasting your lectures in the form of an article, you should connect them expressly and openly with the present crisis, and make them, in effect, a pamphlet on that.' Mill urges that it should appear under Cairnes's name and in many reviews instead of just one.[14] In his reply, Cairnes echoes Mill's sentiments, and language: 'I subscribe most cordially to your opinion that the present is a case for a crusade of all civilized humanity.' Interestingly, he also adopts for the first time in correspondence with Mill the latter's form of signature, styling himself 'J. E. Cairnes'. (Mill's letters were invariably signed 'J. S. Mill'.) Hitherto, Cairnes had written 'John E. Cairnes'.[15]

The friendship, in short, ripened over political issues. Cairnes's extravagant praise for *Representative Government* was enthusiastically reciprocated by Mill for *The Slave Power*. The book was dedicated to Mill, first, because the mere appearance of Mill's name, Cairnes wrote with more fervour than logic in the dedication, shows that the author is qualified to speculate on the subject. Ultimately, Cairnes concluded, he could not resist 'the opportunity of connecting my name in public with that of one from whose works I have profited more largely than from those of any other living writer.'[16] The lavish, not to say slavish, preface did not deter Mill from reviewing the book in the *Westminster Review*, where he called its author, in effect, the leading political economist of the day.[17] Revealingly, after offering some suggestions to enhance the book's distribution, he confided to Cairnes that

> I do not think there is an opinion or a sentiment in the book with which I substantially disagree; and this is so very generally the case when I read anything you write, that I feel growing up in me, what I seldom have, the agreeable feeling of a brotherhood in arms. This feeling being one of the pleasantest which life has to give, I owe you thanks privately as well as publicly for adding as much to it as you have done by your present volume.[18]

The surfacing of that long-dormant feeling apparently obliterated any objections Mill might have had to the historical materialism the book's argument rests on. That its thesis owed much to Buckle was not acknowledged by either the writer or reviewer.

For Cairnes's part, one needn't subscribe to a psychological determinism that sees all relationships re-enacting the conflicts – or attempting to redress the injuries – of early childhood to recognize that Mill, at least initially, provided him with the warm endorsement that his own father appears to have withheld not only for his views but for his abilities. As Mill's opinions were valued over those of any other public figure, it is difficult to overestimate the gratification Cairnes derived.

Needless to say, much of Cairnes's extensive correspondence with Mill does not concern political questions. In November 1861 Cairnes provided Mill with a detailed critique of 'Utilitarianism', the first four chapters of which had just appeared in two instalments in *Fraser's Magazine*.[19]

Of greater moment was his very extensive contribution to the sixth edition of Mill's *Principles* between October 1864 and March 1865. A second significant exchange on economics occurred in May and June of 1869, following Mill's review of Thornton's *On Labour*. At that point, Cairnes found Mill's disavowal of the wages fund doctrine unexceptionable, but, with some trepidation, questioned Mill's treatment of supply and demand (which, in fact, takes up the better part of the review). Cairnes's reservations may well have stimulated the reassessment of classical value theory that appears to have been behind the writing of *Some Leading Principles of Political Economy*.[20]

Cairnes returned to the problem of recasting the concept of cost of production in letters in May and June of 1872, as he was revising the section on value theory in *Leading Principles*.[21] But the correspondence in late 1864 is by far the most extensive. Some of the initial points Cairnes makes do concern the explicitly political resonances of Mill's *Principles*. Cairnes, unhappy with the 'Fourth fundamental theorem' of capital, which caused Mill much posthumous grief ('Demand for commodities is not demand for labour') wants Mill to clarify and sharpen his attack on 'unproductive consumption'. In another such instance, Cairnes hopes that Mill will shoot down a recent 'refutation' of Malthus.[22] And on a more narrow application – of the implications of capitalization for taxation – Cairnes attempts to convince Mill that landlords ought to be more thoroughly squeezed. (In this endeavour, he inadvertently edges toward a marginalist understanding of 'equality of sacrifice'.)[23] Though he effusively thanked Cairnes, Mill was more interested in the additional empirical evidence he could deploy than in theoretical refinements.[24] He sought, in particular, more information about Ireland. Cairnes obliged him, right before Christmas, with a treatise of some 6800 words, culled from notes by Longfield, and works by Thornton, Goldwin Smith and others.

Ireland was of pre-eminent concern for Cairnes, naturally, and he was convinced that an equitable resolution of the land question would immediately defuse support for Fenianism.[25] But preceding a settlement of the land question, Cairnes hoped for a satisfactory conclusion to the still more contentious university education question.[26] It is difficult to appreciate the extent to which this issue exercised him – and other advanced Radicals – during his final years. Fawcett, in his moving obituary for Cairnes in the *Fortnightly*, after noting, significantly, that 'probably the most distinguishing merit of Mr Cairnes as an economist was the remarkable skill with which he applied the principles of economic science to the solution of political problems',[27] went on to devote a substantial section of the essay to Cairnes's role in the education debate. 'To him more than to any other man', Fawcett claimed,

> is the cause of united or undenominational education in Ireland indebted for having escaped the manifold perils by which it was at one time threatened.... Although he was a thorough Liberal in politics, he never wavered in the opinion that it was far better that the political party to which he belonged should suffer a damaging defeat, rather than that the higher education of Ireland should be handed over to the control of an Ultramontane priesthood.[28]

Not coincidentally, Cairnes's feelings toward Fawcett grew warmer precisely as the education issue began to bulk large in his consciousness.[29] Mill, of course, had a great many other fish to fry, and while generally concurring in Cairnes's analysis of the question, did not share anything like his enthusiasm for the issue.[30] As early as August 1865, Cairnes expressed his regret about Mill's 'disposition to conciliate a party who in the name of freedom of education are seeking to get control of the education of the country into their own hands in order to corrupt and pervert it'.[31] Mill's coolness, after a January 1866 'rapprochement', eventually elicited the first brusque critique by Cairnes of any position Mill had adopted.[32] In June of 1867, he confided to Courtney his disappointment in Mill's lack of zeal on the education question.[33] Three months later, Courtney himself felt the sting of Cairnes's lash on the issue:

> I have read your remarks on the Irish Education question with profound sorrow. The situation is gloomy indeed, not the less so that the gloom, as it seems to me, proceeds mainly from the view taken of it by yourself and so many other liberals.[34]

Cairnes did not give up on Mill: 'I fear I have almost, if not quite, worn out your patience on the subject of Irish education, and yet I am going to tax it once more'.[35] His disappointment with Mill on Irish questions only intensified after he read *England and Ireland*.

The militancy of Cairnes's secularism suggests an imperfectly metamorphosed Calvinism. 'For my part', he cavalierly assured Mill in 1868,

> I should greatly prefer separation [of England and Ireland]. That would issue, in the first instance, in a sanguinary civil war, but in the upshot the more energetic and progressive elements of society would come to the top; and, the hurly-burly done, the conditions of progress might be established.[36]

The late-twentieth-century reader hardly knows whether to be more impressed by the close parallel between Cairnes's insouciant remarks and the broken-eggs-and-omelette defence of Soviet Communism in the 1920s and 1930s – or with Cairnes's (seemingly unconscious) appropriation of a line from the second witch in *Macbeth*. His casual bloody-mindedness, in any case, gives one pause.

However, this is certainly not to argue that Cairnes's position on the extremely complex university question is indefensible. At stake in the proposals put forward by the government in 1865 and 1866 was the very existence of the Queen's University system in Ireland, including, of course, the Galway campus where Cairnes had been teaching since 1859. A leading purpose behind the establishment of these colleges, he argued, was to overcome sectarian strife.[37] Moreover, Cairnes shows, Catholics were attending these colleges in significant numbers despite clerical anathemas, and even in the face of episcopal decrees denying the sacraments to matriculating students.[38] His very Millian argument on behalf of the collegiate system, as opposed to the creation of a second central examining university like London University, is also telling.[39] And certainly Cairnes's objections to the 'gagging clauses' of Gladstone's 1873 Bill are not without merit.[40]

Nonetheless Cairnes's willingness to see the entire Irish Question resolved by force is not the exceptional, choleric departure from a non-militant perspective that it might be taken for. At the beginning of the American Civil War, in keeping with his economic determinism, Cairnes actually argued that if the expansion of slavery were contained, the institution would collapse.[41] However, he soon came around to

Mill's view that unconditional conquest was necessary.[42] Bolstering his revised argument with a lengthy quotation from Mill, Cairnes made the case in the second edition of *The Slave Power* that,

> it is consistent with political morality . . . that in certain cases the principles of constitutional government and those of non-intervention should be set aside, and that a government should compel a portion of its subjects, or a people should intervene to compel another people, to accept a form of government at variance with the wishes of those on whom it is imposed.[43]

Of greater moment, though, is Cairnes's own role in the repudiation by a significant number of Liberals of the old credo 'Peace, Retrenchment, and Reform'. The abandonment of a non-interventionist foreign policy was a logical concomitant of the repudiation of the doctrine of *laissez-faire* on economic and social issues.[44]

An important document in this transition is Cairnes's defence, in the *Fortnightly*, of a 'national' army.[45] The very fact that it is addressed to Liberals is significant: he seeks to counter objections with which he professes considerable sympathy.[46] Briefly, Cairnes attempts to reassure Liberals that rather than a national army infecting the body politic with militarism, universal conscription would ensure that the army would only be deployed defensively; professional standing armies, on the other hand, 'concentrate and . . . intensify, the military spirit, producing all the evils and dangers of an armed caste, out of sympathy with civil society'.[47] Just as on Irish education Cairnes attacked the idea of 'free trade in education' on moral grounds – that it leads to cramming and not character development[48] – so, too, in defending universal conscription, he rails against the 'peace-at-any-price principles' of Manchester,[49] the belief that contract is always superior to status[50] and, still more fundamentally, the notion that the state has no right to compel the services of its citizens.[51] He assures wary readers that 'what we should expect is, that the will would go before the law, and that good citizens would perform, spontaneously and cheerfully, what the law declares to be for the good of all'.[52] Compulsion is necessary to detach a few free riders. While he does not rest his case on it, Cairnes also emphasizes the benefits accruing to the individuals conscripted.[53] He quotes approvingly a Swiss official who avers that 'we see in it [universal conscription] a republican institution of capital importance, a school of equality, a means of union amongst all citizens, and a powerful instrument of national life'.[54]

Cairnes, in short, was assisting in the reshaping – the 'moralizing' – of Liberalism. Mill's high regard for him as chief lieutenant in the campaign to improve mankind seems justified.

How did Cairnes come to transcend, or shed, his interest in the salvation of the individual through faith and replace it with a commitment to the salvation of society through politics? Cairnes may have drifted from Evangelicalism during the long period he was a student at Trinity. The disillusionment may have come earlier. Among other books Cairnes read late into the night after working all day in his father's brewery, Stephen singles out Gibbon.[55] But in any event, Cairnes wrote nothing for publication – and there is nothing in his surviving correspondence – touching on his beliefs.

One expects, naturally, to see the subject surface during moments of crisis. As is well known, the doctrine of conversion was central to Evangelicalism. This transformation characteristically began with an acknowledgement of one's depravity and an appeal to God's grace. One was most likely to experience the call during or after a brush with death, either in the form of a serious illness or bereavement.[56] From the mid-1860s Cairnes was afflicted by a debilitating illness the most conspicuous symptom of which was a progressive paralysis of the joints.[57] Stephen describes the ailment as 'rheumatic gout', Fawcett as 'inflammatory rheumatism', and dates its commencement from 1866. (Today it would likely be considered rheumatoid arthritis, the result, possibly, of rheumatic fever in childhood.)[58] Cairnes and his doctors attributed the ailment to a fall from a horse in 1860. The therapies recommended were no more efficacious than the diagnosis was accurate. These consisted largely of bathing in the mineral waters of various spas. In 1868 he apparently submitted to surgery. Whatever this may have consisted of, it was judged successful, but only briefly.[59] By about 1871 Cairnes was totally paralysed. Eventually, being wheeled in a Bath chair, and then simply being carried outside, proved too excruciating, and for some time before his death he was confined to his bed.[60]

All memorialists remark on his great stoicism.

> It was very seldom that I saw him suffering from depression; and only once I noticed in him anything approaching to a tone of despair. It was at the time when he found it necessary to give up

> teaching his two boys, and he seemed to conclude that if he could not do this, there was nothing else left that he could do.

Generally, though, 'his cheerfulness was so remarkable that in his society his friends almost forgot his affliction, and his conversation could not have been more bright and lively if he had been in the enjoyment of perfect health'. His

> charm, vivacity, and humour... made all his friends look forward to their visits to him as one of their greatest pleasures. When any of his friends heard a good story, probably the first thing they thought of was – 'How Cairnes will enjoy it!' It used to be proverbial among us, that laughing with him over some joke or hearing him tell some amusing story, we often lingered so long at his house that we generally had to run to the railway station, and not unfrequently missed the last train.[61]

Cairnes continued to dictate articles during his last three years, his final contribution, in the *Fortnightly*, appearing four months before he died. Judged purely by his publications, his output during this period far exceeded that of his entire previous career. Two collections, *Political Essays* and *Essays on Political Economy, Theoretical and Applied*, appeared in 1873. The following year *Some Leading Principles of Political Economy, Newly Explained*, was published and in 1875 Cairnes issued a second edition of *The Character and Logical Method of Political Economy*.

Cairnes's first allusion to his illness to Courtney occurs in 1863, when he reports having 'renewed an old sprain in my knee'.[62] He does not refer to the disability in correspondence with Mill until four years later.[63] It is only a couple of weeks after the letter to Mill – in June of 1867 – that he first describes the ailment as a 'disease'. A crucial turning point in his teaching career now occurred. If a summer stay at Bareges in the Hautes-Pyrénées did not restore his health, he resolved to resign his university position.[64] It didn't, but a compromise was reached whereby Leslie took over Cairnes's teaching assignments during the 1867–68 academic year.[65] In the event, it was not until April of 1872 that he was obliged to resign his professorship.[66]

For 18 months after the June letter to Mill, he avoided referring to his rheumatism in correspondence with his mentor. Then, in November of 1868, he sounded a note of real pessimism: 'in no instance has the improvement been maintained for more than a few days. The result is that my hopes of being ever able to make myself useful in the world – outside at least of my domestic circle – decline daily'.[67]

What is remarkable in Cairnes's correspondence is how infrequently the paralysis is alluded to. As Fawcett's obituary suggests, one quite forgets, as Cairnes savages Carlyle and Harrison, or takes issue with Mill's theory of value, that he was altogether immobilized and in considerable pain.

More remarkable still is Cairnes's letter to Courtney in which he relates the sudden death of a much beloved son. He withholds the news until the second paragraph, after effusively, and somewhat coyly, thanking Courtney for forwarding some material.[68] Following a brief but affecting description of the boy, he immediately launches into a lengthy discussion of the Irish Education question and other issues. Even given the mores of his day, Cairnes's restraint (or denial) seems excessive.[69]

On no occasion during his long illness does Cairnes console himself with thoughts of Divine Providence. There are no speculations on an afterlife, no meditations on Job or the Passion. The only allusions to God and Christianity are ironic.[70] The word 'evil' crops up occasionally, but almost exclusively in reference to *The Times*. There is one discussion of theological controversy. This concerns a lecture by D'Arcy Thompson – presumably at Queen's College Galway – which scandalized most of the audience, an outcome Cairnes appears to have relished.[71]

Cairnes, like so many first-generation agnostics, appears to have lost neither the attachment to duty nor the self-censoriousness widely attributed to the Nonconformist (and Evangelical) conscience. As we've seen, he lamented his disability only insofar as it made him useless to the world.[72] 'So long as one can work', he wrote to Mill, 'life is tolerable.'[73] After a very rare complaint to Courtney ('one cannot reconcile oneself at once to the prospect of an aborted career'), Cairnes immediately apologizes for 'this piece of egotism'.[74] He had reproached himself in similar terms for yielding to the impulse to call *The Economist*'s attention to Jevons's pamphlet verifying his own speculations about the effect of gold discoveries on prices. 'I resisted the temptation for several days', he writes, 'but at last in a weak moment I gave way, and now I... regret it.'[75]

Obviously no simple analysis of the relation of Cairnes's religion to his politics, and consequently, his economics, is likely to be satisfying. Cairnes himself was highly critical of Carlyle's crude gospel of work, though primarily because it appeared to terminate in the doctrine 'might makes right'.[76] The fervent Calvinism of Cairnes's youth had disappeared by the time he emerged as a political economist of repute. But as Cairnes himself urged in a letter to Mill, laws of 'co-existence' rather than 'succession' obtain in both the organic and social spheres.[77] It is unlikely that the character traits that led Cairnes to Calvinism vanished without a trace, or were superseded. While it would be reductive to describe his politics as merely a surrogate religion, there are grounds for believing that the complete absence of religious beliefs is not unrelated to the intensity of Cairnes's passion for politics – a passion he sustained to the end.[78] If this is the case, it helps explain why his political agenda may have impaired his receptivity to marginalism and other departures from classical economics that rejected or ignored the Malthusian law of population and the Ricardian law of rent.

II

As early as 1864, Mill hailed Cairnes as the nation's premiere political economist.[79] But by the time he published his opus a decade later, Cairnes clearly did not reciprocate Mill's esteem. The issues he takes exception to are fundamental – how cost of production is defined, how markets are cleared – and Cairnes's demurrals are, to say the least, forcefully expressed, as noted in Chapter 5. What accounts for the shift from the profound reverence Cairnes expresses early in the 1860s?

In some instances, notably his celebrated elaboration of the notion of non-competing groups, Cairnes's criticisms are the result of the play of a logical mind over a flawed system. But in other instances – and generally where his objections are most heated – Cairnes is defending a doctrine the abandonment of which will undermine the moral principles political economy upholds. In his disagreements with Mill on both natural and market price – that is, how both cost of production and supply and demand are defined (not trivial issues) – Cairnes sees himself as defending political economy from misuse by the enemies of advanced liberalism. The incentives to self-sacrifice, to hard work and thrift, are undermined if long-run cost and short-run demand are misconceived.

It is worth noting, first, the two chief accomplishments Cairnes credited Mill with shortly after the latter's death. 'Hasty readers' beguiled by Mill's modesty[80] have concluded Mill was unoriginal, Cairnes warns; in fact Mill bequeathed political economy a more accurate conception of wages and a more rigorous, and limiting, understanding of the scope of political economy.[81] Cairnes also defends Mill in the one instance where he has been widely accused of deviating from orthodoxy – on the land question. In fact, Cairnes argues, Mill's attack on the 'unearned increment' accruing to land-owners 'with the growth of society'[82] is derived directly from Ricardo's theory of rent. But, Cairnes claims, Mill *has* introduced a new and valuable premise: 'the influence of custom as modifying the action of competition'.[83] With this contribution, Millean political economy plainly furnishes grounds for legislation.[84]

Cairnes is quite unfazed by the inconsistency of this claim with his earlier argument that Mill enhanced the scientific credentials of the discipline by stipulating its rigorous non-partisanship.[85] Cairnes plainly has in mind the most numerous class of writers claiming the sanction of political economy for their policy recommendations – *laissez-faire* Liberals like Lowe.[86]

Similarly, Mill's first innovation, which consisted simply in having revealed that the minimum of wages is not merely 'a physical but a moral minimum, and as such, is capable of being altered with the changes in the moral character of' workers,[87] has transparent political implications: one must work to raise working-class morals. Political economy cannot be invoked to justify low wages.

After grappling unsuccessfully with Jevons (see Chapter 11), Cairnes's chief concern in Part I of *Leading Principles* is to reinforce the important classical postulate that demand and supply are not only interdependent, but identical. They are 'fundamentally the same phenomena regarded from different points of view – different faces of the same facts'.[88] The most important implication is that 'Political economy furnishes no... palliation of unmitigated selfishness'[89] and 'that no public benefit of any kind arises from the existence of an idle rich class': '... what they consume in luxury and idleness is not capital, and helps to sustain nothing but their own unprofitable lives'.[90]

To defend the proposition that supply and demand are one and the same, Cairnes must first refute Mill's criticism that one is 'a quantity' and one 'a desire', and that there can therefore be no ratio between them.[91] Demand is thus 'effective demand': 'the desire for commodities or services, seeking its end by an offer of general purchasing power; and Supply... the desire for general purchasing power, seeking its end by an offer of specific commodities or services'.[92]

The semantic difference has implications for the way market price is determined. Cairnes objects to Mill's excluding extra-marginal buyers and sellers – those whose highest and lowest bids, respectively, are lower than the lowest and higher than the highest offers of their counterparts. Cairnes argues that 'supply and demand outside the market are among the conditions which determine price within the market', and Mill 'pointedly excludes from consideration conditions which are essential to the solution of that problem'.[93] Though Mill's version is of course closer to the contemporary understanding of how markets are cleared, Cairnes is struggling to accommodate some important concepts: (1) differing elasticities of demand[94] and (2) the role of time and information in influencing price.[95] Market price, for Cairnes, is ultimately a function of the skill of 'dealers'.[96] Following Whately, he compares them to a ship's captain 'who, taking account of the stock of provision at his disposal, and the length of his intended voyage, adjusts to these conditions the rations of his crew'.[97]

The second important disagreement with Mill is also raised in Part I and concerns 'natural' rather than 'market' price. Cairnes strenuously resists Mill's reduction of cost of production to wages and profits.[98] Cost must be understood, he insists, as sacrifice: while costs *to the capitalist* are measured in wages, real costs consist of labour and abstinence.[99] Mill is guilty of having shifted his perspective from humanity at large to the employer.[100] The political import is clear: high wages are perfectly compatible both with high profits and with expanding international markets.

Cairnes's linguistic purity yields some benefits. (He recognizes, for one thing, that producers are rewarded by the *value* of the commodities they produce.)[101] But though he acknowledges 'risk' as a part of cost,[102] 'the utility or skillfulness of the services rendered' is not, naturally, and Cairnes thus detaches himself from the vanguard of the discipline.[103]

Perhaps Cairnes's most celebrated refinement of Mill's principles also occurs in Part I: his recognition of the effect of 'non-competing' groups of workers on the value of the commodities they produce. This emendation was not directly politically inspired; it was a rearguard effort to defuse increasing criticism of cost-of-production-based values.[104] Of course in defending Ricardian political economy, at the cost of small concessions, Cairnes was defending the policies and values it validated, as he knew full well.[105] Cairnes begins by rejecting the argument that competition *nowhere* prevails (even by 1874 a quite familiar refrain): if labour is relatively immobile, capital is not, and the rising generation – or parents on its behalf – also respond to incentives.[106] But competition effectively reduces the exchange value of commodities to their cost of production only among 'labourers belonging to the same industrial group', of which Cairnes claims there are approximately four.[107] Cairnes acknowledges, however, that most commodities are the joint product of different 'groups'. Thus 'in strictness, we can seldom say that the values of two commodities are in their whole extent governed by their costs of production.'[108]

So after taking pains to be more rigorous than Mill in defining cost of production, and insisting that it is the sole determinant of value, Cairnes finds that he must seriously qualify the applicability of cost of production. International values, it turns out, govern exchanges between non-competing groups. International values are derived from reciprocal demand – the demand of the group in question for the products of all other groups compared with their demand for the products of that group.[109] Lacking Marshall's scissors – and his period analysis – to cut this particular Gordian knot, Cairnes goes through various contortions to reconcile cost of production and reciprocal demand.[110]

Cairnes differed with Mill on two other significant issues: the wages fund and socialism.

With regard to the first, Cairnes perceived two separate heresies, both with profound implications for political economy. Thornton's, endorsed by Mill, represented a methodological challenge. Cairnes was able to dispose of it to his own satisfaction with little difficulty. It involves misconstruing what is intended by the term 'economic law'. The law does not oblige an employer, in this case, to spend 'the utmost he can afford to spend on the payment of labour'.[111] There is no compulsion, in short, only a description of probabilities, given human nature – or the character of men in industrialized countries – and, in the case of the wages fund, the range of investment opportunities.[112] Another, and more formidable, methodological objection – that questioning the very meaning of a 'general rate of wages' – Cairnes treats even more summarily.[113] He goes after Longe here, ignoring Leslie's more cogent critique. His objections to Longe's attack are somewhat vitiated by his own conception of non-competing groups.

The second argument against the wages fund, though far more irritating to Cairnes than the methodological criticisms, is less easily dismissed. Longe and others maintained that the aggregate amount available for wages is determined by the demand for commodities. Far from having joined the enemy's camp on this issue, Mill had vigorously denied the claim. Unfortunately, both Mill's exposition of the wages fund and his defence of the notorious 'fourth proposition concerning capital' – that the demand for commodities is not a demand for labour – are deficient, Cairnes acknowledges. The stakes are high: not only is Cairnes opposing in this instance 'the most popular of all popular fallacies', one enjoying 'almost universal vogue', but the repetition of Longe's argument has 'demoralize[d] mankind'.[114] It has, as noted, been deployed to support the claims 'of an idle rich class'.[115]

Regrettably, Mill's formulation of the wages fund doctrine 'is not a solution, but a statement of the problem', however 'clear, comprehensive, and succinct'.[116] It merely expresses a ratio of the supply to the demand of labour: what determines each remains to be investigated.[117] Fortunately, Malthus has satisfactorily explained supply, as, according to Cairnes, the whole world is finally beginning to acknowledge (thanks, in part, to Darwin).[118] Toward the end of his dense, protracted and tangent-ridden examination of the heretical belief that demand for commodities determines the 'fund' expended on labour, Cairnes in effect concedes the argument.[119] He repeatedly claims that demand determines only the 'direction' or, elsewhere, the 'proportion' of expenditure on labour, and invokes the axiom that aggregate demand depends on aggregate supply. But in attempting to explain what actually causes the national product (and hence, the wages fund) to grow, he inevitably comes up with the division of labour. Dutifully following Smith, Cairnes is obliged to concede that,

> the division of labour is limited by the extent of the market.... Where, therefore, the scale of production has not already attained the maximum of efficiency, an enlarged demand for commodities, by permitting its extension, may lead to a more efficient organization of productive forces, and thus accelerate the growth of wealth.[120]

Indeed, 'a demand for a producer's or a dealer's commodities must always be a condition precedent to the realization of his gains'.[121] But

Cairnes's case had already begun to unravel with his acknowledgement at the outset of Part II that 'producers are in effect remunerated out of the values of their products'[122] and that these are governed by reciprocal demand when competition is imperfect. Cairnes, though, never quite appreciates the force of this concession.[123]

By the time Cairnes has completed his analysis, the determinants of the fund appear to have multiplied alarmingly. Though capital is constantly increasing, the share going to support labour, thanks to 'the progress of the industrial arts', steadily, but unevenly, declines.[124] And the wages fund may contract abruptly when circulating capital is converted into fixed on a large scale.[125] Even the price of labour itself affects the size of the fund, and, depending on the ratio of fixed capital to labour, disproportionately reduces or increases it.[126] (Cairnes senses that this 'unexpected consequence' appears to make his search for the determination of the wages fund a circular chase.)[127]

Other emendations follow. In one instance, Cairnes goes some way toward acknowledging the proposition almost as anathema to classical economists as that making wage rates dependent on consumption: the claim that there is 'a real and fundamental connection between money wages and [commodity] prices'.[128] A still more dramatic departure from classical tenets occurs when Cairnes implies, on the basis of a careful consideration of joint inputs – the proportions of fixed and circulating capital and labour that an industry requires – that wages, not profits, are the 'residual'.[129]

The final departure from Mill, on the advisability of socialism, was discussed in Chapter 5. If 'the maxims of abstract justice' cannot be applied to 'the practical problems of the distribution of wealth', neither does the present distribution in itself represent the realization or embodiment of any principle of abstract justice.[130] Having distanced himself from Bastiat, Cairnes proceeds, predictably enough, to defend the market economy on utilitarian grounds.[131] Progress depends on the accumulation of capital, which entails sacrifices – in the form of deferred gratification and risk. These 'will not be undergone without an adequate motive in the form of a compensating reward', and profit depends on private property and 'industrial freedom'.[132] Socialism, for Cairnes, would substitute for the inducement of profits 'benevolence and public spirit' – notoriously weak reeds. When these fail, 'the powers of the State' are invoked and 'disaster and ruin' follow.[133]

Cairnes naturally recommends co-operation, augmenting wages with profits – 'the sole escape'.[134] The greatest boon co-operation confers, for Cairnes, is that in furthering the virtues which it requires – 'self-control and prudence' – it will diminish the great 'Malthusian difficulty' more effectively than 'any amount of direct Malthusian teaching'.[135]

Having dispatched the heresies launched from within the Mill circle with some noisy broadsides, Cairnes sailed for uncharted waters to engage more formidable challengers. Unfortunately, after some dizzying tacking, he wound up captaining the ship of Ricardian political economy into a shallow lagoon. Eventually Marshall installed an engine and it steamed off for another lengthy tour of duty, flying the same hopeful flags (one still did not have to choose between them), Social Reform and Individual Responsibility.

8 Henry Fawcett

I

In his second extant letter to Henry Fawcett, Mill sagaciously observed that his young correspondent's blindness 'will, I am satisfied, be very much in your favour, not only by exciting interest, and neutralizing envy and jealousy, but because it will cause you to be much more and sooner talked about'.[1] Mill was, of course, correct. Though it may ultimately have kept him out of the Cabinet,[2] his blindness probably improved Fawcett's formidable oratorical talents, and secured him the sympathetic attention of much of the nation.[3] It quite possibly also made more palatable his intransigent radicalism, and it certainly made more credible his persistent advocacy of the doctrine of self-help.

Fawcett's blindness obviously also helped – directly and indirectly – to ensure that he has been much more written about than any of the Mill circle, with the possible exception of Morley. His marriage to Millicent Garrett, who was to become a leading feminist for over half a century, means that he will likely continue to be a subject of interest to historians.[4]

Fawcett was born in Salisbury in 1838. His father, William, a draper, came from Westmoreland, via London. The elder Fawcett was a fine orator (purportedly better than his son) and an ardent Liberal, serving as mayor of Salisbury in the auspicious year 1832 and hosting Cobden and Bright when they visited the town a decade later.[5] Fawcett's mother, Mary Cooper, the daughter of a solicitor who was the local Whig agent, was also keenly interested in politics.

Fawcett appears to have been a precocious schoolboy, excelling in mathematics, if not in classics. His first public lecture, delivered at the age of 14, extolled the virtues of steam power, and was buttressed by an abundance of statistical evidence nicely anticipating the enthusiasms and methods of the mature Fawcett. The lecture may also possibly mark the last time Fawcett invoked the Deity on the platform, extolling 'the Great Power' who 'has provided steam for human use'.[6]

The only other mention of God that Stephen records is no less revealing. Writing in 1856 to an old family friend, Mrs Hodding, Fawcett confessed,

> You know somewhat of my character; you shall now hear my views as to my future. I started life as a boy with the ambition some day to enter the House of Commons. Every effort, every endeavour which I have ever put forth has had this object in view.... I feel that I ought to make any sacrifice, to endure any amount of labour, to obtain this position in which I could be of the greatest use to my fellow-men...in removing the social evils of our country, and especially the paramount one – the mental degradation of millions.... I should be racked with remorse through life if any selfishness checked such efforts. For I must regard it as a high privilege from God if I have such aspirations, and if He has endowed me with powers which will enable me to assist in such a work of philanthropy.[7]

The Deity who sanctions steam power also sanctions Fawcett's ambitions, and is thereafter little heard from.

A Cambridge Fellowship was to be the springboard for his political career. (The shrewd Fawcett switched from Peterhouse to Trinity because the latter, 'at its nadir', offered less competition.[8]) An early schoolmaster, a Mr Fearon, a Unitarian and staunch Liberal, may have been a figure of some influence.[9] But Fawcett's ethos was undeniably shaped by Cambridge in the 1850s and 1860s – or of a circle at Cambridge, not exclusively Apostolic, of which Stephen appears to have been near the centre. Stephen, in some of the most memorable passages in his biography, explains and, indeed, summonses Cambridge's *genus locus*:

> Literature was not indeed the strong point of the set. They were typical Cambridge men: believers in hard facts and figures, admirers of strenuous common sense, and hearty despisers of sentimentalism.[10]

> We preferred to mask our impulses under a guise of cynicism rather than to affect more sensibility than we really possessed. I for one should be sorry to see the opposite practice come into fashion.... Staunch utilitarians and political economists, we were always on our

> guard against sentimentalism and keenly alive to the absurdity of excesses in that direction.[11]

Eventually, though, the Cambridge cohort came to recognize 'the great truth that warmth of heart is not incompatible with, but essential to, a thoroughly masculine nature'.[12]

Cutting across the hackneyed Utilitarian/Romantic dichotomy, Collini has usefully characterized the resident spirit as a kind of Muscular Liberalism.[13] Energy, independence and candour were the virtues supremely valued, and were embodied in the highest term of approbation, 'manly'.[14] A characteristic temperament rather than a coherent set of principles thus distinguished mid-century liberalism from its predecessors and, especially, its New Liberal successor.

But Cambridge Liberalism had its creed, and Fawcett's Bible, clearly, was Mill's *Political Economy*. Stephen joked that Fawcett had read no other book.[15] This was not in fact true (as Stephen hastily assures the reader), and 1859 saw the publication of two books that may have affected Fawcett nearly as profoundly: Darwin's *Origin of the Species* and Mill's *On Liberty*. Two years earlier Fawcett had been enormously impressed by the first volume of Buckle's *History of Civilization*.[16] The prospect of a 'scientific' history was exhilarating – its determinism and its optimism were probably equally attractive. It appealed to his hostility to the aristocracy and to his delight in penetrating pretences to unveil the real operative forces at play.

How much more impressive an achievement then was Darwin's hypothesis, suggesting as it did the laws governing the development of life itself.[17] Particularly telling were the conclusions Fawcett emphasized: (1) the process is progressive – things improve, or at least get more complex; (2) the process is, nonetheless, brutal. Success requires trial and struggle – 'an exterminating war throughout the whole of nature must ceaselessly be waged';[18] and (3) best of all, God is reduced to a first cause.[19] Species and individuals create their own destinies. Life is an examination. 'This is the doctrine of Malthus applied to the whole animal and vegetable kingdoms', he exults.[20] Fawcett is aware, of course, that Darwin had only put forward an hypothesis; further study of the geological record will ultimately confirm or refute it.[21] Still, attacks on the *Origin* had frequently been ill-informed and unfair, and perhaps not the least pleasure in the task Fawcett took upon himself in summarizing the *Origin* was that it enabled him to calmly and dispassionately advocate toleration.[22]

Tolerance meant a hearing for beliefs he found congenial. At the essay's close, Fawcett abandons his pretence of neutrality, expressing the hope that public opinion about evolution will itself evolve: like the 'convert' Dr Hooker, '[o]ther minds may perhaps pass through similar stages of primary doubt and ultimate belief'.[23]

The desire to champion toleration was in part a Cambridge legacy, but also obviously owed much directly to Mill. Stephen fully shared Fawcett's somewhat contemptuous indifference to matters theological, even as he understated it.

> It is strange to turn from Cambridge of this period to the Oxford so vividly described by the historians of the Newman generation. It is like passing to the history of a remote century of a different civilisation. ... We had, of course, our High-Churchmen and our Evangelicals... [b]ut there was no active spirit of theological investigation. The cardinal virtue in such matters, according to us, was a common sense which might be taken to imply a liberal and tolerant spirit or simple indifference. Indifference was certainly the characteristic of... Fawcett himself.[24]

But the phrase 'cardinal virtue' belies both the disinterestedness and the lack of interest implied by indifference. Fawcett was, in fact, a zealot for toleration.

His reverence for Mill was legion: 'no teacher could ever boast of a more ardent and attached disciple'.[25] While he was often chaffed for being a man of one book, Mill's *Principles*,[26] it was *On Liberty* that Fawcett hailed as 'the greatest work of our greatest living writer'. He confided to the Manchester schoolboys to whom he was awarding prizes in October 1866, that 'as I read his noble, I might almost say his holy, ideas, I thought to myself, If everyone in my country could and would read this work, how infinitely happier would the nation be!' The second adjective, despite, or because of, his hesitation, is not insignificant. 'How much less of the energy of the nation', he continues,

> would be wasted in contemptible quarrels about creeds and formularies; and how much more powerful should we be as a nation to achieve works of good, when, as this work would teach us to be, we were firmly bound together by the bonds of a wise toleration![27]

Toleration is thus not grudging forbearance, but an active force uniting those who practise it. And sectarianism is sinful chiefly because it wastes energy. After the accident that blinded him, Fawcett displayed a remarkable stoicism and cheerfulness. (He later claimed that within ten minutes he had resolved to 'stick to his pursuits as much as possible'.[28]) 'There was only one thing, he told his sister, which he dreaded – namely, a loss of energy.'[29]

More specifically, intolerance wasted energy by interfering with market processes that worked to the benefit of individuals and the nation. Stephen's characterization of the objectives of university reform, the first cause Fawcett embraced, is revealing: intentionally or not, he adopts the language of political economy. The reformers wished,

> to do away with all restriction which hampered the full efficiency of the prizes offered to intellectual excellence. The function of the University was education; the mainspring of the educational system was the rewards obtainable by success in examination; the more attractive the prizes, the more open the field, the greater would be the success of the system.[30]

In other words, the production of first-rate dons depended on increasing capital and extending the market.

At this point – 1858 – religious tests were no longer imposed either for degrees or scholarships at Cambridge. Fawcett was obliged to turn to Trinity College, Dublin, where tests were still in force, in order to agitate for secular education. Then, in 1873, Gladstone's Irish Universities Bill provided him an opportunity to launch a full-tilt anti-sectarian crusade.

As in the discussion of Cairnes's views, it is not necessary to adjudicate the conflicting arguments of the debate to recognize that Fawcett demonstrated an exceptionally strong commitment to first principles. In so doing, he carried with him only a tiny fraction of the party.[31] For Stephen, because Fawcett 'thought comparatively little of the importance of the religious differences', he opted for establishing a system the Church establishment vehemently opposed.[32] In truth, it was not that he 'thought little' of religious differences as much as he hoped that secular institutions would gradually reshape beliefs: when Catholic students were exposed to the chilly waters of rationalism, their superstitions would dissolve. When faith confronted reason, the outcome could not be in doubt. Tolerance was a formidable means of social change, and it was certainly not to be extended to institutions that did not themselves practise it.

It was hardly less wicked to compromise with the intolerant. Millicent Fawcett's only allusion to her husband's religious beliefs in her memoir comes at the end of her discussion of the University Bill. 'What right had any educational institution, he urged, to be called a university in which history, theology, and philosophy were forbidden to be taught? In his view, this was almost a sin against the Holy Ghost.'[33]

Fawcett's actual religious beliefs are difficult to disinter. There is not even the scant nod to religion Cairnes offers in *The Character and Logical Method of Political Economy*.[34] Fawcett's political ambitions obviously inhibited any desire he may have felt to divulge his thoughts on the subject. But after his death, his wife acknowledged that he had not been a Christian.[35] And Stephen informed his fiancée that 'Fawcett doesn't believe in one of the 39 articles, except perhaps that wh. says that a Xtian may swear'.[36]

There was no transcendent rival, in short, to the Improvement of Mankind. This was to be achieved, above all, by applying the principles of political economy as established by Mill, and by extending the dominion of toleration. Toleration, in turn, would ensure a speedier and more widespread acceptance of secularism and the *Principles*. And the work of 'the Holy Ghost' would be accomplished.

II

The two most significant problems that remained for Radicals after 1870 were (1) the continued poverty of the working classes and (2) the persistence of pauperism. Why, in short, a quarter of a century after the repeal of the Corn Laws, had wealth not diffused more widely? 'No subject, in the whole range of economic science, can be of greater practical interest.'[37] 'Fawcett's sympathy with the poor and the helpless was not only deep and genuine', Stephen claimed; 'it was the mainspring of his most energetic political action.'[38] And Fawcett's *Manual* was fundamentally a political book. In disseminating Mill's doctrines to a wider audience, it would enhance the influence of the *Principles* on public policy. (The book made no pretences to advancing the science.) The *Manual* itself, moreover, explicitly sought to apply the *Principles* to current social problems. Successive editions incorporated Fawcett's articles on topical issues. And in enabling Fawcett to secure a professorship at Cambridge – the book's original *raison d'être*[39] – it was intended to launch his own political career, permitting Fawcett himself to apply Mill's lessons in Westminster.

The aristocracy remained a key political problem, naturally. For Fawcett, it was simply a case of political power thwarting economic development. The propensity of government to interfere in the economy might, however, survive aristocratic dominance, and so Fawcett was not overly sanguine about the benefits of extending the suffrage.[40] Nonetheless, apart from its inevitability (and the justice and expediency of enfranchising women), universal suffrage could not but help diminish aristocratic privileges that denied to the other classes the prosperity and the ensuing intellectual and moral advances that greater freedom would confer. For if Fawcett had his doubts about an untutored electorate, he was supremely confident in the ability of workers to raise themselves through their own exertions. He was a far greater advocate of self-help and enemy of bureaucracy than any of the other Millites, not to mention the purer Benthamites still in circulation.

Of course, by the 1870s much had already been done to abridge the aristocracy's power. The Corn Laws were gone, the army, the civil service, and the universities had been thrown open. Even 'primogeniture', Fawcett conceded, 'is maintained much more by custom than by law'.[41] Nonetheless, despite the fact that cases of intestacy (when primogeniture was mandated) were rare, law affects custom, and abolishing primogeniture and entail would facilitate the transfer of land, and thus stimulate the redistribution of wealth.

But the removal of aristocratic prerogatives was insufficient in itself. Like Mill, Fawcett had two paramount objectives: that agricultural labourers should become land-owners – peasant proprietors – and that workers should become capitalists – co-operators or profit-sharers. Wages needed to be augmented by rent or profits. Furthermore, 'the magic of property turns sand into gold'.[42] Having a stake in the outcome of enterprises would promote values and behaviour conducive to greater productivity and greater savings, and, additionally, would educate the urban working classes about the complexities of managing a commercial or industrial firm, thus averting unnecessary strikes and reducing the appeal of dangerous panaceas. 'All remedies... must be inadequate which do not establish a complete union between capital and labour: this is effected when the capital which industry requires is supplied by the labourers themselves.'[43]

Given his rigid and reductive version of the wage fund, co-operation was especially imperative if workers were to escape from the familiar vicious circle: '... directly the labourers obtain any advance in wages[,] they call into operation an influence which, sooner or later, must exert a tendency again to reduce wages'.[44] Hasty and improvident marriages had two evil effects: 'In the first place, an increase in the supply of labour tends to diminish wages; in the second place, as population increases, food becomes dearer, the cost of living is augmented, and wages possess less purchasing power.'[45] The law of supply and demand is inexorable: attempts to keep wages above their 'natural' level (which varies from industry to industry) inevitably lower the rate of profit and send capital fleeing to more remunerative investments, thus diminishing the wages fund, the sole source of the demand for labour.[46]

Fawcett was aware that arguments for co-operation and, especially, for peasant proprietorships risked dismissal on the grounds of both practicability and economic principles. He took some pains to address potential objections. He conceded that mechanized farming has created significant economies of scale – larger farms, *caeteris paribus*, are likely to be more productive.[47] Nonetheless, Fawcett argued, the lack of 'a pecuniary motive to work with energy and skill'[48] on the part of hired labourers more than offsets the efficiencies of larger-scale production. Ultimately, extra-economic considerations were paramount: the farm labourer's

> life is... one of dull routine. It may be said that he is spared many anxieties with which the labourer who is his own master has to contend. But... these cares and anxieties are the most valuable instruments of education, and... without them the human faculties can never be adequately developed.[49]

Desirable as peasant proprietorships were, they should not be introduced coercively. Given his hostility to the existing distribution of land, it was natural that he should wish to distinguish his position both from that of the followers of Henry George (after 1880) and from the socialists. The nationalization of land – and other instruments of production – would have disastrous consequences for several reasons:

1. It would be 'flagrantly unjust' not to compensate present owners. Moreover, it 'would be impossible to say where this wholesale appropriation would stop'. The large landowner and the peasant proprietor would not be its only victims.[50]

2. If current owners *were* compensated, however, the 30 years' purchase price would approximately equal three times the national debt.[51]
3. If the government leased the land at market prices, there would have been no point to the confiscation, but if leased on other terms, 'patronage and favouritism' would determine allocation, and 'the demoralizing corruption that would ensue would be more far-reaching and more baneful in its consequences than even the pecuniary loss which the scheme would involve'.[52]

There was no immediate prospect of state socialism in England. However, a number of schemes to ameliorate the situation of the working classes were objectionable on similar grounds – that thrift and industriousness would be taxed to reward sloth and improvidence, and additionally, that investment in home industries would be discouraged. (For an ardent free trader, Fawcett was unusually suspicious of foreign investments.)[53] The programmes Fawcett opposed on these grounds included public works (though India was partially exempted); compulsory disability insurance; and free education. Worst of all, however, was the existing Poor Law system, which 'is undoubtedly based on socialism'.[54] Involuntary poverty was, of course, distinguished from voluntary. The former included the children of dissolute parents and the victims of financial crises and such natural causes as bad weather, natural disasters and the depletion of resources.[55] (Business cycles, for Fawcett, were caused exclusively by over-speculation.) Voluntary poverty, on the other hand, resulted from a deficiency of will, and was far more common. As a result, Fawcett claimed,

> the leniency and want of firmness with which it has been treated may probably be regarded as the most powerful of all the agencies which have produced the widespread distress which afflicts even the most wealthy countries… . Indiscriminate almsgiving always in the end demoralizes those whom it is intended to benefit, and intensifies the evils which it seeks to alleviate.[56]

The economic problems facing the country were then to be resolved by allowing agricultural labourers to be landlords and urban workers to become capitalists, and by forcing the poor to become members of the working class. Behind these solutions was the belief pithily expressed by Fawcett's friend and biographer, 'Whoever professes to raise the position of a class without elevating its character is a charlatan'.[57]

9 William Thomas Thornton

William Thomas Thornton's name today is associated almost exclusively with the attack on the wages fund doctrine that elicited Mill's famous 'recantation'. Two things are noteworthy about the episode: (1) Thornton was Mill's long-time friend and former East India House colleague; and (2) Thornton's assault was something less than overwhelming. Some contemporaries and, eventually, historians of economic thought have expressed surprise that so ineffective a barrage yielded such a dramatic surrender.[1] The two facts, though – Thornton's friendship with Mill and his easy triumph – are connected.[2] The capitulation was staged, and Mill's purposes have long been recognized: apart from doing a good turn for his friend, he hoped to discredit a doctrine he perceived had come to be used against trade unionists.[3]

Our interest in the present chapter, however, is less in Mill's response than in what initially motivated Thornton's apostasy. For his objective was not merely to demolish the wages fund doctrine (the critique of which originally consisted of a mere footnote),[4] but to discredit classical political economy in its entirety. The science rested on an understanding of the effects of supply and demand that Thornton believed was fundamentally unsound. The scope of his argument did not escape him: finding himself 'immediately in collision with Mr Mill', Thornton later acknowledged, he felt 'a little as Saul of Tarsus might have felt if, while sitting at the feet of Gamaliel, he had suddenly found himself compelled by a sense of duty to contradict his master'.[5] Unquestionably, political principles inspired Thornton's attack no less than they did Mill's capitulation. For though he was hardly uncritical of 'the wrongful claims of labour' (his subtitle), Thornton hoped to vindicate both the rights and efficacy of trades union activity. However, the source of Thornton's objections to the wages fund lay deeper than his political beliefs and the Millite legislative agenda. I will be arguing that Thornton's religious beliefs were not incidental to his wholesale rejection of classical economics. Thornton, unlike his fellow Millites, was a Theist; he devoted considerable time and energy to proving the existence of a beneficent Creator.

I will examine Thornton's religious beliefs below, but a revealing comparison can be made initially with Fawcett, the Millite *ne plus ultra*.

Like many other rationalists who came of age intellectually in the 1850s, Fawcett was profoundly influenced, as noted, by Buckle and Darwin. It was exhilarating to discover that the competition for scarce resources inexorably compelled life itself, and the human species in particular, to progressively improve. The implicit mandate for politicians was wonderfully clear: eliminate legislation which attempted to interfere with the working of natural laws. Thornton had a very different – and, characteristically, far lengthier – response to Buckle and Darwin. He sought, briefly, to defend freedom – and, hence, morality – against Buckle,[6] and to rescue the concept of an intelligent and (at one time) active Deity against the materialism Lewes and Huxley distilled from Darwin.[7] In a series of prolix essays, Thornton endeavoured to illuminate 'the rational solidity of so much of every religion as consists of theism'.[8]

Behind Thornton's wholesale rejection of the fundamental premises of Ricardian political economy – as behind his attacks on 'Huxleyism' and 'Scientific Atheism' – is a need to defend human freedom. '[T]hat ever-changing chameleon, human character' ensures that prices are indeterminate. Appraisals of the prospective demand for a given good or service inevitably diverge, and on this ultimately hinges his objections to Ricardian notions of supply and demand.[9]

I begin with an extended discussion of Thornton's attack on fundamental propositions of classical political economy because, first, this is what he is remembered for today, and, second, to emphasize the enormity of his breach with Mill. The remainder of the chapter is, in effect, an attempt to illuminate the source of Thornton's vigorous dissent from his friend – his religious beliefs – and to reconstruct Thornton's distinctive conservative radicalism.

I

While historians have generally expressed surprise at Mill's acquiescence in the wages fund controversy, Britain's leading economist (from Mill's death to his own) purported to be amazed that anyone could have ever believed in the hoary old tautology in the first place.[10] Jevons's contempt was contagious: writing ten years after Mill's recantation, Sidgwick noted the 'growing tendency... to treat it [the wages fund theory] as exploded'.[11] Indeed, 'killing the wage-fund "theory" became a favorite sport', Schumpeter observed.[12]

Subsequently, however, the theory began to enjoy a renewed respectability. At the very least, as noted earlier, it was a first approximation of a theory of capital.[13] But still more recently, Thornton's attack has itself experienced a revival of interest and respect. Thornton has been defended as a precursor of disequilibrium theory,[14] of efficient contract theory (modelling union–employer bargaining),[15] and as so trenchant a critic of the assumption of equilibrium outcomes from market transactions as to provoke Jevons into countering with a misguided mechanistic analysis of supply and demand.[16] These claims, in turn, have elicited renewed scepticism about Thornton's aims and accomplishments.[17]

There is certainly evidence that Thornton's contemporaries took his attack seriously. J. L. Shadwell, the only student of Cairnes's to publish a full length treatise, which he did with Jevons's encouragement,[18] begins the preface to his *A System of Political Economy* by noting that he 'commenced studying POLITICAL ECONOMY at the time when the publication of Mr Thornton's works on Labour had just given so rude a shock to the common belief that the science, so far as it dealt with the subject of Value and Wages, was complete'.[19] He compares Thornton's attack on the doctrine to Dollinger's on Papal Infallibility.[20] Biagini has documented the extent of the appreciation of Thornton's accomplishment, albeit belated, in the working-class press of the mid-1870s.[21] Thomas Burt, the miners' leader and subsequent MP, felt *On Labour* marked a turning point in the development of economic thought, and George Howell urged workers to read the book closely.[22]

Thornton indicts classical political economy's representation of the working of supply and demand on two grounds.

1. First, price is not determined at the equilibrium of supply and demand because increased demand does not, in fact, raise prices. Nearly all of his examples are meant to illustrate this conundrum. Conveniently for his argument, Thornton stipulates that the additional consumers in all his scenarios have identical demand schedules. Thus, new buyers for horses stubbornly offer the same £50, and no higher, that the previous buyers did.[23] So, too, potential customers for gloves are unwilling to offer more than 10 shillings a pair.[24] Needless to say, if one envisions a market where no one

is willing to offer a higher price than the initial bid, prices will not rise.
2. Conversely, Thornton argues, suppliers generally feel no compulsion to keep lowering prices until the market is cleared. If a corn importer were obliged to sell his entire supply the moment his ship docked, he might not get 20 shillings a quarter for wheat normally worth 60 shillings. Fortunately (for their own solvency, at least), most suppliers are able to reserve prices.[25]

But what determines the reserve price? How do merchants decide when to decline offers? After suggesting that the upper limit of any price is set by utility to the consumer and the lower by utility to the dealer (the only mention of utility in an extensive discussion), Thornton eventually concludes that 'competition' determines price.[26] But what, then, fuels competition? After more laborious exposition, Thornton decides that it is 'the least favorable estimate' of 'prospective supply and demand' by dealers offering the same product in the same market.[27] Thornton's argument is thus circular. His rejection of supply and demand is based, at bottom, on the indubitable fact that most markets aren't cleared in the short run, if clearing a market is defined as the sale of everything each seller wishes to dispose of or every buyer wishes to purchase. Market prices have floors and ceilings, and the floor, as Mill himself notes, is determined by the prices sellers reserve. Bids by buyers beneath this price are extra-marginal. And what determines reservation prices are estimates of future demand. Thus, demand is quite meaningful for those whose livelihood depends on satisfying it. And their assessments of future demand affect supply, as price adjustments are communicated to secondary and tertiary producers, who respond accordingly.[28]

Nonetheless, Thornton's example of what can happen in the absence of reserved prices is illuminating. He compares an 'English' and a 'Dutch' auction. In the first case, a conventional auction, consumers bid against each other. In the 'Dutch' auction, however, the dealer quotes the price, moving downward until he gets offers. In Thornton's example, a buyer willing to pay 8 shillings for 100 herrings would pay that amount in a Dutch auction, whereas if he were the only bidder willing to go even as high as 6 shillings, he would get his fish for the lesser amount at an English auction.[29] In his response, Mill quite reasonably dismisses the possibility that such discontinuities would exist in a large wholesale market. Other knowledgeable bidders would likely push the final price close to 8 shillings (assuming the initial bidder was informed). But in any case, lowering the price would hardly fail to increase demand.[30] All the same, Thornton's demonstration that institutional practices can affect outcomes when prices can't be reserved has some merit. Though it takes him a while to advance his argument, Thornton's next step is obvious: labour, like fish, is an anomalous commodity, in that it is difficult for workers to reserve prices. The first reason he offers, however, is not legitimate: labour, he argues, 'will not keep. Today's labour cannot be sold after today, for tomorrow it will have ceased to exist.'[31] While this is certainly true, it is true of all services (as well as a number of perishable products). Thornton's next observation, however, is unexceptionable: most labourers have nothing but their labour to live on. Without savings, they can't 'stand out' for higher prices, as other sellers do.[32] While normally customers' needs for commodities are more urgent than those of the dealers to sell, this is not true of the labour market, Thornton argues. The labour market, furthermore, is notoriously distinguished by combinations rather than competition.[33] '[T]he price of labour', he concludes, 'is determined not by supply and demand, which never determined the price of anything, nor yet generally by competition, which generally determines the price of everything else, but by combination among the masters.'[34]

The wages fund doctrine is a special case of the law of supply and demand. Having proved (to his own satisfaction) that supply and demand do not affect price as postulated by classical political economy – that price is indeterminate – Thornton was in a position to reject on this basis the central claim of the wages fund doctrine: an increase in capital will not necessarily result in higher wages; an increase in the number of workers will not necessarily reduce wages. But Thornton doesn't adopt this argument. Instead, he makes two other claims: (1) that the idea of a fund is illusory because individual employers do not, in fact, allocate a predetermined amount for wages. Since there are no actual individual wage funds, there can thus be no aggregate fund. (2) In his second edition, utilizing the more sophisticated argument marshalled by Mill, Thornton emphasizes the absurdity of postulating unitary elasticity for wage capital. Employers are very much influenced by the price of labour. They do not mindlessly spend an amount previously allotted, but purchase only as much labour as they need.[35]

Despite the recent defences of Thornton noted earlier, most economists would not find persuasive Thornton's arguments against both the wages fund and the dynamics of competitive markets.

Cairnes's methodological objection to Thornton's argument also remains valid: Cairnes argued that Thornton misunderstood the meaning of economic 'law', which recognizes tendencies but, unlike Acts of Parliament, does not *compel* anyone to do anything. Nor, as Mill made abundantly clear, do isolated exceptions invalidate a law. They are likely a consequence of countervailing 'disturbing causes', governed by their own laws of operation.[36]

Apart from the problems already alluded to (the fact that Thornton acknowledges, implicitly, that estimates of future demand influence price by determining the reservation price, and the fact that Thornton's examples are specious, assuming highly atypical coincidental and vertical demand curves), Thornton fails to deal with both the principal classical and (obviously) marginalist objections to his arguments.[37]

Behind Thornton's enterprise is a deep-seated objection to the classical conundrum that 'the price [of labour] cannot be permanently raised unless the supply be first checked, and the supply cannot be checked unless the price be first permanently raised'.[38] That is, only an increased standard of living will induce workers to limit families, and thus raise their standard of living. With unconscious malice, Thornton calls the paradox a 'millhorse circle'.[39]

But his objection to the wages fund is essentially an assertion of freedom, the key query in his article being, 'Is there any specific portion of any single individual's capital which the owner must necessarily expend upon labour?'[40] Celebrating his overthrow of the laws of supply and demand, he exults that,

> [i]t is no small gain to have discovered that no such despotic laws do or can exist; that, inasmuch as the sole function of scientific law is to predict the invariable recurrence of the same effects from the same causes, and as there can be no invariability where – as in the case of price – one of the most efficient causes is that ever-changing chameleon, human character or disposition, price cannot possibly be subjected to law.[41]

How did Thornton come to hold beliefs so anathema to the Mill circle, while remaining so near its centre?

II

Thornton's background is rather more exotic than that of the rest of the Mill circle: he was half-Turkish. His father, Thomas, had married Sophie Zohrab, the daughter of a merchant, while he was residing in Constantinople.[42] William, born in Buckinghamshire on Valentine's Day, 1813, was their youngest son, and Thomas died just a little over a year after his birth.

The senior Thornton was very much a self-made man. His own father was a Yorkshireman who had established himself in London as an innkeeper. Thomas (whose date of birth is unknown, but was likely around 1765) no doubt inherited some of his father's congeniality. While serving as a manager in a British factory in Constantinople, he befriended various Ottoman officials and European ambassadors, and acutely observed Turkish social and political institutions. When he returned to England after 14 years, he published *The Present State of Turkey* (1807), a highly sympathetic account of the Empire, which established his reputation as an authority on the Near East and a champion of the Turkophiles (largely Tories, needless to say). Much as James Mill earned a place at East India House by the labours of his pen, Thomas Thornton was appointed counsel to the Levant Company in consequence of his book, but died before he could accept his commission.

William's uncle, Sir Edward, had a still more distinguished career. Like his brother, he too served abroad most of his active life. Admitted as a sizar to Cambridge, he became 3rd Wrangler and a Fellow, but then entered the diplomatic corps under the patronage of a couple of Tory officials. He was especially active as a minister plenipotentiary during the Napoleonic wars, and eventually attained the rank of ambassador, at one point rescuing the King of Portugal during an insurrection.

Like his father and uncle, William was blessed with a sociable nature and a love of foreign travel. He was to make as good use of his wanderings through Belgium and northern France as did his father of his more exotic sojourn.

William also seems to have inherited something of the innate Toryism of his grandfather, father and uncle (innkeeping, as well as

Turkophilia, suggesting the latter predisposition). Thornton was unquestionably influenced by the anti-liberal Carlyle and Kingsley. He addresses a plaintive poem to the latter ('To the Author of Alton Locke'), rebuking him for having treated Thornton with contempt, failing to recognize a 'yoke-fellow' fit 'to work beside you in our Master's field'.[43] Thornton's preface to *Old Fashioned Ethics and Commonsense Metaphysics* consists almost entirely of a string of unattributed quotations from Carlyle, 'one of the most frequent "companions of my solitude" ', including the famous phrases from Chapter 7 of *Sartor Resartus* that could only have made Thornton's best friend wince to reread:

> Has the word Duty no meaning? Is what we call Duty no divine messenger and guide, but a false, earthly fantasm, made up of Desire and Fear? In that Logic-mill of thine hast thou an earthly mechanism for the Godlike itself, and for grinding out Virtue from the husks of Pleasure? I tell thee, Nay![44]

His second collection of poems is dedicated to William Aytoun, the Scottish poet, satirist, longtime contributor of conservative articles to *Blackwoods*, and, ultimately, Tory pensioner.

William Thornton's early career no doubt owed something to the influence of his uncle and, posthumously, of his father. But another well-connected relative, his cousin Sir W. H. Thornton, provided more immediate assistance, inviting the 14-year-old William to reside with him in Malta, where Sir William was installed as auditor-general. After three years, young William was offered a position by the Counsel General of Constantinople. He spent six years in the Ottoman capital, returning to England in 1836 to assume a clerkship in the East India House, a vacancy created, coincidentally, by the death of James Mill.[45] Thornton worked there for the remainder of his life, eventually being given charge of the Public Works department in 1856 and becoming first secretary for Public Works when the company was taken over by the government two years later. We glimpse him summonsed (in January 1870) to meet with the Duke of Argyll, Secretary of State for India, who was anxious that a state-run railway system be inaugurated in India. The Duke was pleased and surprised to discover that Thornton supported such a project.[46] Three years later the Duke helped Thornton secure a CB.

Apart from its role in determining the kinds of issues he would become familiar with, and, perhaps, imparting something of a bureaucratic cast to his thinking, Thornton's position at the East India House served his career as an economist in at least a couple of ways.

First, of course, it enabled him to meet John Stuart Mill. After their initial discussion of Thornton's *Overpopulation*, they conversed daily. 'And what talks we had on such occasions, and on what various subjects!'[47] Apart from the intellectual stimulus and camaraderie, and the boost to his literary career, the friendship also facilitated his rise at East India House. Mill insisted that Thornton be named Assistant Examiner as a condition of his accepting the post of Chief Examiner in 1856, and then performed Thornton's duties for a year after the latter's breakdown, enabling him to retain his position. Apart from being worth at least £600 a year, the job – ten to four, Monday to Saturday – appears to have permitted Thornton to work on his own essays at the office, as well as enabling him to take at least two month's vacation each year.[48]

What sort of an individual was Thornton? Few accounts have survived, but, inevitably, Thornton's own writing reveals something of his personality. He is, particularly in the prose of his later works, avuncular, discursive and sometimes charmingly diffident (as when he cheerfully acknowledges that he has not read Comte, though still prepared to dissect his social thought).[49] He is attentive to his audience, quite aware that some of his propositions may seem audacious, but if the reader will be sufficiently patient, he or she will slowly be brought to see the light. His favourite rhetorical persona is that of the genial and patient defender of common sense against supposed experts. Thornton's modesty and self-consciousness distinguish his prose sharply from Mill's, Morley's and Cairnes's, and while no less fond of sarcasm than the latter, his thrusts are more good-natured. He delights in the *reductio ad absurdum*, whether the target is McCulloch's belief in economies of scale in agriculture, Fawcett's belief in a wages fund, or Lewes's belief in determinism and materialism. Classical allusions pepper Thornton's prose, but his appeal is almost always to experience, to empirical evidence, and to the reader's reasonableness and sense of justice.

Virtually the sole surviving descriptions of Thornton are, luckily, Leslie Stephen's, who considers Thornton's influence on Mill 'remarkable'.[50] 'The excellent W. T. Thornton', Stephen notes, '...was one of the few friends who communicated freely with [Mill] during his seclusion.' 'Thornton's extreme amiability', he adds in a footnote, 'his placid and candid, if slightly long-winded, discussions of his favourite topics, won the affection of his young hearers, and has left a charming impression upon the survivors.'[51] Stephen himself, however, on at least one occasion was less than charmed by Thornton's verbosity. Dining at the Political Economy Club on 7 December 1866, he wrote to his fiancée Minnie Thackeray:

> I am suffering the torments of the damned from the God-forgotten Thornton, who is boring on about supply and demand, when I would give anything to be with you. He is not a bad fellow, but just now I hate him like poison.[52]

In private correspondence, Stephen was far more critical of Thornton's abilities.

> I have just received a note from W. T. Thornton in wh. he says that he hopes for my sake I did not write a review of him in the PMG. If I did, he says, I show that a long practice of reviewing has made me incapable of fairness even when I mean to be fair. That is... courteous as he obviously thinks that I did write the review. As it happens, I did not but I half wish that I had. My unfairness in regard to him is that I have never told the public what a fool he is, but I shant tell him so.[53]

Bain observes that 'one of Mill's chief friendships in later years was with Thornton, who differed from him in a great many things, but the differences were of the kind to bring into lively exercise Mill's argumentative powers', and compares him to Sterling, also a genial and loquacious stimulus.[54] Morley, in his copious *Recollections*, is content merely to list Thornton as one of the luminaries at the 'ideal symposia' he attended at Blackheath Park,[55] and Packe also has surprisingly little to say of Thornton, apart from drawing on a couple of letters and on his essay on Mill at East India House.

Mill himself does not mention his friend in his *Autobiography*, in keeping with its character, nor is he alluded to in Helen Taylor's addendum. Nonetheless, Mill's letters to him, always commencing 'Dear Thornton', reveal the depth of his attachment. '[H]e is a person I particularly respect and like', Mill confessed. 'In perfect candour, sincerity, and singleness of mind, few men come near him.'[56] Thornton was one of the very few visitors welcomed at Avignon after Harriet

Taylor's death. (Thornton was, indeed, the first non-relative to whom Mill wrote following his wife's last illness.) Thornton's letter to Fawcett from Avignon remains the fullest description of Mill's 'dear little cottage'[57] at St Veran, and of Mill's and his step-daughter's daily routine there.[58] Helen Taylor was particularly fond of Thornton, and worked assiduously preparing what Mill describes to his friend as '*your* room'.[59]

Apart from their revealing his affectionate feelings for Thornton, and some interesting details of his domestic life, Mill's letters confirm Bain's impression: the two friends enjoyed intellectual sparring. Anticipating the 1862 visit, Mill tells Thornton that he looks forward to 'having out the subject of Darwin & many others'.[60] In other letters he remonstrates with his friend over Thornton's lack of scepticism about 'spiritualism',[61] and his faith in *The Times*'s and *Saturday Review*'s accounts of the American Civil War.[62] Several of Mill's letters contain extended arguments about utilitarianism.[63]

There is something in the characterizations of Thornton that suggest bachelorhood, an impression reinforced by his fusty and bemused literary persona. And indeed, neither the *DNB* nor the extant obituaries mention a wife or children.[64] Nonetheless, his correspondence and poetry[65] make clear that he was married and had a daughter, Evelyn (referred to as Eve or Ellen), and a son, Edward Zohrab, an officer. The family resided at 7 Cadogan Place, a not unfashionable address just west of Sloan Street, between Knightsbridge and Belgravia. When Thornton's daughter died in March 1876, Helen Taylor assured him that he was 'one of those who will find in the disinterested care for the happiness of others and the progress of our fellow creatures the only comfort, the consolation, or at least the anodyne for grief'.[66] Like most members of the Millite circle, he himself was frequently in poor health, even apart from the year-long breakdown in 1856. As a result, Thornton travelled abroad regularly, sallying off to investigate peasant holdings between periods of recuperation at the spas.[67]

Thornton's life in London appears to have been divided between the East India House, the Garrick and Political Economy Clubs, and Mill's Sunday dinners at Blackheath. His private life nowhere intrudes upon his books and articles.

I have delayed considering Thornton's education and religious beliefs. The two are naturally related, and are quite as unorthodox as his youthful sojourns in the Near East. Thornton's only formal education, which ceased around the age of 14, was at the Moravian settlement at Ockbrook. It has been impossible to determine the circumstances under which he was sent there, but Thornton's family may well have been Moravians. His grandfather, Thomas, originally came from Yorkshire, where the oldest and largest Moravian settlement in Britain had been established at Fulneck.[68] A John Thornton of Fulneck was a Moravian missionary who supervised trading operations at the Church's outpost in Labrador, the kind of career congenial to the peripatetic Thorntons of Thomas's and William's generations.[69] The first Moravian chapel in Britain was established in 1738 in Fetter Lane, London, and remains the site of the Church's United Kingdom headquarters. So a Moravian migrating to London could well have remained an active congregant.

While the reputation of some Moravian boarding schools attracted parents of other denominations, this was less likely in England than America.[70] Famous non-Moravian graduates of Moravian academies – like H. H. Asquith and Reginald McKenna, among others – generally didn't matriculate until at least the 1860s.[71] The Ockbrook school, moreover, was only established in 1799; it is unlikely that it was widely known beyond Moravian circles when Thornton was enrolled some 20 years later.[72]

What were Moravian beliefs and practices when Thornton was being educated at Ockbrook? Very briefly, the Church was originally established by Bohemian Hussites, but did not survive the persecutions of the Thirty Years' War. It was revived in the early eighteenth century, largely through the efforts of Count Nicholas von Zinzendorf, a Saxon nobleman influenced by the Lutheran Pietists at Halle. The sect's theology was very much Christ-centred. Like Pietism, Moravianism was what Zinzendorf termed a 'heart religion' based on 'Heart-Truths'.[73]

But Zinzendorf, who has been called the greatest German theologian between Luther and Schleiermacher, de-emphasized the concern with sin and repentance characteristic of Pietism and, later, of Evangelicalism.[74] He preferred the term 'redemption' to 'atonement'.

Other key Moravian beliefs of some significance here were the emphasis on Christian fellowship (both for individual salvation and as an agency of Church renewal) and on good works.[75] And in opposition to Wesley and his followers, Zinzendorf denied the perfectibility of man, and, by extension, the importance of self-denial: 'We ridicule all mortification. No purification precedes perfect love.'[76] Thus, though life in the settlements was regimented and communal, it was not ascetic. The bakery at Fulneck was famous, the 'love feast' – the meal preceding communion – much emphasized. Great stress was placed on music in church and community.[77]

The organizational principles Zinzendorf bequeathed the church were distinctive in at least two important ways. First, in keeping with his ecumenical outlook – 'in necessitariis unitas; in non-necessitariis libertas: in utrisque caritas'[78] – Zinzendorf opposed the establishment of a separate church. Those Moravians not descended from the Bohemian Brethren were advised to retain their affiliations within their national churches.[79] He himself remained a Lutheran. At the same time, Moravians were to form themselves into separate communities, modelled on Herrnhut, the refugee village founded on Zinzendorf's estate in 1722.[80] A number of enterprises flourished in the settlements, called 'diaconies', but there was no collective ownership; individuals were salaried employees, with the Church retaining profits.

Much has been written about the influence of Moravianism on John Wesley, who first encountered Moravian missionaries on his voyage to Georgia in 1735.[81] The influence on Thornton remains more speculative. He does not discuss his debts in any surviving letter or published work. Nonetheless, it is not unreasonable to assume that his Moravian education at Ockbrook affected him in at least three ways.

First, being raised in and to some degree identifying with a tiny Protestant sect of pre-Reformation origin – one that had suffered persecutions in the seventeenth century that dwarfed the disabilities subsequently imposed on English dissenters – Thornton is likely to have imbibed a sceptical attitude toward religious authority, and, quite possibly, toward other, temporal authorities as well.

Second, living and working in an economically self-sufficient community, where all property was owned and administered by the Ockbrook Elders Conference, undoubtedly stimulated his thinking about economic subjects. He would likely have regarded the existence of private property and the market from a fresh perspective. Insights into the Moravian system's drawbacks may conceivably have intensified his defence of private property in *On Labour* and elsewhere. It was not, in any case, an institution he was likely to take for granted.

Finally, Moravian beliefs themselves may have had some impact. While there is no evidence that Thornton continued his affiliation with Moravianism and he does not appear to be especially interested in Christ, the very fact that he does address theological questions, in several long poems and essays, not to mention the tenor and content of these meditations, distinguishes him sharply from the rest of the Mill circle and testifies to the durability of the faith he imbibed at Ockbrook. He had no doubt that the universe was created by a beneficent God who is 'present everywhere, is ever nigh,/ Attentive to His meanest creature's cry', whom we must serve in this life and with whom we will be reunited in Heaven.[82]

For the Theist in the second half of the nineteenth century, proving God's goodness was no less important than demonstrating his existence.[83] Thornton's most sustained attempt to reconcile God with evil is 'Modern Manicheism', the title poem of his second volume of poetry. When, after some 115 pages in his essay collection criticizing materialism and atheism, Thornton resolves to state his own views, he confesses that he can do no better than to reproduce the long poem first published 16 years earlier.[84]

The poem tells of a prophetic vision in which 'a Voice' informs the poet that God had intended good things for man; he had planned a home where there would be no 'care, nor want, nor anguish'.[85] The poem 'Labour's Utopia' provides a more graphic account of this intended abode. What went wrong? The Voice turns first to Matthew 7:9–11,[86] then Matthew 13:25–28, invoking the parable of the householder who 'found/ Tares that amid the stifled wheat had grown. / Then knew he well, how entering unawares,/ This, while men slept, an enemy had done'.[87] The devil is abroad. God would like very much to do him in, but is not sufficiently powerful. This realization should not cause despair, but, rather, 'a thrill of joy impart'.[88] God needs more than praise and homage – he needs our help, and this is a gratifying prospect. You do God service by clothing the naked, feeding the hungry, tending the sick and wounded. 'Thus, in a Sacred Band, associate', the Voice urges.[89] As an earlier sonnet exhorts, it is the supreme privilege to join 'that great conflict, which, against the powers/ Of darkness, angels and archangels wage,/ labouring God's pure dominion to extend/ O'er realms still held in demon vassalage'.[90] If you are unable to perform 'outward acts', you can still subdue the 'Passions' in 'each recess of thine own breast'.[91] Here the Voice abruptly ceases, without having explained the relationship between subduing passions and rendering good works, among other things.

When Thornton argues for the existence of God, he turns from poetry to prose and from inner voices to nature.[92] The design of the universe – and man's intelligence, imagination and innate moral sense – testify to the existence of a Creator. Thornton's argument cannot detain us. He attacks 'Huxleyism' initially on epistemological grounds, with much slippery logic, concluding that 'life' exists apart from matter and predates it and is ultimately 'some species of spirit or mind'.[93]

Eventually unsatisfied with the easy triumphs of semantic legerdemain, Thornton turns to the physical world and discovers (*contra* Darwin, Spencer and, especially, Lewes) that nature presupposes intentionality, and, therefore, an extra- and super-human intelligence.[94]

Thornton accepts most of Darwin's conclusions,[95] but repeatedly argues that there has to have been a first cause: matter was originally organized by some immaterial agency.[96] Borrowing from Darwin himself, Thornton describes in detail that favourite organ of Theists, the eye, and expresses incredulity that it could be caused 'by the mere restlessness of elemental forces'.[97] Nor can 'variation causing alterations', Darwin's causal explanation,[98] account, argues Thornton, for the mathematical precision with which some bees construct hives, evidence also drawn from *The Origin of Species*.[99] Thornton urges repeatedly that the notion of an intelligent creator provides the simplest and most probable explanation.[100]

Thornton's Theism provides the basis for his scepticism about Ricardian political economy. Our freedom negates any 'laws' about human behaviour, and this freedom is derived from God. Calvinism misrepresents God as thoroughly as Huxleyism misinterprets nature. In claiming that all outcomes are predetermined, Calvinism unites 'hideousness and absurdity'.[101] God is Moloch.[102] The very attempt to construct a social science is tainted by the same presumption. There are no constants. Each generation is influenced by preceding generations; neither men nor circumstances repeat themselves, and hence there are no 'laws of human nature'.[103]

Thornton's Theism also leads him to question the validity of two other no less fundamental Millite doctrines – the Religion of Humanity and Utilitarianism. While admitting that an adherent of the Religion of Humanity can be virtuous – and adducing as evidence the 'sublime' virtue of Mill, without naming him (and thus unknowingly returning his compliment) – Thornton argues that '"creed", "conviction", and "sentiment"' do not a religion make: there must be an object of worship to revere and to love. 'The Human Race', Thornton has little trouble showing, is a poor substitute.[104]

The burden of Thornton's critique of Mill's Utilitarianism is that his friend's altruistic version of Benthamism leads to a proliferation of 'rights' that impose unwarranted obligations on others – that is, it makes 'duties' of what are properly regarded as 'virtues', Mill's own accusation against Calvinism.[105]

The conclusion is somewhat ironic in view of the fact that Thornton begins his discussion by insisting on the existence of natural rights. These turn out to be precious few, however: the rights, essentially, to person and property, to 'deal in any way one pleases, not noxious to other people, with one's own self or person' and 'to dispose similarly of the produce either of one's own honest industry' or of that over which rights have been 'honestly acquired'.[106] Rights are not bestowed directly by God, but derive from debts. They are the consequence of antecedent acts in which obligations have been contracted.[107] However, both the freedom and inclination to work on someone else's behalf are a result of God's will.

Having conversed with Mill daily for over a dozen years and at frequent intervals thereafter, Thornton is naturally concerned that his belief in 'natural rights' may earn him 'in philosophic quarters a sort of civil contempt'.[108] In particular, he answers at some length the charges Mill made in response to *On Labour*, specifically, his claim that 'rights' are invariably derived 'intuitively'.[109] Thornton accuses Mill, with some justice, of assuming that his only opponents are 'intuitionists'. Seizing on the same line from Mill's 'Utilitarianism' that Jevons was to ridicule six years later, Thornton notes that his friend is at least as deserving of the designation 'intuitionist' as he himself, for Mill has claimed that 'the moral faculty, if not a part of our nature, is a natural out-growth from it, capable, in a certain small degree, of springing up spontaneously'.[110] Utilitarians, Thornton argues, derive the 'greatest happiness principle' intuitively – that 'social happiness' is superior to 'individual happiness' is simply taken for granted.[111]

Although he believes that Utilitarianism is fundamentally 'wrong' – that is, morality and utility are not identical – the bulk of Thornton's argument in fact questions its utility. Specifically, it fails to adequately acknowledge human fallibility.[112] Actions are to be judged wholly on their consequences, but it is exceedingly difficult to calculate the consequences of one's actions. 'Meaning to cure, we may only too probably kill; meaning to kill, we may not impossibly cure.'[113]

In particular, Thornton notes the facility with which people use Utilitarian premises to rationalize self-interested behaviour, and, in one of his more prescient passages, argues that those individuals acting on behalf of what they genuinely perceive as the public good may well pose an even more serious threat to society.[114] While no second Robespierre darkens the horizon, Thornton remains concerned about the ease with which coercion by the majority can be legitimized on utilitarian grounds, remaining truer to the Mill of *On Liberty* than its author. He reiterates his claim from *On Labour* that there are 'private rights independent of utility which no public needs can cancel'.[115]

The charge of fallibility extends even to perfectly rational and well-intentioned utilitarians. Absent his bedrock of natural rights, Thornton claims, rights proliferate and, inevitably, conflict.[116] The substitution of 'legalised privileges' for rights makes the task of adjudicating claims exceedingly difficult.

Ultimately, then, the failure to distinguish virtue from obligation results in coercion. Despite his attempt to represent his anti-utilitarianism as derived from simple ratiocination, it offers at bottom a religious understanding of morality: virtue exists apart from and prior to utility, much as spirit pre-exists matter.[117]

Even Thornton's early works, orthodox as they are in some respects, demonstrate how encompassing mid-century radicalism could be. Despite the repeated invocation of the wages fund and the sustained and vehement defence of Malthus in *Overpopulation* (1846),[118] that book, along with its sequel *A Plea for Peasant Proprietors* (1848), reveals a deep substratum of Southeyan values. It was possible to reconcile second-generation philosophic radicalism with principles and policies that would have sorely vexed the earlier Mill circle.

One is accustomed to analyses of Victorian socialism and Cobbettian radicalism which emphasize the way they mirrored conservative critiques of industrialization.[119] It is surprising, however, to see what is fundamentally, despite Thornton's reservations, a utilitarian-based hostility to aristocratic privilege accompanied by such unabashed fondness for a 'country' ethos and traditional morality.

The pastoral vision that stands behind Thornton's argument is made explicit in the poem 'Labour's Utopia'. Agrarian, not civic virtues are extolled; the yeoman is celebrated, not the artisan or merchant. Hestia, not Hermes or Athena, presides.[120] Similarly, in *Overpopulation*, a measure of nostalgia for the independent Saxon invaders who would brook no all-powerful lord[121] and for 'the golden age of the working class'[122] – from the late fourteenth to the early sixteenth century –

co-exist with an intransigent defence of the New Poor Law[123] and an equally vehement and still lengthier argument on behalf of free trade.[124] Indeed, Thornton hopes that the 'repeal of the Corn Laws might thus cause the race of large capitalists to disappear from the occupation of the soil, and to be replaced by small farmers'.[125] Their piety is nearly as attractive as their prudence, to which it contributes.

10 Thomas Edward Cliffe Leslie

T. E. Cliffe Leslie's attack on classical political economy differed appreciably from Thornton's in duration and intensity. Thornton never followed up on his criticism of supply and demand; Leslie's assault on Ricardian orthodoxies was not only far sharper but more sustained. Apart from the 16 articles published as *Land Systems and Industrial Economy of Ireland, England & Continental Countries*,[1] half of his output was devoted to economic theory or to the history of economic theory.

Leslie's grievances against classical political economy were, of course, those of an historicist, and will be summarized below. Nonetheless, they complement Thornton's. For both 'heretics', at bottom, classical political economy claims to know things that are unknowable. For Thornton, prices – specifically the price of labour – cannot be predicted with any accuracy: prices have less to do with supply and demand than with how effectively employers are able to co-operate among themselves and, more generally, with the unpredictability of economic decisions. While he was concerned for a time with assessing the effect of gold supplies on prices, the recurring refrain sounded by Leslie as well was the indeterminacy of wages and profits. But compared to Thornton, Leslie's accusations were based on a considerably more detailed critique of the capacities of economic actors and on a more thorough and systematic examination of wage and profit rates. Where for Thornton, greed and, especially, whimsy upset nice calculations of equilibrium, for Leslie it was simply ignorance that rendered such equations otiose.

I will first look at the substance of his charges in a little more detail. Then I will consider the intellectual and political influences shaping his version of historicism. I will next discuss what is known of his personal life and upbringing, and will assess the way in which his religious and ethical beliefs may have contributed to his critique of classical political economy.

I

'*Contra qui*' is often a useful question, and Leslie never disguises the identity of his adversaries: it is principally David Ricardo and, nearer at hand, the heir of and spokesman for reductive Ricardianism, Robert Lowe. While Leslie acknowledges that 'the more sagacious adherents to the mere deductive method ... probably decline to accept Mr Lowe as their representative', nonetheless 'his exposition is a *reductio ad absurdum* of their own system'.[2] Leslie takes some pains to establish an impressive pedigree for inductive economics. Both Adam Smith and J. S. Mill combine induction with deduction. Ricardo is the aberration.[3]

Ricardo and Lowe are guilty of two sets of erroneous assumptions. The first concerns human nature and the second human understanding. (Leslie himself does not employ this dichotomy.) Economic motives, in the first instance, are misleadingly reduced to self-interest; economic events, in the second case, are regarded as more intelligible than they in fact are. Leslie, albeit unsystematically, addresses both sets of misapprehensions and their mischievous consequences.

The first error consists in the premise that it is sufficient for economists to view individuals as selfish and lustful and lazy, that is, governed by pecuniary self-interest, the sexual drive (euphemistically, 'the population principle') and a strong preference for leisure over work. But the desire for wealth, Leslie argues, includes 'a multitude of different passions, ideas, and aims, varying in different ages and countries, and with different classes and different individuals; and each having its own peculiar effects on the nature, production, and distribution of wealth'.[4] Wealth simply consists of too many and too diverse commodities.[5] The range of mankind's tastes – and the fact that these evolve continuously – gainsays any attempt to systematize about the desire. As early as 1862 Leslie devoted an entire essay to inveighing, with some wit, against the notion that 'love of money' is a meaningful, let alone deplorable trait. Moralists 'confound, in their horror of a mere abstraction, the love of health, cleanliness, decency, and knowledge, with sensuality, avarice, and vanity'.[6]

If the pursuit of wealth encompasses numerous and disparate motives, the sexual drive is capable of assuming nearly as many different guises: it is 'widely varying ... [and] inseparably interwoven with religious and moral ideas and historical causes'.[7] And the aversion to work, the third motive of interest to classical economists, is even more worthless as an analytic tool. While a savage may indeed put a high premium on leisure, 'with the progress of civilization a love of exertion for its own sake grows up, and employment becomes necessary to the happiness of a great number of men'.[8] Because he rejected any cost-of-production theory of value, Leslie – unlike Marshall – could accept with equanimity the fact that men live to work, as well as work to live. Never one to forego an additional paradox, Leslie also argues that an aversion to labour has itself spurred production. Love of wealth and love of ease are not 'antagonizing principles'.[9]

Leslie objected still more strenuously to assumptions about the extent of the knowledge possessed by workers, employers and investors.

Ironically, it was only in an early capitalist social order that accurate predictions could be made about wages and profits, as these were dictated by customs and traditions little subject to change. In the savage state, from which Ricardo purportedly derived the labour theory of value, exchanges in fact seldom took place at all within communities, and there were no measures of labour and sacrifice.[10] In an advanced commercial economy (*contra* Bagehot), exchanges are too numerous and various to allow the kind of information required by Ricardian postulates to be disseminated to economic actors (quite apart from the fact that 'tradition, custom, law, political institutions, religion and moral sentiment' continue to exert profound influences on economic behaviour).[11] Thus, only in the small, stationary economy – in 'well-known and long-established employments, in the same neighborhood, undisturbed by speculation...' – can labour and capital respond effectively to the stimulus of prices.[12]

Leslie's most sustained attack on Ricardian assumptions about the mobility of labour and capital occurs in 'The Known and Unknown in the Economic World'. He argues that Mill's theory of international values and Cairnes's application of it to non-competing groups in the domestic economy need to be still further extended. The effect of the migration of labour and capital in response to fluctuations in wages and profits is 'uncertain, irregular, and inconclusive'.[13] Classical equilibria, of course, depend on the free movement of labour and capital in response to demand, as signalled by prices. But if wage and profit rates cannot be accurately assessed, they will not tend to be equalized, quite apart from the intentions of workers, employers, entrepreneurs and investors. Merchants and manufacturers have a clear interest in concealing profit rates, while customs and traditions drastically limit the options economic actors entertain: farmers 'as a rule do not go out of farming until they are ruined'.[14] 'Instead of the world of light, order, equality, and perfect organization, which orthodox political economy postulates, the commercial world is thus one of obscurity... [and] confusion.'[15] New technologies, the extension of credit and political events, particularly wars, wreak havoc on predictions.[16] The huge losses sustained during the depression in trade in the late 1870s attest, for Leslie, to the speciousness of assumptions about the foreknowledge and rationality of investors.[17] And the numerous rival explanations for the depression testify both to the rudimentary state of the science and to the fact that fluctuations can be precipitated by myriad causes.[18] There are, to summarize, no equilibria. Ubiquitous 'frictions' prevent the equalization of wages or profits. 'International values' prevail everywhere; cost of production does not determine value.

There are several important implications, particularly for distribution, Ricardo's main preoccupation.

1. Profits are not increased solely by a fall in wages.[19]

   All the sophistry in the literature of Socialism has not given birth to a more mischievous fallacy than that contained in the Ricardian dogma: 'The rate of profit is never increased by a better distribution of labour, by the invention of machinery, or by any means of abridging labour.... These are causes which operate on price and are beneficial to consumers; but they have no effect whatever on profit. On the other hand, every diminution in the wages of labour raises profit.'[20]

2. Wages are not determined by population, the wages fund and calculations of subsistence-level income.[21] Rather, they are a consequence of productivity and the relative strengths of trade union and employer combinations. Only where the latter are ineffectual does competition among employers determine wage rates – as Thornton argued.[22] Competition within a trade rarely occurs, however, unless there is competition from outside the trade – typically from mining or manufacturing.[23] Leslie urges co-operation, naturally, though without the zeal of Mill, Thornton, Cairnes or Fawcett, and suggests that to increase productivity is more effectual than merely to extort larger shares.[24] What Leslie is mostly at pains to emphasize, though, is that the conditions regulating wages don't lend themselves to any

universal rule.[25] He repeatedly stresses the disparity in income by region within single occupations – a disparity that has increased markedly over the past century, rather than diminished.[26]

3. Rents, in turn, have little to do with returns to the most marginal lands under cultivation. The most important cause of disparities in rent appears to be the size of individual farms, itself a consequence of laws, customs and the kind of produce the land most readily yields.[27] Bigger is not necessarily better: a recurrent motif in Leslie, as in Thornton, is that small farms yield higher rent because they are more productive.

The Ricardian conclusions with direct bearing on public policy are thus summarily dismissed.

II

Leslie's writings on English and Irish land systems reveal quite clearly both his intellectual debts and his politics. He was explicit about the former: '...whereas Mr Mill in his youth attended the lectures of Mr Austin, the author had the good fortune to attend those of Sir Henry Maine at the Middle Temple, and to learn first from them the historical method of investigation'.[28] Based in part on Leslie's intellectual antecedents, both Coats and Koot have argued convincingly that British historicism is an indigenous plant, and not a German import.[29] Leslie's insistence that he was an historicist long before he'd read Roscher, Nasse or Schmoller would seem to be correct. And while Comte's *System of Positive Philosophy* (not, Leslie adds pointedly, his 'System of Positive Polity') 'is a work of prodigious genius',[30] Comte's influence on the formation of his thought, he maintains, was minimal. That influence was felt indirectly nonetheless during his long friendship with the Comtist J. K. Ingram, the Trinity College polymath whose Presidential Address before Section F (Economic Science and Statistics) of the British Association for the Advancement of Sciences, at its 1878 meeting in Dublin, became something of an historicist manifesto.[31] Leslie also greatly admired his older contemporaries, the Belgian economist Emile de Laveleye and Leonce de Lavergne, economist, philosopher and politician from La Creuse in central France – but chiefly for their empirical work, and for the cordiality and respect with which they treated him.[32]

Maine's influence is clearly evident in Leslie's articles on 'The Land System of England, 1867' and 'The English Land Question, 1870'.[33] Leslie's former teacher is quoted extensively in the first of these. The burden of Leslie's argument is that legislation since the eighteenth century has reversed a long tradition of judicial practice which undermined feudal constraints on land tenure.[34] The result has been catastrophic. Today, Leslie argues,

> every grade of the rural population has sunk; the landed yeomanry are almost gone; the tenant-farmers have lost their ancient independence and interest in the soil; the labourers have lost their separate cottages and plots of ground, and their share in a common fund of land.[35]

The evil effects of the return of 'feudal' land legislation is not confined to the countryside. It has stymied industry and commerce by arbitrarily restricting it to sites without natural economic advantages, and has resulted in the great overcrowding in the cities that has rendered living conditions deplorable for so many. The story is familiar: driven by insecurity of tenure or the loss of commons, the hundreds of thousands of migrants to urban centres have found that rentals are so high – owing to the fact that alternative sites have not been developed, a consequence, again, of laws of succession – that families are obliged to huddle together in demoralizing proximity in unsanitary rooms.[36] But it is in Ireland that the land system has most cruelly retarded prosperity, and the first three essays of *Land Systems* treat the Irish Question.

Without attempting to evaluate the merits of Leslie's arguments, there can be little question that these are essentially political articles. Published primarily during the late 1860s in *Fraser's* and *Macmillan's*, as well as the *Fortnightly*, the essays collected in *Land Systems* – Leslie's most empirical work – are clearly intended to influence public policy. His evidence, in fact, consists primarily of rather cursory overviews of economic history (mostly without citations), supplemented by occasional anecdotal material. Some of the articles are transparently controversial.[37] All are topical, all normative. (Leslie's accounts of his visits to northwest Germany, northern and central France, and Belgium are naturally far more descriptive.)

As with the other Millites, one cannot in the end prove that Leslie's politics 'preceded' his economics, or that his theoretical positions were policy-driven. But the most cursory analysis of the structure of the essays, their deployment of evidence, their rhetorical devices, supports the conclusion that the Irish barrister was not without a brief. See, for example, of innumerable instances, Leslie's strategic equation of the Irish land legislation of 1866 with 'true' *laissez-faire* principles, which require the state to provide the security private enterprise cannot itself produce.[38]

This is hardly scandalous, needless to say. Until Marshall's shadow lengthened, economy was political economy and political economy was political, Senior's and Mill's demurrals notwithstanding. A chief objective remained to illuminate the ways in which legislation either helped or hindered the production and distribution of wealth.[39]

For an historicist, then, Leslie was a liberal.[40] He was always a staunch supporter of free trade, a liberal touchstone for over a century. (He qualified this with regard to Ireland.) But, as one would expect, no more than Cairnes was he a libertarian or Cobdenite liberal. His Hobbesian conception of human nature forbade the possibility:

> The existence of law in civilized society is based upon experience that the natural state of independent human beings is mistrust, violence, and warfare; that they covet the same objects, are not, nor can be just to each other in their competition; and that they are prone to employ the tyranny of force to obtain submission to their partial wills.[41]

Like Cairnes, Leslie wrote glowingly on the virtues of a citizen army and compulsory military training.[42] The qualified nature of his liberalism is also revealed in his support of the income tax. Radicals, of course, had long campaigned against indirect taxes, but by the early 1870s the income tax had also become the focus of radical and trade union hostility. It was perceived as unequal, increasingly affecting working-class and lower-middle-class incomes, and reducing employment. Perhaps most onerous was the intrusion into private life that Schedule D sanctioned.[43] Leslie, however, decisively rejected a key argument of income tax opponents, that its inquisitorial nature was contributing to lowering public morals. While commercial dishonesty is generally lower today, this is not attributable to the deceptions taxpayers are induced to practise, he told Mill. Rather, 'the speculative characteristic of modern trade, the immense prizes to be won, the far sharper competition in business' are to blame. Indeed, protests against the tax are the result of 'the selfish and shortsighted desire to throw off one's own contribution to the State, at whatever cost to the country'.[44]

Leslie's opposition to the campaign for the repeal of the Contagious Diseases Acts is also revealing about the timbre of his liberalism. Just as the State should require military training and tax the income of its citizens to support this enlarged army, so it ought to protect its soldiers from venereal diseases, the claims of individual rights on these issues notwithstanding. However, the rather extraordinary letter in which he discloses his position on the CD Acts to a pained Mill is probably as revealing about his personality as it is about his politics, and it is best to treat it under that head.

The extent of Leslie's sympathies with feminism is nicely indicated in an aside to Ingram: 'I hold that men don't know what women are fit for or ought to do, and have no right to exclude them from any career on *a priori* grounds'. But he hastens to add, 'Though I myself believe the domestic career the best for such of them as can get a husband, which all cannot'.[45] Characteristically, Leslie objects to the methodology of anti-feminists more than to their conclusions.

Leslie's feelings about Ireland were similarly circumscribed. Mill chided him in 1870 for not going further in his legislative recommendations.[46] Eleven years later, he and Morley had a falling-out over Forster's Land Act, which Leslie thought hasty and ill-advised.[47] 'I don't [delight] in the glories of "ould Ireland", or care one fig about her', he confided to Ingram. 'I wish the name Ireland was never [adopted] and that she were called what she is – West Britain.'[48]

Thus, though unquestionably a liberal, and of the non-Cobdenite genus, Leslie's liberalism was more cautious and guarded than Mill's on the two social issues of paramount importance for the latter – land reform and the emancipation of women. Leslie's misogynism and Ulster background no doubt played a role. But his attack on a priori economics, while certainly intended to undermine the rationale for *laissez-faire*, could be readily turned against extensions of government based on abstractions too remote from daily life in the real world, too impervious to local contingencies. It could act as a brake on reform, in short. Overly simplistic interventionist/libertarian, Old Liberal/New Liberal dichotomies are of limited use in triangulating Leslie's politics. And this is before one factors in the 'agrarian radicalism' appealing to both Thornton and Leslie – their admiration for the independent yeoman-farmer.

A species of conservatism, it is worth recalling, was deeply embedded in (non-philosophic) radicalism: the ideal of an independent yeomanry remained an important element in mid-Victorian radical thought, an enduring legacy of classical republicanism.[49] Leslie shared this faith. His essay on Auvergne is especially revealing. It offers an extended contrast between social conditions in the plains and the mountains of the Puy-de-Dome, the province's major *department*. What interest Leslie are differences in the distribution of landed property: in the mountains, estates are significantly larger than in the Limagne valley. After discussing purely economic reasons for the (counter-intuitive) difference, Leslie discloses what he feels is its chief cause: in the mountainous areas 'family feeling and religious sentiment' are far stronger.[50] These beliefs result in a kind of voluntary primogeniture – younger sons and daughters enter religious orders in large numbers.[51] Younger siblings also commonly 'emigrate', working part of the year in distant cities. What is noteworthy about Leslie's treatment of what is, of course, a tried-and-true dichotomy – the piety and conservatism of the mountains, the secularism and materialism of the plains – is his evident admiration for the former, even when it issues in a perverse outcome, by Millite standards: the consolidation of large estates. Indeed, Leslie claims that the Auvergnat practice sheds light on the origins of English primogeniture, which evolved from custom (enforced by itinerate royal courts) and not from judicial fiat. There is no celebration of 'the money-making and commercial spirit' which results in 'individualism . . . and the disintegration of the family',[52] or of the confidence in the powers of man as opposed to those of nature. Nor, more surprisingly, are the virtues fostered by small proprietorship underscored. No doubt some of his warm feelings for the *montagnards* result from their enabling him to contradict truisms of political economy, the essay's chief objective. But it is difficult to imagine Mill, Cairnes or Fawcett responding similarly.

The sentiments recur in 'A Visit to La Creuse', where the 'gentle but manly virtues' of the peasantry are being obliterated by Imperial policy, which is transforming the region's young men 'into a crowd of restless roving town operatives and dissolute garrison soldiers'.[53] The extinction of 'Jacques Bonhomme' is deplorable not just for France but for Europe. And Leslie concludes his first article on Westphalia with the dire warning that 'of England . . . though not of Germany, Herr Riehl's maxim is true, that the custom of the peasant is the sole foundation of present order, the sole safeguard against future anarchy. And the peasant is driven to town.'[54]

III

Leslie was born in Wexford, Ireland, in 1825, the second son of a rector who held two livings and owned some property in Ireland.[55] Leslie's mother, Margaret Higgonson, was the daughter of an Anglican clergyman. The Rev. Edward Leslie resided in England and himself undertook Thomas's education. Like Mill, the boy was taught Latin, Greek and Hebrew at what Ingram calls 'an exceptionally early age'.[56] Leslie attended King William's College on the Isle of Man, and then, at only 15, entered Trinity College, Dublin, where he was a classmate of Cairnes, five years his senior, and W. E. Hearn, the Australian economist whose *Plutology* Jevons was to much admire. The Whately Professor when Leslie matriculated in 1842 was J. A. Lawson, a proponent, like his predecessors and the Chair's founder, of the subjective theory of value, holding that 'it is a proposition always true, and of universal application, *that the exchangeable value of all articles depends upon their utility*, that is, upon their power to gratify the wants and wishes of man'.[57]

Nothing is known, unfortunately, of Leslie's relation with Cairnes as an undergraduate, though the disparities in age, temperament, religious background and education make it improbable that they had much to do with each other. A likely influence at College was the precocious Ingram, who received his BA a year after Leslie entered. Leslie may have participated in the Dublin Philosophical Society that Ingram, also the son of an Anglican clergyman, founded in 1842. This important friendship continued as long as Leslie lived, introduced him to Comte, and fortified his disenchantment with orthodox political economy. Leslie did much to propagate Ingram's historicist manifesto.[58] In turn, Ingram, with Bastable, edited and introduced an updated collection of Leslie's economic essays six years after his death, *Essays in Political and Moral Philosophy* being then out of print.

Leslie was an outstanding student, receiving a classical scholarship in 1845 and graduating with a Senior Moderatorship and gold medal in ethics and logic in 1847. He entered Lincoln's Inn in 1848 and was called to the bar in 1857. In the interim, in 1853, he accepted an appointment to the chair of jurisprudence and political economy at Queen's College, Belfast. The chair paid very poorly, though it permitted him to spend most of each year in London.[59] He was obliged to do a considerable amount of examining, and Mill was of assistance in helping him secure this work.[60] In part induced by his financial difficulties (a second son, he does not appear to have inherited any of his father's property), but in part because he found the forms congenial, Leslie began writing essays and reviews in the late 1850s, for *Fraser's*, *Macmillan's*, the *Athenaeum*, the *Academy* and the *Fortnightly*. In the end, reviewing became an essential part of what he had come to view as a one-man crusade for historicism:

> It is exceedingly tiresome going over old ground.... I should be glad now to stop reviewing at least until after my next book is out. Yet I am afraid to refuse the work lest some champion of the old method should cut in and give a triumph to its followers.[61]

Leslie's personal life was somewhat tragic. It was shadowed by chronic illness and, apparently, unhappy relations with women. The problems were exacerbated by a strong sense of persecution. Or perhaps the slings and arrows, real and imagined, were a welcome distraction. Editors, publishers, printers and, especially, exponents of deductivist economics harried and harassed him – or worse, in the case of the latter, studiously ignored him. Leslie believed he was neither a heretic nor usurper, but was fighting to restore the legitimate methodological claimant to the throne, the inductivist approach:

> Fawcett, finding that he could not be king himself over political economy, resolved to be a king-maker and crowned Cairnes. He hoped thereby to establish a buttress against assaults on his own wretched old system of economics, and indeed his hope was not frustrated. But I receive constantly proof that the structure is giving way.[62]

Pessimism was more typical: Leslie's world was divided into allies and enemies, and the former were few and ineffectual.

> The old hacks are all against me and, not being able to confute what I say, try to silence my doctrine. The young university economists, on the other hand, like Toynbee, seem unable to write; and content themselves with letting College students read what I write.[63]

Leslie's anxieties about the typography and timing of his publications almost exceed his concern with their reception. Printers are repeatedly reviled: 'What stuff can a printer be made of who sacrifices an author in this way to his own indolence and carelessness.'[64]

Leslie's letters contain frequent complaints of his poor health, though the exact nature of the malady is hard to determine.[65] Insomnia also played a part. Sleeplessness, he confided to Helen Taylor, is 'one of the chief difficulties now'.[66] He took exception to her wishing to attribute his malaise to 'brainwork', arguing that he had always been afflicted by it.[67] Migraines might have been another symptom. Leslie complains to Mill about 'violent and depressing headaches', emphasizing that he looks forward to 'gaining rather than regaining complete health'.[68] However, alternating with references to his symptoms are recurrent confessions of laziness.[69] Like Thornton, he seems to have thrived abroad.[70] One gathers from his letters that his happiest moments were spent on the continent. He seems to have found the company of Levaleye and Lavergne especially congenial. The fact that he felt that he was appraised at his true worth only on the continent no doubt helped restore his sense of well-being there.[71]

It was on the continent, however, that Leslie's career suffered a serious reverse. In Nancy during the summer of 1875 he lost what he claimed was a nearly completed manuscript on English economic and legal history (of which the essay 'The History and Future of Interest and Profit' is presumably an excerpt).[72]

In June of that year, Leslie may have sustained a loss nearly as devastating. He appears, during the late spring 1875, to have conceived an affection for Helen Taylor which transcended that of an ardent disciple for the daughter, and fellow-acolyte, of a deceased master. The interest was not reciprocated.[73] By summer he seems to have been edging toward a proposal of marriage to Mill's step-daughter. This is obviously somewhat conjectural, but there is a short series of exchanges – culminating in Taylor's precipitous departure from London – which suggest the degree of Leslie's infatuation with her.

In December of 1874 – after expressing pleasure that Taylor liked his recent article on Auvergne – Leslie complains, characteristically, of his treatment at the hands of an editor, in this instance Peter Taylor, Radical MP and proprietor of the *Examiner*. He asks Helen Taylor to convey to her namesake Mill's high opinion of Leslie's writing.

In January 1875, his anxieties about his health elicited the bromide from Helen Taylor – 'that brainwork takes too much out of the physical system to be consistent with strong health'[74] – to which Leslie took exception. 'Imperfections of my constitution' were to blame, not 'my occupation'.[75] Exchanges about various subjects follow; they agree to disagree about Russia. (Taylor, not surprisingly, is a Russophile, Leslie a Russophobe.) In May, though, after assuring Taylor that his review of Macleod[76] was so severe primarily because the latter was attacking Mill, Leslie dramatically crosses over into a darkly confessional mode. 'I must get out of town.... My time is distracted here with the multifarious trouble which each day brings.' The 'notoriety' he has achieved, he confesses, 'entails such penalties that I sometimes wish I could give up altogether the attempt altogether [*sic*] to publish my ideas'.[77] Then in a letter later that month he becomes especially solicitous: he expresses regret at not having heard a recent lecture Taylor had delivered and, moreover, regrets that she 'should undertake a physical labour – which speaking in public is – which you are hardly equal to venturing with safety'.[78] He notes in passing that he is glad Spencer confirmed his own (apparently unexceptionable) opinion that 'Mr Mill had great mental powers and natural endowments'.[79]

A week later he writes her a mysterious and provocative letter. Apparently he had himself hand-delivered the previous letter, along with yet another, special letter. These are his words: 'With the letter I put a letter in your box, but could not make it go down, and it stuck up visibly so that someone passing might have taken it out. I rang the bell, but it was not I think answered.' Leslie then pleads for half an hour of her time: 'perhaps you will kindly tell someone to let me in'.[80] The sexual undertones rumble beneath the paranoia.

The suitor was not admitted. Taylor, in a letter the following day, chose to respond only to the comments about Mill, to which she reacted with a fury seemingly disproportionate to Leslie's anodyne observations. It is worth quoting at some length.

> I never for a moment denied that Mr Mill had great natural abilities, nor did he deny it himself, but I venture to think we both knew the character of his mind and the probable extent . . . of his original mental powers more accurately than any one who only saw him for an hour or two from time to time. I also think that the habits of both his mind and mine led us to be closer observers and more accurate recorders of the effect of circumstances than most people are. Hence I think that our united testimony is of some weight when we say that his exceptional talents were due largely to the exceptional care taken to develop them. Nay I even go so far as to think that the denial of this is an absurd paradox, which needs . . . strong prejudices to be accepted.[81]

Apart from the display of hostility to Leslie, Taylor, clearly, is claiming Mill for herself. Not only is she privy to information to which an outsider like Leslie would have no access, but she was, in effect, Mill's equal. She was a full partner in his quest for self-knowledge; their 'united testimony' carries rather more weight than Mill's solo efforts at introspection. But not only is she a uniquely insightful observer of

Mill's mental peregrinations; by implication, James Mill, her mother and herself must be credited with moulding and shaping the eminently malleable, if promising, intellect of J. S. Mill. Radical politics are generally predicated on an environmentalist epistemology, and her perception that Leslie was attacking this no doubt intensified her response, but the personal animus is unmistakable.

In any event, Taylor appears to have fled to the continent shortly after rebuffing Leslie's attempt to see her. His next letter to her begins plaintively. 'It was a pleasure at last to get a glimpse of your handwriting. No one deserves a holiday better than you, so I must not complain that you went as fast as you could to Avignon for it.'[82]

A poignant letter follows in October.

> I became very ill in France at the end of August, and much to my regret was unable to go southward.... I had hoped to visit Avignon and find you there. In addition to this disappointment and to much bodily suffering, I had the great misfortune to lose almost the whole manuscript of a book which had cost me much labour, which I had expected to publish by Christmas. I must now give all the time I can spare from professorial and examining duties to repair my loss.[83]

It is impossible to assess the impact of the two calamities. Some of Leslie's best essays appeared after 1875.[84] Nonetheless, he never published a monograph, or a systematic treatise. And he never married.

That he very much wanted to was no secret. In a rather unusual public disclosure, Leslie concluded an 1863 article on 'The Celibacy of the Nation' with the confession that he was one of 'those who...wish to be happily married themselves'.[85] The article is itself revealing. It is, in effect, a plea that the unmarried, a group Leslie argues is more numerous than is sometimes appreciated, ought by rights to be honoured. Celibacy, he argues, 'without vows or compulsion is a form of human existence which is commonly to be seen only in civilized society, and which becomes commoner as civilization goes forward and spreads'.[86] Presently, 'a goodly number of us are what the sneering world calls "old bachelors" and "old maids", as if celibacy were something stale and antiquated, instead of being something quite fresh and modern'.[87] The benefits conferred to the nation by celibacy consist, of course, in postponing the Malthusian day of reckoning, when population will have outstripped resources, competition will have driven down wages and driven women back to the kitchen and nursery, and England will have become 'all town and market garden'.[88]

Interestingly, at the outset of the article, Leslie – like Thornton and in contrast to Fawcett – takes issue with Buckle, who claims that 'marriages have a fixed and definite relation to the price of corn' and are not determined 'by the temper and wishes of individuals'.[89] Leslie leaps to defend individual freedom. To the extent that the price of corn does influence the marriage rate, this suggests that men are, in fact, susceptible to 'personal feelings', resisting the lures of marriage until they can support wife and children. Middle- and upper-class men, however, do not consult the price of bread when they wish to choose a spouse.

Leslie's candid announcement of his desire to marry, coupled with the repeated plea (only partly tongue-in-cheek) that the unmarried be honoured as saviours of the nation, reveals a certain ambivalence. But the most suggestive statement of Leslie's feelings about women occurs in a lengthy letter to Mill detailing reasons for his reluctance to join Mill in supporting Josephine Butler's Ladies' National Association for Repeal of the Contagious Diseases Acts. Mill himself was rather guarded in his approval of the campaign. As indicated in Chapter 3, he was very concerned that the London Committee for Women's Suffrage not be tainted by an explicit association with Butler's crusade, and he went to great lengths to try to weed out individuals unreliable on this issue.

Leslie begins by disputing the belief he ascribes to the Association that 'all vice comes from men'. While acknowledging, somewhat mysteriously, that prostitution is a consequence of 'bad laws made by men', he objects to generalizations about the sexes. The LNA is guilty of 'a new form of the old fallacy of distinguishing moral and intellectual character by sex', thus violating a principle close to Mill's heart. In fact, 'there are plenty of bad women in the world'. After detailing other objections, mainly the matter of protecting innocent wives and children, he returns to the character of prostitutes:

> there is a class of women about whose pursuits there can be no sort of doubt. The places they frequent, their very looks are conclusive.... I hold that human beings following such an occupation subject [?] themselves to any measures [the public requires] for its own safety.

Women, he objects still later, are not

> all injured innocents. Now in fact they are good bad and indifferent, just like men, and some of them are very bad indeed, perfectly

abominable. In respect of the service in question, I know of cases where they were not the tempted but the tempters from the first.[90]

All this may merely reflect a recent unpleasant encounter with a prostitute. But the intensity and frequency with which the sentiments are expressed suggest a fairly acute degree of distress. Leslie himself begs Mill to excuse him 'for indicating in so perfervid a manner some many reasons for protesting against a Protest which has [attracted] names of so much respect as Miss Taylor's'.[91]

Obviously the relationship of personality to social theory is a much-vexed issue.[92] No one would wish to urge a very strong or unilateral causal relationship between Leslie's illnesses and his difficulties with women, on the one hand, and his methodological approach on the other. Nonetheless, there may be an affiliation, in Leslie's case, between a love of paradox, a distrust of general laws and self-assured pronouncements, and a relationship with one's own body and with the opposite sex that is unpredictable, frustrating and occasionally disturbing. Once again a contrast with Fawcett may be instructive. The bluff, hearty and healthy – though blind – parliamentarian revelled in *ex cathedra* declarations. Fawcett's disability, as indicated, may have toughened him mentally, making him less receptive to nuance and more taken with inexorable laws that seemed to cut through false sentimentality and idealism.

As with Mill himself, then, the fact that happiness was so problematic may have induced Leslie to question received formulae about its attainment. The role of religion in accelerating and deepening that discontent is, regrettably, a matter of speculation. As with Thornton, the religion in which he was raised appears to have been a temperate, non-Calvinist Protestantism not likely to inspire the kind of evangelical secularism of Cairnes, Morley or Mill, or to have made Comte appealing. Leslie was descended from a distinguished conservative Anglican family. Among his ancestors was John Leslie, 'the Fighting Bishop' of Raphoe and of Clogher, who defended his fortified palace first against the Irish, then the Cromwellians. One of the last royalists to submit to the Commonwealth, he lived to be one hundred, marrying at the age of 67 the 18-year-old daughter of the dean of Raphoe, with whom he had ten children. The seventh, Charles, from whom Leslie was descended, was the celebrated non-juror. An able and tireless controversialist, Charles Leslie engaged in polemics with papists, Quakers, Baptists, Jews, deists and, especially, the latitudinarian Whig divines. Interestingly, he wrote a critique of Locke's *Treatises on Government* in which he attacked the ahistoricity of Locke's assumptions.[93] Charles Leslie's pen frequently got him into trouble, and he was obliged to flee to the continent a couple of times, where he badgered the Pretender to pledge to maintain the Church of England.

That religious beliefs need to be taken seriously by any economist – that they constitute a motive as powerful as the 'desire for wealth' – is a claim repeated throughout Leslie's *oeuvre*, though perhaps nowhere as tellingly as in an attack on Cairnes in 'Political Economy and Sociology'. When Cairnes acknowledges that religious considerations ought 'to be taken account of precisely in so far as they are found, in fact, to affect the conduct of men in the pursuit of wealth', he concedes more than he intends, Leslie suggests, alluding sweepingly to the impact of the medieval Church and the Reformation.[94] Leslie then contrasts Cairnes's concession with his subsequent dictum that 'the economist starts with a knowledge of ultimate causes', and 'is... at the outset of his enterprise, in the position which the physicist only attains after ages of labourious research'.[95] 'The followers of the deductive method', Leslie concludes, 'are, in fact, on the horns of a dilemma.' Either they must assume 'that men are activated by no motive save the desire of pecuniary gain' or they must argue 'that they [the economists] have an intuitive knowledge of all moral, religious, political, and other motives influencing human conduct, and of all the changes they undergo in different countries and periods'.[96]

Leslie's own religious and ethical values are revealed most clearly in his 'Utilitarianism and the Summum Bonum'.[97] At first sight, the essay seems to be making a case for relativism – that 'virtue' is determined by the state of a given society. For the opening argument that ends ought not to be considered apart from means quickly resolves into another extended endorsement of Sir Henry Maine's approach. Leslie has little difficulty in parading before his antagonists (Mackintosh joins Buckle in the hot seat) the widely diverse practices that have been regarded as virtuous. But far from throwing up his hands before the catholicity of tastes, Leslie resorts to the grand stratagem of the Victorian social sciences, gliding effortlessly from 'is' to 'ought' by arguing that what is more recent, being more highly evolved, is superior. Mores have evolved from cruelty and collective responsibility to kindness and individuality. Macaulay is enlisted to confirm the growth of humaneness and civility.[98] If morals are to continue to progress, can Utilitarianism help out? No, says Leslie: happiness cannot serve as an end. The moral progress of mankind – the true *summum bonum* – requires the cultivation of a sense of duty. A belief that pleasure and freedom from pain are ultimate objectives, even granted the ability to calculate the consequences of one's actions, will not ensure the self-denial and self-sacrifice that virtue entails. Only a concept of honour will do.

In the end Leslie opts for something of an aesthetic definition: 'the chief quality in the character of virtue is, in truth, not usefulness, but excellence, rarity, nobleness'.[99] Leslie then rather arbitrarily seizes on the second of these: scarcity, it turns out, is the true source of value in morals as in markets.

Leslie's claims, in fact, are not presented very coherently or systematically; as usual, he is more effective as a critic than a constructive theorist. Like Thornton – and countless critics afterward – Leslie goes for one of the more gaping chinks in Mill's armour, the Socrates/pig proof. Naturally enough, this offends his historico-relativist sensibilities: 'There is an illusive semblance of simplicity in the Utilitarian formula. The tendency to produce happiness seems to be an easy test; but it assumes an unreal concord about the constituents of happiness and an unreal homogeneity of human minds.'[100] Furthermore, bodily and mental pleasures cannot be weighed against each other, nor, even within a homogeneous group, can one individual's pleasure be measured against another's.

Ultimately, there is an appeal to God, or at least a denial of the Utilitarian understanding of His plans: there is no evidence that He 'desires above all things the happiness of his creatures, and that this was his purpose in their creation'.[101] Rather, science teaches that the purpose of creation is 'the development, improvement, and elevation of the faculties of terrestrial beings'.[102] And in the happiest world conceivable, there would be no scope for the development of 'the noblest faculties', or for the practice of 'the noblest virtues'. 'Heroism, self-sacrifice, and compassion, imply the existence of pain and suffering.'[103] Even the growth of intelligence increases unhappiness.

In the end, Leslie returns to his relativism, and to his profound distaste for reductivism. Human good is simply too multifarious. 'It is innocent pleasure . . . but it is also improvement; it is enjoyment, but it is also discipline, energy, and action.'[104] And the ongoing moral progress of mankind makes any pronouncement about the *summum bonum* premature.

Leslie's critique of utilitarianism is not as penetrating or encompassing as Thornton's. His objections – especially when he stresses the variability and immeasurability of happiness – are closer to Fitzjames Stephen's. Somewhat surprisingly, Leslie does not question the utility of utilitarianism – its assumptions about our capacity to determine the consequences of our actions – and he has nothing to say on the actual genealogy of morals. Clearly 'nobility' and 'scarcity' are hardly more reliable guides than 'utility', and are no less historically conditioned.

Leslie, then, is rather less religious than Thornton. God is seldom invoked, and when we wish to determine His purposes, we consult science. There is nonetheless an unmistakable religious dimension to Leslie's critique of classical political economy. It consists chiefly in a recoil from intellectual vanity. For at the core of his methodology is a denial of man's omniscience: political economists cannot pretend to know intuitively the various and changeable motives that influence economic behaviour.

11 Conclusion

I would like to begin by looking briefly at the largely unedifying encounter of Mill and his followers with marginal utility theory.[1]

Superficially, it might appear that Mill would have welcomed the appearance of Jevons's *Theory of Political Economy* in 1871; he might even have been expected to have anticipated its arguments. Such, of course, was not the case.[2]

Marginalism, in the first place, was not politically helpful. Jevons, 'a man of some ability', unfortunately has,

> a mania for encumbering questions with useless complications, and with a notation implying the existence of greater precision in the data than the questions admit of. His speculations on Logic... are infected in an extraordinary degree with this vice. It is one pre-eminently at variance with the wants of the time, which demand that scientific deductions should be made as simple and as easily intelligible as they can be made without ceasing to be scientific.[3]

Cairnes was, typically, still more pointed about the problems introduced by generalizing Ricardian rent. If we accept a theory of value that fails to recognize 'a fundamental distinction between land and the ordinary products of industry', then 'any reform in land' is 'without scientific warrant'.[4] Cairnes complained to Mill more generally about the most pernicious 'characteristic of the French school' (and the anathema would apply with no less force to Jevons): the 'tendency to vicious generalization which, instead of elucidating, darkens the problem'. To regard 'abstinence as a form of labour, rent as a form of interest', to make capital 'cover land as well as wealth in general' is to render the science unintelligible – and, hence, apolitical.[5]

When Cairnes actually tackled Jevons, with Mill's warm approval, the result was disastrous: Cairnes was unable or unwilling to understand what was meant by 'marginal'. Jevons, he claims, is reiterating Say's heresy.[6] As a result, he feels the disagreement is largely verbal, and at the core of the new theory is a tautology: value depends on utility and utility is what affects value.[7] Cairnes's difficulty, revealingly, begins with his conceiving of *sacrifice* rather than scarcity as the co-determinant of value.[8] He then proceeds to confuse value with utility:

> a woolen coat sells for less now than it did a century ago; therefore it is less useful now than then .... [E]very improvement in production, just in proportion as it cheapens a commodity, diminishes its utility; while every thing that raises the cost enhances the utility.[9]

One looks in vain for the kind of classical critique one might have anticipated – a straightforward demonstration (*à la* Marshall) that Jevons's 'catena' is circular: that is, that a commodity's marginal utility ultimately depends on its cost of production, because that will determine its scarcity.

Fawcett and Thornton ignored Jevons, though one can well imagine what they might have thought. The most serious effort to grapple with the new approach was made by Leslie; his is the most sympathetic reading. Leslie's personal feelings for Jevons no doubt enhanced his respect for the latter's work. The two were on excellent terms.[10] Still, Leslie's endorsement is something of a surprise; one would expect an historicist to be hostile to the assumption that economic transactions ought to be rendered mathematically.

This is not the case, first, because Leslie holds no brief for the cost of production theory of value,[11] and is no less dismissive of Ricardian rent.[12] (It is not coincidental that his commitment to the politics both doctrines supported was more modest than that of the orthodox Millites.)

Unlike Cairnes, Leslie grasps, roughly, the concept of marginal utility,[13] at least in so far as it accords with his belief that 'value depends mainly on the limitation of supply'.[14] Nonetheless, as one would anticipate, he rejects the claim that prices are determinate. Economic transactions don't culminate in equilibria: ulterior conditions defeat the attempt to apply mathematics.[15] While Ricardo's system might be rendered mathematically, this is not to its credit.[16] Smith's propositions, more worldly and acute, defy differential calculus.[17] Exceptions are made, however, for currency questions.[18] In a letter to Jevons, Leslie enlists the authority of Ingram, 'an excellent mathematician' who received his fellowship in mathematics, in support of the view that 'we must be content to be logical' in economics. 'I only wish', he cannot resist adding, 'the greater part of the hitherto accepted theory were so much as logical .... Cairnes to my mind had a singularly illogical way of working out his results.'[19]

Leslie naturally has reservations about how Jevons has radically limited the purview of political economy, but consoles himself that the difference is largely one of classification. He does take strong exception to the attempt to exclude population questions, however, and if this problem is admitted, the membrane between 'economic sociology' and 'economics' ruptures.

Paradoxically, then, radical politics resulted in reactionary economics.[20] For unless one subscribes to the view that either everything of value in neo-classical economics was perfectly well explained by classical political economy, or that both systems were equally worthless, or, alternately, that it was marginal utility theory that 'shunted the car of Economic Science on to a wrong line', then clearly the success of economics as both a science and a profession lay in the acceptance of marginalism, allowing the deployment of differential calculus to analyse the outcome of exchanges.[21]

I

Ricardian political economy offered its adherents a powerful and encompassing moral system.[22] Values ultimately define the borders that divide what is forbidden from what is permitted, on the one hand, and what is merely permitted from what is admired and encouraged, on the other. And apart from the kind of activities that are condemned and sanctioned, value systems can be distinguished by the breadth of that band of behaviour that is simply tolerated, that is neither proscribed nor esteemed. Not only did Mill's version of classical political economy unequivocally condemn certain behaviour and exalt other behaviour, but there were few economic activities it was neutral about – the band representing the merely tolerable was narrow. This was precisely Mill's chief objection to Calvinism – and to Comte.[23] What Mill wrote of Comte's creed was no less true of his own: 'the most prejudiced must admit that this religion without theology is not chargeable with relaxation of moral restraints. On the contrary, it prodigiously exaggerates them.'[24]

To summarize the moral system of Millian political economy, the line in the sand divides those who are productive from those who are unproductive. Condemned are (1) recipients of rent, (2) consumers (more technically, the consumers of 'unproductive' labour), and (3) the sexually profligate.

1. Landlords reap where they did not sow, thanks to the law of diminishing returns, 'the most important proposition in political economy'.[25] As population increases and marginal lands are

farmed, rent rises and landlords profit 'as it were in their sleep, without working, risking or economising'.[26] Even without the law of diminishing returns, Ricardian classical political economy revealingly overestimates 'the natural powers of the soil' and purports to discriminate between these powers and capital investments in land in a way that is untenable, and between agricultural products and manufactured goods in a way that is no less tendentious.

2. A second proposition that Mill labours hardly less energetically to sustain carries an equally strong moral charge – his fourth theorem of capital: 'a person who buys commodities and consumes them himself, does no good to the labouring classes; and that it is only by what he abstains from consuming... that he benefits the labouring class'.[27] Mill's argument that 'the demand for commodities is not the demand for labour' can be defended, to be sure, but largely by deft translations and liberal exegeses.[28] However well-developed Mill's demand and supply analysis, he ought not to be confused with Marshall. The latter's elaboration of consumer surplus would never have occurred to Mill. Consumers and their desires are relegated to the periphery for what appear, again, to be largely normative reasons. 'Saving, in short, enriches, and spending impoverishes, the community along with the individual.'[29] Semmel's explanation for Mill's inability to apply utilitarianism to economic theory in a plausible and fruitful way may be the most convincing of the many hypotheses advanced: virtue trumped utility.[30] Ironically, marginalists – who have been accused of hedonism and relativism – were able to moralize at greater length than their predecessors (if no more effectively) insofar as they felt entitled to target consumption: 'the man who wishes to serve his fellows will see that responsibility in consumption is one of the duties that lie nearest him .... [H]is consumption should be weighed and planned – not casual or automatic – in short... it should be ruled by conscience.'[31]
3. The condemnation of desire reaches its apogee, naturally, in the law of population. The two great drives – for food and sex – enrich idle parasites while they pauperize labourers. It is difficult to overemphasize the importance of Malthusianism for Mill. Coming to Mill's economic writing after reading discussions in the secondary sources, one is hardly prepared for the repeated insistence on the necessity for prudence and self-restraint – much as a reader approaching the New Testament after first making the

> acquaintance of modern theology would be astonished at the extent to which Christ and the early Christians were preoccupied with the imminent end of the world. It is hardly an exaggeration to claim that Malthusianism is Mill's grand theme: if he hoped readers would distil a single lesson from the *Principles*, it was surely the desirability of self-restraint. 'Civilization in every one of its aspects is a struggle against the animal instincts.'[32] Mill objects not merely to the effects of sexual intercourse, but to the act itself, which involves 'a degrading slavery to a brute instinct in one of the persons concerned, and most commonly, in the other, helpless submission to a revolting abuse of power'.[33]

Redemption comes, then, through abstinence. The upper class must renounce thievery, the middle class, acquisitiveness, and the working class, sex.

A different sort of salvation was offered to intellectuals: the opportunity to enlist in the effort to elevate the labouring population. For Mill's, of course, was a Malthusianism with a difference: if the consequences it described were grim, they were hardly inexorable. 'Nothing more would probably be necessary to secure [prudence] than an opinion generally diffused that it was desirable.'[34] The campaign to nullify the 'law of population' became an energizing and gratifying crusade.[35] And political journalism, in particular, was valorized.[36]

If the Millite doctrines offered its believers something like the comfort and sustenance of a religion, it is logical to seek in the religion of the dissenters the grounds for their dissent. If Thornton and Leslie were the leading opponents of classical political economy in the 1860s,[37] the former attacked, I have argued, in the name of freedom, and the latter on behalf of irrationality. The criticisms of each seem to be impelled by a kind of homespun scepticism – a distrust of systems and systematizers – commonly associated with a certain strain of Tory thinking, though perhaps no less characteristic of the non-philosophic radical tradition. Behind the scepticism appears to be the belief in a transcendent principle, if not a Supreme Being. Thornton's is the besieged, heroic God of Manicheism; Leslie's deity is more obscure. (It is significant that for Thornton disequilibrium is the consequence of employers' greed and consumers' whimsy, while for Leslie it results from the ignorance of the economic actors.) Performing one's 'duty', not merely maximizing utility, is the imperative in each case. Both writers insist upon something like natural rights: Thornton's emanate from his concept of obligation, Leslie's from the ancient traditions of a people or region.

Not surprisingly, political questions do not appear to have the same urgency for the Millite 'heretics' as for the 'loyalists'. Methodologically more radical than Mill, politically Thornton and Leslie were to his right. Mill was more alive to the full implications of Thornton's attack on the wages fund (which he may well have suggested to his friend) and to the radical political resonances of Leslie's anti-Ricardian arguments than was either theorist himself.

II

This raises the second and perhaps still more controversial question that I've addressed: what influence did the Millites have on Mill's economic writing during his last half-dozen years? The impact of his heterodox followers – Thornton, specifically – on Mill's *religious* thought may well have been significant. In 'Utility of Religion' Mill had somewhat condescendingly recommended Manicheism as a stimulus to 'pleasing and encouraging thought' in those for whom the Religion of Humanity was too austere.[38] But writing to Florence Nightingale at least two years later, he appears to have himself accepted Manicheism. Mill confesses that

> no religious theory seems to me consistent with the facts of the universe, except (in some form or other) the old one of the two principles .... It may be, that the world is a battlefield between a good and a bad power or powers, and that mankind may be capable of sufficiently strenuous cooperation with the good power, of deciding, or at least accelerating, its final victory.

With Thornton clearly in mind, he goes on, 'I know one man, of great intelligence & high moral principle, who finds satisfaction to his devotional feelings, and support under the evils of life, in the belief of this creed.'[39] The fact that Manicheism had seemed reasonable to his father no doubt enhanced its appeal to Mill.[40]

In 'Theism', while again applauding the salutary effect of a belief in (Thorntonian) Manicheism,[41] Mill now openly accepts it as an intellectually plausible hypothesis as well. Darwinism may indeed have the last word (though it cannot account for the commencement of organic life, he claims);[42] but 'the adaptations in Nature afford a large balance of probability in favour of creation by intelligence'.[43] However, 'the author of the Kosmos worked under limitations... he was obliged to adapt himself to conditions independent of his will.'[44] There is no basis, though, for attributing these limitations to a malevolent intelligence; rather, they are likely to have resulted from the poor 'qualities of the material' or from the Deity's own lack of skill.[45] Mill concludes that,

> such evidence as there is, points to the creation, not indeed of the universe, but of the present order of it by an Intelligent Mind, whose power over the materials was not absolute, whose love for his creatures was not his sole actuating inducement, but who nevertheless desired their good.[46]

This was not far from Thornton's beliefs; it was light years from Morley's.

If Mill's religious beliefs shifted late in life, his core values did not. However, his practice of the Religion of Humanity led him to modify some of the Ricardian premises on which it rested. Not surprisingly, Thornton and Leslie, in contrast to their heterodox colleagues, offered very little criticism of their mentor: each, with some justification, claimed Mill as a supporter of his departures.[47] Indeed, Mill's economic writing during his final years consisted mostly of warm endorsements of their respective books (and of a volume by Leslie's first mentor, Maine). On the other hand, Mill chose not to call attention to any publication by Cairnes, Fawcett or Millicent Fawcett.[48] Both of the Fawcetts, Mill confided to Croom Robertson, were 'a little doctrinaire', inclined 'to see a principle in its full force, and not to see the opposing principles by which it must be qualified'.[49] They and Cairnes were not of much use in counter-attacking those who disparaged trade unionism and land reform on economic grounds.

Before briefly recapitulating Mill's arguments, it is important to re-emphasize the distinction between what Mill *knew* and what he *wrote*. Examining the arguments he actually chose to make is a different exercise than appraising Mill's system in its totality, and assigning him to the proper niche in the pantheon of great economists, or proving that he fully anticipated neo-classical demand and supply analysis. Characteristically, Mill's claims are generally carefully qualified; however unwarranted some of his historical observations, he never lapses into crude errors on matters of theory. Nonetheless, he manages to suggest that certain outcomes are plausible which clearly contravene his own prior claims and, sometimes, common sense.

On the wage fund, he implies that wage increases: (a) won't affect wage capital in the long run; (b) won't limit employment, or reduce wages in other occupations; and (c) won't be transferred to consumers, even in specific trades in the short run. All three propositions – or insinuations – conflict with classical assumptions. Unwilling to abandon the latter, Mill indulges in the equivocations described in Chapter 5. These largely consist of blurring distinctions between long run and short run, and between aggregate and partial or sectional outcomes. Ultimately, he accepts what he concedes to be the monopolistic practices of unions, on the grounds that they are necessary to maintain a 'morally-fit' subclass.

Mill's adaptation of Leslie's arguments in order to attack opponents of land reform raises two additional problems. (a) Mill contradicts classical political economy's predictions about efficiency. The concept of economies of scale was hardly at the heart of classical political economy; to deny that they obtained in some instances was not to jeopardize the system. But such a denial calls for empirical evidence that Mill was unable or unwilling to provide. (b) The second problem is also methodological. It consists of Mill's appeal not to the utility of small-scale farming, but to extra-economic considerations. His citing historical precedent – tribal customs – as legitimating certain practices is, again, not itself problematic, provided he acknowledged what he was doing. However, this approach blatantly contradicts propositions he simultaneously advocated with great energy elsewhere.

III

What, then, do Mill's departures in religion and economics have in common? Is it entirely coincidental that the desire to defend the possibility of God's existence surfaced in tandem with the desire to launch new defences of trade unions and land reform?

There seem to be two plausible explanations. A somewhat cynical interpretation would suggest that the two initiatives reveal a new opportunism, inspired by impatience. Mill was seeking to make classical political economy more attractive to an audience that had become increasingly important – the educated, self-improving worker. It was through the agency of this individual that the Malthusian message would be diffused. It was through his agency as well that the claims of revolutionary socialism would be rebutted, and the path left open for the evolution of trade unionism into co-operation.

The book Mill was working on when he died, published in the *Fortnightly Review* in 1879 as 'Chapters on Socialism', appears to have been addressed to this audience. The heart of it – or what we have of it – is a careful, elementary exposition of (1) how competition benefits the working classes;[50] (2) how capital supports labour, and earns a profit that is entirely legitimate;[51] (3) the way in which the management of the nation's entire productive resources by the State would be at best grossly inefficient, and, at worst, eliminate the freedom that is essential to the development of character.[52]

In order to gain the ear of this influential stratum of the working class, Mill may well have felt that he needed to make his support of political economy for unions more explicit. Though hardly quite so consciously, Mill may also have felt that he needed to establish his own *bona fides* as a supporter of religion. So just as he gave his *imprimatur*, as a political economist, to trade union activities, he wished to demonstrate that the religious beliefs of his audience did indeed have the warrant of modern philosophy or at least, as in the case of trade unionism, were not explicitly condemned by expert opinion.

Mill had learned something from the Westminster electorate in 1868: it was chiefly his support of Bradlaugh, he felt, that had cost him his seat.[53] A parliamentary career was one thing, the improvement of mankind quite another. His desire to be an effective spokesman for ideas he felt were of the utmost importance to human progress may have induced him to make the allowances and accommodations that were so offensive to Morley.

To be a little more specific about Mill's strategy in 'Theism', he hoped to enlist two religious impulses on behalf of his great campaign: (1) the idea of imitating Christ, and (2) the idea of assisting in God's work.

> [I]t is Christ, rather than God, whom Christianity has held up to believers as the pattern of perfection for humanity. It is the God incarnate, more than the God of the Jews or of Nature, who being idealized, has taken so great and salutary a hold on the modern mind. And whatever else may be taken away from us by rational criticism, Christ is still left.[54]

Claims about the divinity of Christ were what was later interpolated – though Mill expresses this sentiment obliquely.

Then, in his final paragraph, he once more turns to Thornton. Deliberately refraining from using the term Manicheism, Mill commends the

> elevated feeling...which is not open to those who believe in the omnipotence of the good principle in the universe, the feeling of helping God – of requiting the good he has given by a voluntary co-operation which he, not being omnipotent, really needs.[55]

This can hardly have been calculated to seduce the orthodox. Nonetheless, Mill may have felt that there existed a large body of believers who, precisely because they were sensitive to social evils, did not truly conceive of God as omnipotent, and would welcome both Mill's lucid precis of their *ad hoc* creed, and his endorsement of that creed.

A somewhat less cynical assessment of Mill's final years is that he simply grew more hopeful. This was Morley's view. The *Fortnightly*'s editor spoke disparagingly, in an essay on George Eliot, of 'the pale belief and dim starlight faith of his posthumous volume'.[56] Mill's remarkable 1870 letter to Lord Amberley has been mentioned. The Catholic Church has altogether exaggerated 'the force of the natural passions'. The sexual drive 'will become with men, as it already is with a large number of women, completely under the control of reason'.[57] Meanwhile, incredibly, the Malthusian spectre was withdrawing.[58] One can only speculate, however, whether Mill's clear recognition of this fact would have resulted in the radical revision of the *Principles* its acknowledgement called for, had he lived another half-dozen years. As a young man, Mill had distributed literature on artificial means of birth control. Even if feasible, this may now no longer have been necessary.

The resurgence of Mill's belief in the ability of peasant proprietorships to enrich and moralize agricultural labourers is further evidence of his optimism – or the strength of his desire that England retain Ireland.[59] And his faith in co-operation remained undiminished, despite the fact that the movement to establish producers' co-operatives was foundering.[60]

Perhaps the most significant area in which Mill's optimism increased was in his appraisal of the State's ability to discharge economic functions. Specifically, as noted, he hoped to involve the State in the purchase and management of land. He had always reserved for government the right to expropriate landlords, with compensation.[61] But only in the late 1860s did he call for the State to invoke that right. The proposals, in *England and Ireland* (1868) and the *Programme of the*

Land Tenure Reform Association, with an Explanatory Statement (1871), were, as noted, not very detailed. In Ireland, rents would be fixed at their current rate plus the commission's estimate of their increase 'from any other source than the peasant's own exertions' – 'unless special circumstances made it unjust to require so much'.[62] (These circumstances are never specified.) The more ambitious proposals of the LTRA authorize the state to determine and then appropriate from the landlord any 'increase in value to which he has contributed nothing'[63] – Henry George's 'unearned increment'. The State is additionally empowered to purchase the land of those who object to what is elsewhere called a 'tax... on the future increase of his rent'.[64] The State is further called upon to outlaw any future conversions of public to private land, to take over land 'owned by public bodies or endowed institutions' and 'the soil' of large cities, and to purchase additional land for the purposes of experimenting with collective farms.[65]

The distance these proposals carried Mill from his orthodox disciples is nicely revealed by an article Henry Fawcett wrote for the *Fortnightly* in 1872, the year after the LTRA manifesto. Fawcett is arguing against the wholesale nationalization of land and does not mention Mill, but his sentiments are clear: 'It is not more but less State intervention that is needed'.[66] Fawcett's suggestions for land reform stop with changes in the law that would facilitate the transfer of land. Most of the article documents how 'the whole community would be demoralized and degraded by... an incalculable amount of jobbery, intrigue, and favouritism' were the State to set rents.[67]

It is probably fair to observe that, just as the youthful distributor of birth-control handbooks would have smiled at the mature Mill's belief that sexual passion was on the wane, so the middle-aged author of sections 2 to 7 of Chapter 11, Book V, of the *Principles* (consisting of six strenuous 'objections to government intervention')[68] would have been less sanguine about the motives and interests of individuals who act on the State's behalf, even if selected competitively.

One can only speculate about the explanation for the analogous shift in Mill's religious beliefs – his guarded hope that a God may exist who was well disposed to mankind, possibly offering an afterlife. The prospect of being reunited with Harriet Taylor was no doubt a strong motive. 'The only consolation possible is the determination to live always as in her sight', Mill wrote shortly after his wife's death, then cancelled the line.[69] 'Her memory is to me a religion', he declared in the *Autobiography*.[70]

If the hope of again living in the presence of the object of his worship was a powerful inducement to the sentiments expressed in 'Theism', no less important was the reassurance that in some way their joint work could be resumed. For Mill argues that, in any future life, just as we will be who we have made ourselves, so we may continue to improve ourselves by improving mankind.[71]

Thornton had expressed similar sentiments in a poem in his first collection.[72] If the longing to again see and serve Harriet Taylor may have inspired the optimism and the (albeit qualified) credulity of Mill's last forays into theology, his best friend Thornton, I have argued, exercised at least as significant an influence. The latter's admirable life, and the warmth of his friendship, seems to have drawn Mill to his rosy beliefs after Harriet Taylor's death. Ironically, then, her death – both in inspiring the wish to be reunited with her, and allowing Thornton more access and influence – led Mill to modify the far more cynical views on God and immortality they'd once shared.[73]

Hopes about the existence of a deity and the soul's immortality, then, and hopes that the sexual impulse was waning, that instinct was yielding to conscious control, and rivalry to co-operation, may have mutually reinforced one another. God was in His heaven, and had the best intentions, the State was beneficent, and though certainly all was not right with the world, things might be improved more quickly and dramatically than he had hitherto believed.

In the end, it might be fair to say that both impatience and hope inspired the late economic and religious writings that cast Mill adrift from earlier positions, and from his orthodox followers. Hope was fuelled by impatience. The improvement of mankind required the recruitment of skilled workers; trade unions had therefore to be defended. Trade union leaders were demanding land reform.[74] And land reform was urgently needed in Ireland if Fenianism was not to become a potent force, and England further blacken its reputation.

By 1871 Mill felt the end approaching. 'In no very long time I shall be laid in the ground with a very different ceremonial from that', he confided to Bain after Grote's Westminster Abbey funeral.[75] Though his final words were reported to have been, 'My work is done', it is hard to believe that he really felt that.[76] Public opinion, and the institutions affected by it, had come a long way in Mill's lifetime, but there was still, he believed, a great distance to go. If getting there necessitated some departures from earlier positions, if it involved making exceptions and allowances he would once not have countenanced, that was a cost Mill was willing to bear.

Notes

I have used the following abbreviations in the notes; the first 14 items are volumes in *The Collected Works of John Stuart Mill* (Toronto: University of Toronto Press/Routledge and Kegan Paul).

CW 1: J. Robson and J. Stillinger (eds), *Autobiography and Literary Essays* (1981)
CW 2, 3: J. Robson (ed.), *Principles of Political Economy* (1965)
CW 4, 5: J. Robson (ed.), *Essays on Economics and Society* (1967)
CW 6: J. Robson (ed.), *Essays on England, Ireland, and the Empire* (1982)
CW 8: J. Robson (ed.), *A System of Logic, Ratiocinative and Inductive* (1974)
CW 9: J. Robson (ed.), *An Examination of Sir William Hamilton's Philosophy* (1979)
CW 10: J. M. Robson (ed.), *Essays on Ethics, Religion and Society* (1969)
CW 12, 13: F. Mineka (ed.), *The Earlier Letters of John Stuart Mill, 1812–1848* (1963)
CW 14–17: F. Mineka and D. Lindley (eds), *The Later Letters of John Stuart Mill, 1849 to 1873* (1972)
CW 18, 19: J. Robson (ed.), *Essays on Politics and Society* (1977)
CW 21: J. Robson (ed.), *Essays on Equality, Law, and Education* (1984)
CW 28: J. Robson and B. Kinzer (eds), *Public and Parliamentary Speeches* (1988)
CW 30: J. Robson, M. Moir, Z. Moir (eds), *Writings on India* (1990)

HOPE: (C. Goodwin, ed.), *History of Political Economy* (Durham: Duke University Press, 1971–)
JHET: (D. Walker, ed.), *Journal of the History of Economic Thought* (1978–)
Wood: (J. Wood, ed.), *John Stuart Mill: Critical Assessments* (vols 1–4) (London: Croom Helm, 1987)

Hayek: F. A. Hayek, *John Stuart Mill and Harriet Taylor, Their Friendship and Subsequent Marriage* (London: Routledge & Kegan Paul, 1951)

BLPES: British Library of Political and Economic Science, London
  CC: Courtney Collection
  MTC: Mill–Taylor Collection
NLI: National Library of Ireland, Dublin
PRO: Public Records Office of Northern Ireland, Belfast
UCL: Special Collections, University College London Library
Hopkins: Special Collections, Milton Eisenhower Library, The Johns Hopkins University
Yale: Special Collections, Sterling Library, Yale University

Unless otherwise specified, citations of the *Fortnightly Review* refer to volumes in the new series.

1 INTRODUCTION

1. Mill last worked on the *Autobiography* during the early part of 1870. (J. M. Robson and J. Stillinger (eds), 'Introduction', *Autobiography*, CW 1, xxvii.)
2. Morley to Mill, 28 April 1872. Yale, ms. group 350, box 2. Not having published as much as an article on economics, Morley was obliged to argue only that he was 'a competent person and likely to discharge the duties of the post industriously'.
3. The two indispensable book-length studies on the Philosophic Radicals are by W. Thomas, *The Philosophic Radicals: Nine Studies in Theory and Practice, 1817–1841* (Oxford: Clarendon Press, 1979) and J. Hamburger, *Intellectuals in Politics: John Stuart Mill and the Philosophic Radicals* (New Haven: Yale University Press, 1965). Members included Charles Austin, Charles Buller, William Ellis, George Graham, George Grote, Joseph Hume, Sir William Molesworth, John Roebuck and Eyton Tooke. Even allowing for some retrospective bitterness in his appraisal of the group in the *Autobiography*, Mill appears to have been fonder of F. D. Maurice and, especially, John Sterling. (*Autobiography*, 159–63.)
4. Spencer, in fact, he appears to have got to know well only in the 1860s. Other individuals Mill felt close to during that decade include John Chapman, Max Kyllman, John Plummer, Peter Taylor, David Urquhart and Thomas Hare. He also had several foreign friends, including Louis Blanc, Franz Brentano, Gustave D'Eichthal, Theodore Gomperz, Giuseppe Mazzini and Pasquale Villari. Two younger proteges who were not economists were Lord Amberley and George Croom Robertson.
5. Appendix H, *Autobiography*, CW 1, 626. As to Cairnes's reputation, see, for example, the obituary notice of his arch-rival Leslie, 'Professor Cairnes', [1875] *Essays in Political Economy* (2nd edition) [1888] (New York: Kelley, 1969), 60–2.
6. *Autobiography*, CW 1, 33.
7. As acknowledged by the economist whose attack on Ricardian premises ultimately overshadowed their own: 'After the death of W. T. Thornton, he [Leslie] may be said to have led the reaction against the doctrinaire school of economists founded by James Mill and Ricardo', wrote Jevons, in an anonymous obituary of his friend Leslie. (*The Economist*, 4 February 1882, 133.) As to Thornton's success, the testimony of Cairnes's former student, J. L. Shadwell, is telling: 'I commenced studying Political Economy at the time when the publication of Mr Thornton's work on Labour had just given so rude a shock to the common belief that the science, so far as it dealt with the subjects of Value and Wages, was complete.' Shadwell goes on to compare Thornton's assault on the wages fund to Dollinger's attack on papal infallibility (*A System of Political Economy* (London: Trubner, 1877), iii, 20). Leslie, despite his sense of isolation, may have been no less influential: Blaug estimates that by the 1870s 'the dominant view among English economists... was that of the Historical School'. (M. Blaug, *Economic Theory in Retrospect* (4th edn) (Cambridge: Cambridge University Press, 1985), 300).

8. A sizeable literature exists on both 'exogenous' explanations for the development of economic theory and specifically on the role of religion in influencing the evolution of economic thought. See J. Lipkes, *Politics, Religion, and the Fate of Classical Political Economy: John Stuart Mill and His Followers, 1860–1875* (Princeton University, dissertation), 31–46, and accompanying endnotes, for a discussion of some of the relevant works.
9. Marginal utility theory and the marginal 'revolution' will be briefly summarized in Chapter 11.
10. It is important at the outset to disentangle historical and biographical approaches to the question from the technical analyses of philosophers and economists. The latter typically inquire into the consistency of Mill's *oeuvre*: are claims about utility and justice, freedom and necessity, reconcilable? Those undertaking technical analyses of Mill's work are also frequently fond of translating his arguments into the current language of their respective disciplines, and determining what has survived and what has been jettisoned – and, accordingly, how many points ought to be awarded. Intellectual historians, luckily, need not concern themselves with state-of-the-art discourse in economics, political theory or philosophy, and tend not to evaluate an entire *oeuvre* as a complete, or incomplete, system. They are more likely to be concerned with the evolution of thought over time, and the frustrating pursuit of 'influences'. In what ways did Mill shift ground, when and why? Needless to say, this perspective assumes that there were, in fact, important disjunctures, but here Mill himself made the earliest, and largest, claims. At the same time, Mill did not repudiate any work. While he subsequently believed that some earlier essays were unbalanced, and wished to amend everything he reissued, he would not have felt that there were logical inconsistencies either within individual works or between works in his *oeuvre*. So to describe and assess transitions in Mill's thought is not to argue that, in its totality, it is incoherent.
11. *Autobiography*, 237.
12. Carlyle, while he popularized Goethe, Schelling, *u s.w.*, was also himself directly influenced by the St Simonians, to Goethe's distress. (F. Kaplan, *Thomas Carlyle, a Biography* (Ithaca: Cornell University Press, 1983), 155.)
13. *Autobiography*, 169.
14. *Ibid.*
15. *Ibid.*, 169.
16. *Ibid.*, 163.
17. *Ibid.*, 171.
18. J. Schumpeter, *History of Economic Analysis* (New York: Oxford University Press, 1954), 603; J. M. Robson, *The Improvement of Mankind* (Toronto: Toronto University Press, 1968), viii; R. S. Dower, 'John Stuart Mill and the Philosophic Radicals', in F. J. C. Hearnshaw (ed.), *Social and Political Ideas of Some Representative Thinkers of the Age of Reaction and Reconstruction, 1815–1865* (New York: Barnes & Noble, 1926), 114, cited by F. L. van Holthoon, *The Road to Utopia* (Assen: Van Gorcum, 1971), 1.

19. A survey of the view of Mill as a well-intentioned bungler is obviously beyond our scope. See van Holthoon's pithy summary, *Ibid.*, 2–7. The view surfaced before Mill's death, and its validity was conceded, to a surprising degree, by such ardent admirers as Morley and Fox Bourne. See Chapter 4 below. But the opinion is perhaps most clearly and forcefully expressed by Jevons, 'John Stuart Mill's Philosophy Tested', Part IV, *Contemporary Review* 36 (November 1877), 521–38. Other famous critiques of Mill's Utilitarianism in particular are Moore's and Bradley's. (G. E. Moore, *Principia Ethica* (Cambridge: Cambridge University Press, [1901] 1959), 64–81; F. H. Bradley, *Ethical Studies* (Oxford: Clarendon Press, 1927), 103–24.)
20. Relatively recent analyses of Mill's *oeuvre* stressing various inconsistencies include: J. Plamenatz, *The English Utilitarians* (Oxford: Blackwell, 1949); R. Anschutz, *The Philosophy of J. S. Mill* (Oxford: Clarendon Press, 1953); and H. J. McCloskey, *John Stuart Mill: A Critical Study* (London: Macmillan, 1971). For the still more recent case for the coherency and consistency of Mill's thought, see J. Robson; A. Ryan, *The Philosophy of John Stuart Mill* (2nd edn) (Atlantic Heights, NJ: Humanities Press International, 1987); and S. Hollander, *The Economics of J. S. Mill* (2 vols) (Oxford: Blackwell, 1985). Chapters 4 and 5 below seek to modify this revised view.
21. *Autobiography*, CW 1, 111.
22. *Ibid.*, 'Appendix G', 613.
23. A. Bain, *John Stuart Mill, A Criticism with Personal Recollections* [1882] (New York: Kelley, 1969), 167.
24. C. E. Norton to C. Wright, 13 September 1870 in S. Norton and M. DeWolfe Howe (eds), *Letters of Charles Elliot Norton* (vol. 1) (Boston: Houghton, Mifflin, 1913), 400.
25. For a more sympathetic view of Helen Taylor than will be presented here, but one that nonetheless makes no claims for her intellectual originality, see A. Robson, 'Mill's Second Prize in the Lottery of Life', in M. Laine (ed.), *A Cultivated Mind, Essays on J. S. Mill Presented to John M. Robson* (Toronto: University of Toronto Press, 1991), 215–41.
26. Bain, 39.
27. A. W. Levi, 'The "Mental Crisis" of John Stuart Mill', *Psychoanalytic Review* 32 (January 1945), 86–101. Even readers hostile to Freud are likely to concede much of this argument. The cathartic rush Mill experienced was precipitated by a passage in Marmontel's memoirs in which the young author vows to his mother and siblings that he will replace his dead father. They believe him; he is offered his father's bed. The famous tears followed, and Mill was able to resume the role of dutiful son.
28. Hayek, 36–8.
29. Taylor to Mill, 28 (?) May 1849. Hayek, 153.
30. Taylor to Mill, 9 July 1849, Hayek, 156: 'Tocqueville is a notable specimen of the class which includes such people as the Stirlings Romillys Carlyles Austins [*sic*] – the gentility class – weak in moral [*sic*], narrow in intellect, timid, infinitely conceited & gossiping. There are very few men

in this country who can seem other than more or less respectable puppets to us.'

31. Taylor to Mill, 'about 1844', Hayek, 114.
32. G. Himmelfarb, 'The Other John Stuart Mill', in *Victorian Minds* (New York: Harper and Row, 1970), 116.
33. *Ibid.*, 145.
34. G. Himmelfarb, *On Liberty and Liberalism* [1974] (New York: ICS, 1990), 257.
35. Himmelfarb's reading of Mill invites a couple of observations: (1) The import of the two essays for public policy debates during the Vietnam era is obvious, but one cannot help but wonder if the Mill of *On Liberty* might not now seem a little more appealing to those conservatives finding themselves defending First Amendment rights on American campuses, while confronting the natural theology of the radical environmentalist movement; (2) Libertarian liberalism appears to have had more cachet in Britain than in the US in the 1960s and 1970s: the Mill of the early 1830s that Himmelfarb admires is precisely the Mill Cowling and Letwin scourge as 'totalitarian'. See M. Cowling, *Mill and Liberalism* (Cambridge: Cambridge University Press, [1963] 1990) and S. Letwin, *The Pursuit of Certainty* (Cambridge: Cambridge University Press, 1965). It is to be regretted that both Himmelfarb, in her 1974 expansion of 'The Other John Stuart Mill', *On Liberty and Liberalism*, and Cowling, in his long preface to the 1990 edition of *Mill and Liberalism*, chose not to respond to their many critics.
36. *Autobiography*, CW 1, 229.
37. If such a movement can be ascertained with any precision, April 1835 might be a better date, when he published a review of Sedgwick's *Discourse on the Studies of the University*, wherein, Mill says, he 'had an opportunity of putting in practice my scheme of conciliation between the old and the new "philosophic radicalism..."' (*Ibid.*, 209.) Alternatively, 1838 may mark a high water point of his revolt. For in this year he published his essay on Bentham, something he could not have permitted himself before his father's death. Reviewing the essay some 16 years later, he found that he had been rather too harsh on the old man, just as he had overestimated Coleridge, he felt in retrospect, in the companion essay he published in 1844. (*Ibid.*, 1, 227.)
38. *Ibid.*, 225.
39. *Ibid.*, 101.
40. *Ibid.*, 207.
41. *Ibid.*, 221.
42. Mill subscribed £80 to enable Spencer to take over. The journal had been launched a year earlier, in January 1863, as something of a Christian Socialist organ, and Spencer intended to make it the voice of evolutionists. See J. Byrne, 'The *Reader*', in A. Sullivan (ed.), *British Literary Magazines: The Victorian and Edwardian Age, 1837–1913* (Westport, CT: Greenwood Press, 1984), 346–51.
43. Cairnes had grave reservations even about serving as sub-editor. Cairnes to Mill, 23 December 1864, 9 January 1865, and 13 March 1865, vol. 56A, items 19, 21 and 25, MTC, BLPES. Mill accord-

ingly concealed from Cairnes his machinations in the younger man's behalf.

44. The usually prolix Morley's cryptic comment that it was 'by the influence' of his friend Cotter Morison has largely been accepted at face value. See J. Morley, *Recollections* (vol. l) (New York: Macmillan, 1917), 85; F. Hirst, *Early Life and Letters of John Morley* (London: Macmillan, 1927), 63; Everett sees some evidence of politicking in Morley's efforts to cultivate George Eliot. (*The Party of Humanity: the Fortnightly Review and its Contributors, 1865–1874* (Chapel Hill: University of North Carolina Press, 1939), 76–7.) Another valuable eyewitness is co-proprietor Anthony Trollope. (*An Autobiography* [1883] (London: Oxford University Press, 1923), 172.)
45. Mill to Morley, 18 November 1870, 28 November 1870, CW 17, 1774, 1777. Mill admonishes Morley to publish a lecture by Lady Amberley forthwith, and to denounce a surge of Russophobia following Russia's repudiation of the naval clauses of the 1856 Treaty of Paris.
46. Mill to Morley, 28 November 1870, *Ibid*., 1784–5.
47. The lengthy and abstruse *Examination of Sir William Hamilton's Philosophy* was undertaken, Mill claims, because 'the difference between these two schools of philosophy, that of Intuition, and that of Experience and Association, is not a mere matter of abstract speculation; it is full of practical consequences, and lies at the foundation of all the greatest differences of practical opinion . . . ' (*Autobiography*, CW 1, 269).
48. *Ibid*., 72.
49. *Ibid*., 79.
50. *Ibid*., 235.
51. *Ibid*., 163.
52. *Ibid*., 235–6.
53. *Ibid*., 37, 39.
54. *Ibid*., 83.
55. Packe, 69.
56. S. Collini, *Public Moralists, Political Thought and Intellectual Life in Britain, 1850–1930* (Oxford: Oxford University Press, 1991), 121–69; J. Carlisle, *John Stuart Mill and the Writing of Character* (Athens, GA: University of Georgia Press, 1991), and B. Kinzer, 'John Stuart Mill and the Experience of Political Engagement', in Laine, 1991, 182–214. See additionally B. Kinzer, A. Robson and J. Robson, *A Moralist In and Out of Parliament* (Toronto: University of Toronto Press, 1992) for a detailed account of Mill's parliamentary career, particularly as to the ways principles and pragmatism were reconciled.
57. 'Theism', *Three Essays on Religion*, CW 10, 488.
58. 'Pity' overpowers 'Justice', in Morley's formula. (Morley, 1917, 57.)

2 THE POLITICS OF MILL'S POLITICAL ECONOMY

1. Mill to Chapman, 8 November 1844, CW 13, 640–2. What Mill doesn't indicate is the extent to which he was deliberately trying to resuscitate a

system which had been discredited and largely abandoned. For the debates on the persistence of Ricardian economics to 1848 and on Mill's success in reviving it, see S. Checkland, 'The Propagation of Ricardian Economics in England', *Economica* 16 (1949), 40–52; F. Fetter, 'The Rise and Decline of Ricardian Economics', *HOPE* 1 (1969) 67–84; N. de Marchi, 'The Empirical Content and Longevity of Ricardian Economics', *Economica* 37 (1970), 257–76 (Wood, vol. 3, 53–71), and 'The Success of J. S. Mill's *Principles*', *HOPE* 6 (1974), 119–57 (Wood, vol. 2, 122–54); M. Blaug, *Ricardian Economics* [1958] (Westport, CT: Greenwood Press, 1976), 38–63, 165–92; M. Rothbard, *Classical Economics*, vol. 2, (Aldershot: Elgar, 1995), 103–55, 275–97. This chapter discusses Mill's motives in shoring up Ricardo; for verdicts on his fidelity to the system, see note 10, below.

2. W. Grampp, *The Manchester School of Economics* (Stanford: Stanford University Press, 1960).
3. Z. Fink, *The Classical Republicans* (Evanston: Northwestern University Press, 1945); C. Robbins, *The Eighteenth-Century Commonwealthman* (New York: Atheneum, 1968 [1959]), J. G. A. Pocock, *Politics, Language and Time* (New York: Atheneum, 1973), 80–147; J. G. A. Pocock, *The Machiavellian Moment* (Princeton: Princeton University Press, 190), 333–552.
4. 'Fonblanque's *England Under Seven Administrations', London and Westminster Review* vol. 7 (April 1837), CW 6, 353.
5. J. Hamburger, *Intellectuals in Politics: John Stuart Mill and the Philosophic Radicals* (New Haven: Yale University Press, 1965), 31, 32.
6. W. Thomas, *The Philosophic Radicals* (Oxford: Clarendon Press, 1979), 10.
7. Thomas, 2. 'Benthamism' was even more pejorative. (*Autobiography* CW 1, 81.)
8. *Ibid.*, 172.
9. 'The Cattle Disease Bill', 14 Feb. 1866, *Hansard* 3rd Series, V. 181, cols 488–92, CW 28, 49.
10. Space does not permit a consideration of the debate on the extent to which Mill was a Ricardian. Schumpeter, dissenting from a century-long consensus, argued that there was something like a clean break. 'The economics of the *Principles* are no longer Ricardian.' (J. Schumpeter, *History of Economic Analysis* (New York: Oxford University Press, 1986 [1954]), 529, 603–4.) This has been modified in subsequent decades by other commentators, who nonetheless stress Mill's original contributions. (M. Blaug, *Economic Theory in Retrospect*, 4th edn (Cambridge: Cambridge University Press, 1985), 219. R. Ekelund and R. Hebert, *A History of Economic Theory and Method* (New York: McGraw-Hill, 1997), 170–4; P. Schwartz, *The New Political Economy of John Stuart Mill* (London: Weidenfeld and Nicolson, 1972), 235–6; G. Stigler, 'The Nature and Role of Originality in Scientific Progress', in *Essays in the History of Economics* (Chicago: University of Chicago Press, 1965), 11.) Hollander goes furthest in the opposite direction, arguing for continuities, broad and fine, between Ricardo and Mill. (S. Hollander, *The Economics of John Stuart Mill*, 2 vols (Oxford: Blackwell; 1985); S.

Hollander, 'Ricardianism, J. S. Mill, and the Neo-Classical Challenge', in J. Robson and M. Laine (eds), *James and John Stuart Mill: Papers of the Centenary Conference* (Toronto: University of Toronto Press, 1976), 68–70.) While other writers regret Mill's loyalty (M. Blaug, *Ricardian Economics* (New Haven: Yale University Press, 1958), 227–9; Schwartz, 49; Rothbard, 278.), for Hollander, Mill's 'refusal to innovate for the sake of innovation' was all to the good – Jevons's (and Walras's) departures were net losses for the discipline. (Hollander, *Economics*, vol. 2, 917, 931, 935, 938–9.) Where Mill does break with Ricardo, it is in public policy issues – with mixed results. (Schwartz, 67–234, 239–40.) Though ostensibly derived from his spurious distinction between production and distribution (the only theoretical advance Mill claimed for the *Principles* – and which he dutifully attributed to Harriet Taylor), the social reforms he advocated – as Hollander notes – were grounded in good Ricardian theory. (Hollander, *Economics*, vol. 2, 917–19.) I go somewhat further, arguing that not only was Mill a Ricardian, but it was precisely the public policy implications of Ricardianism that made him defend the system so tenaciously – until his final decade. Ricardian principles expressed in appealing scientific axioms a morality he found profoundly congenial, and to which he dedicated himself to propagating.

11. D. Ricardo, 'On the Principles of Political Economy and Taxation', in P. Sraffa (ed.), *The Works and Correspondence of David Ricardo*, vol. 1 (Cambridge: Cambridge University Press, 1966), 66.
12. James Mill, *Elements of Political Economy* [1844] (New York: Kelley, 1965), 31. Mill Senior's role in pushing radical applications for Ricardian rent should not be overlooked, including the possibility of a tax on the 'unearned increment'.
13. Ricardo, 17, 24; G. Stigler, 'Ricardo and the 93 Per Cent Labor Theory of Value', in *Essays in the History of Economics* (Chicago: University of Chicago Press, 1965), 326–42; H. Barkai, 'The Empirical Assumptions of Ricardo's 93 Per Cent Labour Theory of Value', *Economica* 34 (1967), 418–23.
14. Ricardo, 74–5.
15. *Ibid.*, 77.
16. *Ibid.*, 35, 48, 162–3, and *passim*.
17. *Ibid.*, 120–2.
18. D. Ricardo, 'Essay on the Influence of a Low Price of Corn on the Profits of Stock', in Sraffa, vol. 4 (1951), 21.
19. *Principles of Political Economy*, CW 2, 174.
20. *Ibid.*, 230.
21. *Ibid.*, 416, 417.
22. *Ibid.*, CW 3, 819–20.
23. *Ibid.*, CW 2, 78.
24. *Ibid.*, 83; for a starkly Calvinist explanation of the difference between productive and unproductive consumption, see James Mill, 221–2.
25. *Autobiography*, CW 1, 177.
26. While the phrase itself doesn't appear in the *Principles*, it was likely to have been borrowed from Mill, who uses the two words in the same paragraph (CW 3, 821), and discusses the concept at length. Article IV

of the Land Tenure Reform Association's Programme, drafted by Mill, speaks of 'Taxation of the Future Unearned Increase of the Rent of Land'. 'Land Tenure Reform', CW 5, 690n.

27. E. P. Lawrence, *Henry George in the British Isles* (E. Lansing: Michigan State University Press, 1957) and C. A. Barker, *Henry George* (New York: Oxford University Press, 1955); but see the criticism of J. Saville, 'Henry George and the British Labour Movement: A Select Bibliography with Commentary', *Bulletin of the Society for the Study of Labour History* 5 (1962), 18–22, who claims George's influence in Britain has been exaggerated.
28. *England and Ireland*, CW 6, 527: 'What is wanted in Ireland is a commission . . . to examine every farm which is to let to a tenant, and to commute the present variable for a fixed rent. . . . The time is passed for a mere amicable mediation of the State between the landlord and the tenant. There must be compulsory powers . . .'
29. See in particular his letter to Reid, 5 October 1869, CW 17, 1643–4: 'I myself agree in principle with Mr Odger & his friends [who supported nationalization]; but if the [Land Tenure Reform] Assn were to adopt as its purpose the resumption of all the land from its proprietors it could not hope for any support except from a portion of the working classes.' However, writing the next year to Boyd Kinnear, who had just resigned from the Association, Mill hastens to assure his correspondent that it was precisely the *radical* demands in the LTRA's Programme – not that document's moderation – that reflect merely tactical considerations. 'I quite agree with you that public bodies ought not to hold lands', Mill avers, though a trial might be worthwhile to 'convince the working classes that such a system would be unsuccessful or injurious'. (22 July 1870, CW 17, 1749.) Mill's two letters to George himself concern Chinese immigration and the publication of letter number one. (Mill to George, 23 October 1869, CW 17, 1653–4 and 13 August 1870, *Ibid*., 1756–7.)
30. *Principles*, CW 2, 252–3, 278–92.
31. M. Packe, *Life of John Stuart Mill* (London: Secker and Warburg, 1954), 491.
32. Ricardo, *Principles*, Sraffa (ed.), vol. 1, 398.
33. *Ibid*., 93.
34. *Ibid*., 101.
35. *Ibid*., 100; 'There cannot be a better security against a superabundant population.'
36. *Ibid*., 106–7.
37. *Principles*, CW 2, 154–9; 343–54; and *passim*.
38. *Autobiography*, CW 1, 107–9. The credit for converting Malthusianism into an argument for birth control belongs to James Mill and, especially, Francis Place. (D. Winch, *Riches and Poverty: An Intellectual History of Political Economy in Britain, 1750–1834* (Cambridge: Cambridge University Press, 1996), 282–5.)
39. *Principles*, CW 2, 337.
40. *Autobiography*, CW 1, 239.
41. Schwarz, 28, 245–56; Packe, 72n; J. Morley, *The Life of W. E. Gladstone* (vol. 2) (New York: Macmillan, 1904), 543–4; for Mill's feelings about

birth control, see N. Himes, 'John Stuart Mill's Attitude Toward Neo-Malthusianism', *Economic History*, vol. 1 (Jan. 1929), 457–84, and A. McLaren, *Birth Control in Nineteenth-Century England* (New York: Holmes and Meier, 1978), 91–4.

42. *Principles*, CW 2, 372.
43. *Ibid.*, CW 3, 766.
44. *Ibid.*, CW 2, 283–92.
45. *Ibid.*, 378–9.
46. *Ibid.*, CW 3, 768.
47. *Ibid.*, 792.
48. *Ibid.*, 775; 793–4.
49. *Ibid.*, 794.
50. *Ibid.*, 795.
51. *Ibid.*, 775.

3 THE RELIGION OF HUMANITY

1. 'A Sketch of His Life', in H. R. Fox Bourne (ed.), *John Stuart Mill: His Life and Works* (Boston: Osgood, 1873), 25.
2. S. Norton and M. De Wolfe Howe, *Letters of Charles Eliot Norton with Biographical Comment*, vol. 1 (Boston: Houghton Mifflin, 1913), 331. Norton responded with a different, more reverent, equation: 'if one saw much of him, affection would soon equal respect for him'. (*Ibid.*)
3. R. L. Nettleship (ed.), *The Works of T. H. Green*, vol. 3 (London: Longmans, Green, 1889), cxliv; cited by L. Stephen, *The English Utilitarians*, vol. 3 (New York: Putnam's, 1900), 68–9.
4. Jevons to Musgrave, 21 February 1876, in R. D. Collison Black (ed.), *Papers and Correspondence of William Stanley Jevons*, vol. 4 (London: Macmillan, 1977), 167.
5. Marshall to Jevons, 4 February 1875, in Black (ed.), (vol. 4), 100.
6. L. Stephen, 69.
7. J. Morley, 'The Death of Mr Mill', *The Fortnightly Review* 13 (1 June 1873), 670, 671.
8. Fox Bourne, 25.
9. The sobriquet was originally bestowed by Gladstone – and thus with no trace of sarcasm. (J. Morley, *The Life of W E. Gladstone*, vol. 2 (New York: Macmillan, 1904), 544.)
10. H. Spencer, *Autobiography* (vol. 2) (New York: Appleton and Co., 1904), 156–7.
11. W. Thornton, 'His Career in the India House', in Fox Bourne (ed.), 35; Thornton also describes Mill's comic rectitude in refusing a retirement gift from his subordinates: 'I have never seen him so angry. He hated all such demonstrations, he said, and was quite resolved not to be made the subject of them. He was sure they were never altogether genuine and spontaneous; there were always several persons who took part in them merely because they did not like to refuse...' (*Ibid.*, 36–7.)

12. *Autobiography*, CW 1, 289; M. Packe, *Life of John Stuart Mill* (London: Secker and Warburg, 1954), 473–4. The publication of *England and Ireland* in 1868 did not help either.
13. H. Fawcett, 'His Influence at the Universities', in Fox Bourne (ed.), 77–8.
14. A. Bain, *John Stuart Mill: A Criticism with Personal Recollections* [1882] (New York: Kelley, 1969), 150.
15. H. Spencer, 'His Moral Character', in Fox Bourne (ed.), 41–2.
16. Norton, 330.
17. M. Conway, *Autobiography: Memories and Experiences* (vol. 2) (Boston: Houghton Mifflin, 1904), 16–17.
18. 'His feelings . . . were . . . as tender as a woman's. They were wanting not in keenness, but in the massiveness which implies more masculine fibre.' There were compensations: Mill was endowed with an unusual capacity for devotion ('a feminine quality'). Stephen, however, dwells on 'some of the amiable weaknesses which we at present . . . regard as especially feminine'. These turn out to be impressionability and humourlessness. ('Like a woman, he took things – even philosophers – with excessive seriousness.') (Stephen, 72–3.)
19. *Autobiography*, CW 1, 9–27.
20. *Ibid*., 67–9.
21. *Ibid*., 145.
22. *Ibid*., 145–7.
23. *Ibid*., 145.
24. *Ibid*., 147.
25. *Ibid*., 149.
26. *Ibid*., 151.
27. *Ibid*., 153.
28. 'Tennyson's Poems', *London Review* 1 (July 1835), CW 1, 414.
29. *Ibid*., 413; Autobiography, CW 1, 183.
30. *Ibid*., 195.
31. B. and P. Russell (eds), *The Amberley Papers* (vol. 2) (New York: Simon and Schuster, 1966), 375.
32. 'Writings of Alfred de Vigny', CW 1, 466–7; see also 'Inaugural Address Delivered to the University of St Andrews', CW 21, 253–6.
33. I am indebted to the analyses of Mill's conception of poetry in J. Robson, *The Improvement of Mankind* (Toronto: University of Toronto Press, 1968) and F. C. Sharpless, *The Literary Criticism of J. S. Mill* (Hague, 1967).
34. 'Utility of Religion', J. Robson (ed.), *Essays on Ethics, Religion and Society* (Toronto: University of Toronto Press, 1969), CW 10, 422.
35. *Ibid*., 422–3.
36. See in particular Robson, 69–159; Ryan, 30–44; W. Thomas, *Mill* (New York: Oxford University Press, 1985), 30–50; B. Semmel, *John Stuart Mill and the Pursuit of Virtue* (New Haven: Yale University Press), 82–119.
37. *Autobiography*, CW 1, 169, 173, 177; 'Bentham', CW 10, 95–6, 99–100; *Considerations on Representative Government*, CW 19, 390–1. This and the following themes are sounded repeatedly throughout Mill's opus. Illustrations could obviously be multiplied.

38. *Representative Government*, CW 19, 390, 392. This does not imply slavish loyalty or rote learning, needless to say: progress is achieved dialectically, through an active and vigilant opposition. (*Ibid.* 397; 'Bentham', CW 10, 107–9; *On Liberty*, CW 18, 231–2, 253–4, and *passim.*)
39. *Autobiography*, CW 1, 269–70; 'Bentham', CW 10, 107–8; *Representative Government*, CW 19, 386.
40. *Principles of Political Economy*, CW 3, 752–7. Mill's grievance against middle-class culture has an oddly familiar ring: he is concerned that simple, solitary pleasures – in particular the communion with nature necessary for spiritual renewal (admirably fulfilled by his botanizing expeditions) – would be jeopardized. (*Ibid.*, 754, 756.)
41. *Representative Government*, CW 19, 411–12.
42. 'De Tocqueville on Democracy in America [II]', CW 18, 198.
43. The following revisionist works depict, if not an 'authoritarian' Mill, a Mill less concerned with liberation than conversion, for whom the improvement of mankind (which, they emphasize, depends on undermining civil and religious authorities) tends to have priority over the claims of uninstructed individuals to the exercise of freedom: R. V. Sampson, 'John Stuart Mill: An Interpretation', *Cambridge Journal* 3 (January 1950), 232–9; M. Cowling, *Mill and Liberalism* (2nd edition) (Cambridge: Cambridge University Press, 1990); S. Letwin, *The Pursuit of Certainty* (Cambridge: Cambridge University Press, 1965); J. Hamburger, 'Religion and *On Liberty*', in M. Lane (ed.), *A Cultivated Mind* (Toronto: University of Toronto Press, 1991), 139–81. B. Knights, *The Idea of the Clerisy in the Nineteenth Century* (Cambridge: Cambridge University Press, 1978), 140–77, provides a nuanced discussion of Mill's flirtation with a 'clerisy'. Pursuing a somewhat different but related tack is G. Himmelfarb (ed.), 'Introduction', *Essays on Politics and Culture by John Stuart Mill* (New York: Doubleday, 1962) reprinted in *Victorian Minds* (New York: Harper and Row, 1968), 113–54, and *On Liberty and Liberalism* [1974] (San Francisco: ICS Press, 1990). Also related are the following reassessments of Mill's motives and rhetorical strategies: J. Hamburger, *Intellectuals in Politics: John Stuart Mill and the Philosophic Radicals* (New Haven: Yale University Press, 1965); S. Collini, *Public Moralists* (Oxford: Clarendon Press, 1991), 121–69; J. Carlisle, *John Stuart Mill and the Writing of Character* (Athens, GA: University of Georgia Press, 1991). Those responding with a traditional 'libertarian' reading of Mill (and crediting him with candour) include R. J. Halliday, 'Some Recent Interpretations of John Stuart Mill', *Philosophy* 43 (1968), 1–17, Wood, vol. 1, 312–26; C. L. Ten, *Mill On Liberty* (Oxford: Clarendon, 1980), 151–73, and 'Mill and Liberty', *Journal of the History of Ideas* 30 (Jan.–March 1969), 47–68, in Wood, vol. 1, 335–55; J. C. Rees, 'Was Mill for Liberty?' *Political Studies* 14 (1966), 72–7, Wood, vol. 1, 282–9; R. B. Friedman, 'A New Exploration of Mill's Essay *On Liberty*', *Political Studies* 14 (1966), 281–304, Wood, vol. 1, 290–311; and A. Ryan, *The Philosophy of John Stuart Mill* (2nd edition) (Atlantic Heights, NJ: Humanities Press International, 1990), 254–5.
44. Mill to d'Eichthal, 7 November 1829, CW 12, 41; cited by Knights, 164.

45. Mill to de Blignieres, 22 January 1862, CW 15, 768–9; Knights, *Ibid.*
46. Mill to J. P. Nichol, 16 January 1833, CW 12, 136; Knights, 140.
47. Mill to G. d'Eichthal, 14 September 1839, CW 13, 404; Knights, *Ibid.*
48. Hamburger, 'Religion and *On Liberty*'.
49. *On Liberty*, CW 18, 261.
50. 'I have not any great notion of what the "free discussion" men, call the "collision of opinions", it being my creed that Truth is *sown* and germinates in the mind itself, and is not to be struck *out* suddenly like fire from a flint by knocking another hard body against it.' (Mill to Carlyle, 18 May 1833, CW 12, 153; cited by Himmelfarb, *On Liberty and Liberalism*, 47–8.)
51. J. Gray, 'John Stuart Mill on Liberty, Utility and Rights', *Nomos* 23 (1981), 95; N. Thornton, *The Problem of Liberalism in the Thought of John Stuart Mill* (New York: Garland, 1987), 130.
52. See *Hansard*, Parliamentary Debates (3rd Series), vol. 181, cols. 488–92 and cols. 609–20; vol. 184, cols. 2023–6, 2056–7; and vol. 193, col. 1736 and cols. 1789–90, in CW 28, 47–52; 115–19; 328, 333.
53. Both campaigns have been discussed in some detail: see B. Semmel, *Jamaican Blood and Victorian Conscience* (Boston: Houghton Mifflin, 1963); B. A. Knox, 'The British Government and the Governor Eyre Controversy, 1865–1875', *Historical Journal* 19 (1976), 877–900; E. D. Adams, *Great Britain and the American Civil War* (London: Longmans, Green, 1925); A. Weinberg, *John Elliot Cairnes and the American Civil War* (London: Kingswood Press, 1969).
54. Mill to Parke Godwin, 1 January 1869, CW 17, 1535.
55. It also enlisted his animus toward the aristocracy and his love of nature and desire to preserve commons. Additionally, he hoped to draw on (what he perceived as) the growing working-class support for land reform, and, possibly, hoped simultaneously to pre-empt the more radical movement to nationalize land on the part of some working-class leaders. Finally, the applications of land reform to the Irish Question made the conversion of public opinion to his views especially imperative.
56. In the first few months of 1869 alone, see letters of 7 and 8 January, 29 March, and 6 April. (CW 17, 1542–4, 1583–4.)
57. The extent of Mill's commitment can be gauged by the time and energy he devoted to a protracted campaign of internecine warfare among members of the governing committee of this organization. In a remarkable series of 12 letters to Croom Robertson from 13 May 1871 to 18 January 1872, some of which run as long as 1400 words (twice Mill was moved to dispatch two in one day), the two philosophers elaborately conspired to remove the influential Miss Biggs from the Secretaryship of the London Committee. Miss Biggs was apparently the *eminence grise* behind the faction within the London Society that wanted to merge with the Manchester-based National Society for Women's Suffrage, an organization seeking to link the suffrage movement more closely to the campaign against the Contagious Diseases Acts. Mill felt such an alliance would be harmful. However, his language evokes a Nixon White House operative or even a Stalinist aparatnik rather than the Saint of

Rationalism: the rival faction is 'the enemy' (13 May 1871, CW 17, 1818), and 'no opportunity should be lost of getting rid of the different members whose votes are objectionable'. (20 September 1871, CW 17, 1836.) Those favouring the merger 'should be requested to resign, and, if necessary, be removed' (25 October 1871, CW 17, 1846), and Croom Robertson is exhorted to 'use your utmost efforts to weed the Committee of the obnoxious set' (31 October, 1871, CW 17, 1849), for which end a table is prepared and discussed at length listing members that are 'Certain', 'Uncertain' and 'Perhaps hostile'. (6 November 1871, CW 17, 1860.)

The contrast with other committee work is striking. While Mill was certainly interested in the objectives of the Commons Preservation Committee, headed by Fawcett, becoming a member and, on at least one occasion, advising the group on tactics (Mill to Fawcett, 23 November 1870, CW 17, 1782–3), his cool response to an invitation from the local Blackheath affiliate suggests the limits of his involvement. (Mill to Fithian, 6 April 1869, CW 17, 1584.) The Jamaica Committee persisted until May of 1869. (Mill to Chesson, Before 28 May 1869, CW 17, 1606–7.) While Mill served as President from June 1866, and retained extremely strong feelings about the Eyre case, after two juries failed to indict the Governor and his subordinates in March and April 1867, funds and membership declined, along with the Committee's *raison d'être*. (CW 16, 1365n.) Mill's intermittent correspondence on the subject reflects mostly his own dogged commitment to keep the case in the public eye. (Mill to Harrison, 16 June 1867, CW 16, 1281; Mill to Walker, 26 February 1868, CW 16, 1366–7.)

58. In addition to the final two articles he published, the final speech he delivered, and much correspondence during 1871 and 1872 – all on the Committee's behalf – see in particular the letter of 21 April 1872 (CW 17, 1884) for evidence of the extent of his interest in the administrative details of the organization.
59. Mill to Fawcett, 24 October 1869, CW 17, 1659.
60. Of the two, the feminist cause was unquestionably the most important, in part because of its link to the population question. Agreeing with a correspondent that 'the cause of overpopulation . . . is woman's subjugation, & that the cure is her enfranchisement', Mill concludes that this will be 'one of the endless benefits that will flow from that greatest & most fundamental of all improvements in human society'. (Mill to Hamilton-Willcox, 20 January 1871, CW 17, 1801.)

4 MYSTIFYING MORLEY: DEVELOPMENTS IN MILL'S RELIGIOUS BELIEFS

1. H. Taylor, 'Introductory Notice', J. S. Mill, *Three Essays in Religion*, CW 10, 372. (The three essays will be hereafter referred to by their individual titles.)
2. *Ibid.*, 371.

3. *Ibid.*, 372.
4. *Ibid.*
5. A. Bain, *John Stuart Mill: A Criticism with Personal Recollections* [1882] (New York: Kelley, 1969), 133.
6. *Ibid.*, 135–6.
7. J. Morley, 'Mr Mill's Three Essays on Religion' (Part 1), *Fortnightly Review* 16 (November 1874), 637.
8. 'Mr Mill's Three Essays on Religion' (Part 2), *Fortnightly Review* 17 (January 1875), 113.
9. *Ibid.*, 121.
10. *Ibid.*, 123–5.
11. *Ibid.*, 128–31.
12. *Ibid.* 123–4.
13. J. Morley, *Recollections*, vol. 1 (New York: Macmillan, 1917), 106.
14. For 'what, after all, do these concessions amount to? A Probable Deity: a hope of Immortality which cannot be disproved, but for which there is no warrant; a possible revelation, from which miracle is discarded, and which is discredited by flagrant moral difficulties and perversions; a revelation mutilated by the removal of atonement, redemption, original sin, and vicarious punishment.' (*Westminster Review* 103 (January 1875), 28.)
15. *The Dublin Review* 34 (n.s.) (April 1875), 223.
16. *The Edinburgh Review* 141 (January 1875), 33. The two recent scholars who have analysed Mill's religious beliefs have been no more impressed with the logical rigour of his argument, if more sympathetic. For each, Mill's 'religion of hope' is highly problematic, necessitating 'the dissociation of imagination and reason', a 'tragic outcome' for Carr, and a no less untenable severing of morality from metaphysical propositions for Britton. (R. Carr, 'The Religious Thought of John Stuart Mill: A Study in Reluctant Scepticism', *Journal of the History of Ideas*, vol. 23 (1962), 475–95, in Wood, vol. 4, 203; K. Britton, 'John Stuart Mill on Christianity', in J. Robson and M. Laine (eds), *James and John Stuart Mill: Papers of the Centenary Conference* (Toronto: University of Toronto Press, 1976), 21–34.)
17. *An Examination of Sir William Hamilton's Philosophy*, CW 9, 103.
18. Too long to be quoted in its entirety, it begins, 'In sober truth, nearly all the things which men are hanged or imprisoned for doing to one another, are nature's every day performances. Killing, the most criminal act recognized by human laws, Nature does once to every being that lives; and in a large proportion of cases, after protracted tortures such as only the greatest monsters whom we read of ever purposely inflicted on their living fellow-creatures.' ('Nature', CW 10, 385); W. M. W. Call regarded the essay as a more powerful denunciation than anything in Schopenhauer or Leopardi. (*Westminster Review*, 6.)
19. Bain, 136.
20. 'Theism', CW 10, 487–8.
21. *Ibid.*, 486.
22. 'Nature', 375; or, alternatively, the term indicates 'the entire system of things, with the aggregate of all their properties'. (*Ibid.*, 401.)
23. *Ibid.*, 402.

24. Millicent Garrett Fawcett, *What I Remember* [1925] (Westport, CT: Hyperion, 1976), 61.
25. 'Nature', 380; He is also aware that 'naturalness' commonly means an absence of affectation. He grudgingly approves this approbatory use of the word, as a single exception, though he insists that 'sincerity' is a more accurate term. (*Ibid*., 400.)
26. *Ibid*., 397.
27. *Ibid*., 402.
28. *Ibid*.
29. H. Reeve, 'Mill's *Essays on Theism*', *The Edinburgh Review* 141 (January 1875), 12.
30. 'Nature', 393–6. Rousseau is specifically targeted twice in the essay. (*Ibid*., 376, 395.)
31. Morley, 'Mr Mill's Three Essays' (Part 1), 649.
32. *Ibid*., 651.
33. *Ibid*., 649.
34. *Ibid*., 111.
35. 'The Utility of Religion', 405.
36. *Ibid*., 405, 406.
37. *Ibid*., 407. Mill actually introduces 'authority' as a third force along with education and public opinion, but in fact he represents the latter two as the means by which authority exerts its influence.
38. *Ibid*., 413.
39. *Ibid*., 419.
40. *Ibid*., 422.
41. *Ibid*., 421.
42. Morley, 'Mr Mill's Three Essays' (Part 2), 110.
43. *Ibid*., 111.
44. 'Theism', 424.
45. For one striking example, see Mill to Lalor, 27 June [1852], CW 14, 92. On Morley himself, whose intriguing, though somewhat repellant, character – with its mix of rectitude and ambition, independence and subservience – cannot detain us, see D. A. Hamer, *John Morley: Liberal Intellectual in Politics* (Oxford: Clarendon Press, 1968) and John Gross's acerbic portrait (*The Rise and Fall of the Man of Letters* (New York: Macmillan, 1969), 99–112). For his long flirtation with Comtism, see the two fine studies of the university radicals, C. Harvie, *The Lights of Liberalism* (London: Alan Lane, 1976) and C. Kent, *Brains and Numbers* (Toronto: University of Toronto Press, 1978).
46. Morley, 'Mr Mill's Three Essays' (Part 2), 115–16; the quotation from Mill is on p. 488.
47. Morley, 'Mr Mill's Three Essays' (Part 2), 115.
48. *Ibid*.
49. *Ibid*., 116, 117; the quotations from Mill are on pp. 479 and 481, respectively.
50. '...the sublimest dicta in the Gospels [have] exact parallels in the Talmud...' (Morley, 119.)
51. *Ibid*., 119–20.
52. *Ibid*., 120; the quotation is from *On Liberty* CW 18, 256–7.

53. Morley, 'Mr Mill's Three Essays' (Part 2), 120, 121.
54. *Ibid.*, 127.
55. *Ibid.*, 129.
56. Morley to Scully, 3 April 1877, Scully Papers, Rare Books and Manuscripts, University College London.
57. F. W. Hirst, *Early Life and Letters of John Morley* (vol. 1) (New York: Macmillan, 1927), 305–7.

5 CONFOUNDING CAIRNES: DEVELOPMENTS IN MILL'S ECONOMIC THOUGHT

1. See Hollander's criticism of Hutchison's conclusions. (S. Hollander, *The Economics of John Stuart Mill* (vol. 2) (Oxford: Blackwell, 1985), 913–28. T. W. Hutchison, 'The Decline and Fall of English Classical Political Economy and the Jevonian Revolution', *On Revolutions and Progress in Economic Knowledge* (Cambridge: Cambridge University Press, 1978), 58–64.) Nonetheless, while Hutchison may have too closely identified Lowe's economics with Mill's and ignored Mill's professed receptivity to inductive evidence in the *Logic* and the fifth of his *Essays on Unsettled Questions in Political Economy* – the burden of Hollander's charge – there does appear to have been, at the very least, a new willingness on Mill's part to disassociate himself from some important postulates of Ricardian political economy.
2. J. E. Cairnes, *Some Leading Principles of Political Economy, Newly Expounded* [1874] (London: Macmillan, 1883), 48–9. This, like the next criticism, is not a response to specific departures in Mill's articles on Thornton and Leslie. Sidgwick judiciously accounts for the impact of Cairnes's criticisms: 'As a controversialist Cairnes, though scrupulously fair in intention, was deficient in intellectual sympathy; he could hardly avoid representing any doctrine that he did not hold in such a way as to make it almost inconceivable to his readers that it could possibly have been maintained by a man of sense; and when this treatment was applied to some of his master's most important statements, the expressions of personal regard for Mill by which it was accompanied only made the result seem more damaging to a reader who was convinced by Cairnes' reasoning.' (*The Principles of Political Economy* (London: Macmillan, 1883), 5.) What Cairnes wrote, admiringly, of Goldwyn Smith might have been said of himself: 'What a vast fund of scorn is in the man, and what powers of sarcasm.' (Cairnes to Nesbitt, 28 November 1862, MS 8941 (6), NLI.) By contrast, Jevons, so often depicted as the angry revolutionary excoriating 'the noxious influence of authority', is not nearly so critical of Mill. (*The Theory of Political Economy* [1871] (Charlottesville: Ibis, nd), 265; 80–1, 135–39.)
3. Cairnes, *Leading Principles*, 101–3.
4. *Ibid.*
5. *Ibid.*, 182.
6. *Ibid.*, 265.

7. J. E. Cairnes, *Essays in Political Economy* [1873] (New York: Kelley, 1965), 264.
8. Cairnes to Courtney, 5 March 1868, CC, BLPES.
9. Cairnes to Mill, 21 May 1868, Ms HUT 4, Hopkins.
10. *Principles of Political Economy*, CW 2, 230.
11. Granted that some of Leslie's most audacious attacks on Ricardian political economy came after Mill's death. Nonetheless, articles like 'Political Economy and the Rate of Wages' are uncompromising in their dismissal of deductivist economics. (T. E. Cliffe Leslie, *Land Systems and Industrial Economy of Ireland, England, & Continental Countries* [1870] (New York: Kelley, 1968), 359–79.)
12. Hollander, arguing that 'there is no reason why admiration of an individual's work necessarily implies unqualified approval', cites the letter to Leslie in which Mill is most critical of the historicist. (Hollander, 926; Mill to Leslie, 8 May 1869, CW 17, 1599–601.) But this is such a mild rebuke that Hollander is obliged to concede that 'evidently Mill downplayed the significance of Leslie's critique of Ricardian economics'. (Hollander, 926.)
13. Mill to Thornton, 19 October 1867, CW 16, 1318–20.
14. Hollander, vol. 1, 409.
15. Writing in 1879, Sidgwick observed 'a growing tendency...to treat it as exploded'. (*Fortnightly Review* 26 (April 1879), 401.) By the 1880s, 'killing the wage-fund "theory" became a favorite sport'. (J. Schumpeter, *History of Economic Analysis* [1954] (New York: Oxford University Press, 1986), 671.) Cannan's is perhaps the most definitive condemnation: 'The treatment of Distribution in the period under review appears even more unscientific and illogical than the treatment of Production .... The "law of wages" – "wages depend on the ratio between population and capital" – however obvious it may have appeared a hundred, or even fifty, years ago, is now palpably absurd. The "law of profits" – "profits depend on the cost of labour" – is entirely baseless if it be intelligible'. (E. Cannan, *A History of the Theories of Production & Distribution in English Political Economy, from 1776 to 1848* (3rd edn) [1917] (London: Staples, 1953), 301.) Among the doctrine's recent defenders have been Schumpeter: 'Not only was the wage-fund doctrine, properly stated, not "wrong" logically; not only did it emphasize, though too narrowly, certain important aspects of the wage problem; but, in addition to this, it was an analytic tool that...was distinctly useful.' (669); Bowley: 'What appears surprising in the life history of the theory is not that it was adopted, but that it became an object of ridicule.' (M. Bowley, *Nassau Senior and Classical Economics* [1937] (New York: Octagon, 1967), 186.); Stigler: 'Perhaps the most important, and beyond any doubt the most heretical, remark to be made about this theory was that it was correct. The theory was correct: it yielded correct prediction of the effects of changes in wage rates, capital, and population.' (G. Stigler, 'Mill on Economics and Society', *The Economist as Preacher and Other Essays* (Chicago: University of Chicago Press, 1982), 162–3.); and Blaug: 'This doctrine has been so frequently ridiculed that it is difficult nowadays to appreciate its partial validity and, in particular, to realize that it

marks the beginning of an appreciation of the nature of capital as a factor of production.' (M. Blaug, *Economic Theory in Retrospect* (4th edn) (Cambridge: Cambridge University Press, 1985, 185.) In fact, despite Stigler's claim, in one of the earliest – and still one of the best – scholarly treatments of the question, Taussig conceded that 'the old doctrine of the wages fund had a solid basis in its conception, incomplete yet in essentials just', of the payment of present labour from past product.' (F. W. Taussig, *Wages and Capital* (New York: Appleton, 1900), 122–3.)

16. E. Forget, 'J. S. Mill and the Tory School: The Rhetorical Value of the Recantation', HOPE 24 (Spring 1992), 33.
17. W. S. Jevons, *The Theory of Political Economy* [1871] (Charlottesville: Ibis, nd), 256–7.
18. This overview of the theory draws on discussions by James Mill, *Elements of Political Economy* (3rd edn) [1844] (New York: Kelley, 1965), 40–67; J. R. McCulloch, *The Principles of Political Economy* (5th edn) [1864] (New York: Kelley, 1965), 315–59; J. S. Mill, *Principles*, CW 2, 337–79; H. Fawcett, *Manual of Political Economy* (7th edn) (London: Macmillan, 1888), 131–57, 239–55; and Cairnes, *Leading Principles*, 149–88. The analysis is partially indebted to Taussig, 215–63; Schumpeter, 641–3, 667–71; Blaug, 185–7; D. P. O'Brien, *The Classical Economists* (Oxford: Clarendon, 1975), 111–18; and H. Spiegel, *The Growth of Economic Thought* (Durham: Duke University Press, 1983), 389–91.
19. W. T. Thornton, *On Labour: Its Wrongful Claims and Rightful Dues; Its Actual Present and Possible Future* (2nd edn) [1870] (Shannon: Irish University Press, 1971), 84. (Thornton's first edition reprinted his nine *Fortnightly Review* articles in their entirety. His second edition contained very few changes, these mostly consisting of further responses to reviewers in footnotes. The only theoretical change of significance is his adopting Mill's characterization of the wages fund as implying unitary elasticity for the demand for labour.) Longe had made this point in a pamphlet published a year before Thornton wrote. He sent copies to Mill and Fawcett, which were never acknowledged, and came to suspect that Mill had shared its contents with Thornton. Longe went on to make two rather more sophisticated arguments: that even domestic workers were arrayed in non-competitive groups and that 'both capital and labour are the servants of the consumer.... The means through which demand controls production is the mind of the producer. The estimate of the demand... governs the quantity of wealth or capital... employed in productive operations.' (F. D. Longe, *A Refutation of the Wages-fund Theory of Modern Political Economy* [1866] (Baltimore: Johns Hopkins University Press, 1905), 44.)
20. *Principles*, CW 2, 55. For an elaboration of this charge, discussed also by Taussig and W. Breit ('The Wages Fund Controversy Revisited', *The Canadian Journal of Economic and Political Science* 33 (1966), 521), see R. Ekelund, 'A Short-run Classical Model of Capital and Wages: Mill's Recantation of the Wages Fund', *Oxford Economic Papers*, 28 (March 1976), 66–85, Wood, vol. 2, 87–105.
21. 'Thornton on Labour and Its Claims', CW 5, 643–4.

22. Thornton, 89–90.
23. *Ibid.*, 93, 94, 98–9. Even here he doesn't seem to appreciate that there are commodities more perishable than labour.
24. *Ibid.*, 95–6, 101.
25. *Ibid.*, 102–4.
26. *Ibid.*, 59.
27. Mill, 'Thornton', 635–42.
28. *Ibid.*, 645.
29. For a detailed discussion of the last point, see R. Ekelund and R. Hebert, *A History of Economic Theory and Method* (New York: McGraw-Hill, 1997), 190–1.
30. *Ibid.*
31. *Ibid.*
32. *Ibid.*, 644.
33. *Ibid.* Hollander generously assumes that Mill says this because he understood that technical co-efficients were fixed – employers would be unable to acquire the necessary raw materials and machinery to utilize new workers. (Hollander, vol. 1, 412–14.) But Mill never specifies this, and Stigler sentences him to 'an hour in purgatory' for implying that lower wages would not reduce costs and increase sales. (Stigler, 163.)
34. He does raise the objection that a businessman may invest more in other firms if his own wage bill drops – but then declines to answer it. ('Thornton on Labour', 644.)
35. *Ibid.*, 660–1; Mill to Howell, 13 September 1865, CW 16, 1102.
36. *Principles*, CW 2, 397.
37. *Ibid.*, 397n. (i). E. G. West and R. W. Hafer, 'J. S. Mill, Unions and the Wages Fund Recantation: A Reinterpretation', *The Quarterly Journal of Economics* 92 (November 1978), 603–19.
38. *Principles*, CW 2, 397n. (j-j)
39. *Ibid.*, 397–8.
40. *Ibid.*, CW 3, 931n. (p-p).
41. *Ibid.*, 931. For problems in assessing Mrs Mill's impact on the 3rd edition, see Hayek, 184.
42. *Ibid.*, 932.
43. *Ibid.*
44. *Ibid.*, 931–3.
45. *Ibid.*, 933–4.
46. Thornton had argued at some length, and with some heat, that workers had no 'right' to a livelihood: 'It was not the rich who placed the poor on earth and it is not the rich who owe them the means of living here.' (Thornton, 117.)
47. 'Thornton on Labour', CW 5, 656.
48. *Ibid.*, 657.
49. *Ibid.*, 662.
50. *Ibid.*, 661.
51. *Ibid.*, 663.
52. *Ibid.*, 664.
53. *Ibid.*
54. *Ibid.*, 665.

55. *Ibid.*
56. *Ibid.*, 666.
57. West and Hafer, 616. But see R. Ekelund and W. Kordsmeier, 'J. S. Mill, Unions, and the Wages Fund Recantation: A Reinterpretation – Comment', and E. G. West and R. Hafer, 'J. S. Mill, Unions, and the Wages Fund Recantation: A Reinterpretation – Reply', *The Quarterly Journal of Economics* 96 (August 1981), 531–42 and 543–9.
58. A. Marshall, *Principles of Economics* (8th edn) [1920] (London: Macmillan, 1988), 679.
59. P. Schwartz, *The New Political Economy of John Stuart Mill* (London: Weidenfeld and Nicolson, 1968), 96.
60. It is a mistake to assume that marginalism is necessarily hostile to labour, based on J. M. Clarke's blessing of the status quo. The first application of marginalism to the labour market resulted in Edgeworth's famous contract curve, which demonstrated the indeterminacy of negotiations between bi-lateral monopolists, justifying trade union activity. ('[I]n the matter of *unionism*', he concluded, 'as well as in that of the predeterminate *wage-fund*, the "untutored mind" of the workman had gone more straight to the point than economic intelligence . . . reasoning without mathematics upon mathematical subjects.') (*Mathematical Psychics* (London: Kegan Paul, 1881), 45.) Edgeworth's second major application of marginal utility was to supply the rationale for progressive taxation. (*Papers Relating to Political Economy*, vol. 2 (London: Macmillan, 1925), 102.) For an account of the politics of other flesh-and-blood marginalists, particularly Jevons and Marshall, see Hutchison, 'The Jevonian Revolution and Economic Policy in Britain', *On Revolutions*, 94–120. For Jevons, see S. Peart, *The Economics of W. S. Jevons* (London: Routledge, 1996) and R. Bowman, 'Policy Implications of W. S. Jevons's Economic Theory', *JHET*, 19 (Fall, 1997) 196–221. For Wicksteed, see I. Steedman, 'Rationality, Economic Man and Altruism in Philip H. Wicksteed's *Common Sense of Political Economy*', B. Smith (ed.), *Truth, Liberty, Religion: Essays Celebrating Two Hundred Years of Manchester College* (Oxford: Manchester College, 1986). See also I. Steedman (ed.), *Socialism and Marginalism in Economics, 1870–1930* (London: Routledge, 1995).
61. Marshall, 678.
62. Taussig, 248–9; Schwartz, 101; Stigler, 164.
63. West and Hafer and Forget are among the economists who have most fully explored the way Mill's political agenda deflected his arguments. Forget claims that the recantation was a calculated attempt to discredit the 'Tory School'. Even if one accepts the thesis, identifying Mill's target this way is somewhat misleading. The most influential writers using political economy – and utilitarianism – to oppose the reforms Mill regarded as of paramount importance may be more accurately characterized, in the 1860s and 1870s, as conservative Liberals. The exodus to the Tory Party only began in earnest in the 1880s, and, after 1886 such men were more likely to become Unionists. They included many, though not all, of the discrete groups Parry collects under the aegis of 'whig-liberal', but especially the 'party's' non-aristocratic cohort – bankers,

lawyers and journalists like Lowe, Goschen, Fitzjames Stephen, Reeve and Elliot. See J. Parry, *Democracy and Religion: Gladstone and the Liberal Party, 1867–1875* (Cambridge: Cambridge University Press, 1986), 1–149 and J. Roach, 'Liberalism and the Victorian Intelligensia', *Cambridge Historical Journal* 12 (1957), 58–81.

64. Bowley, 177–86, 277–81.
65. Mill reintroduces the great classical bogey, 'unproductive' labour – labour providing services – but promptly claims that money spent on services, while undeniably part of the fund, is so insignificant a fraction that it is legitimate to say simply that wages depend on population and capital. (*Principles*, CW 2, 337–8.) Mill next sets about disputing popular 'fallacies' regarding wages – that they respond to brisk trade, high prices, and the price of food. (The latter is true in the long run, of course. However, it is not capitalists who respond to the price of food, but workers, by either courageously abstaining from sex, or, if middle-class tastes and values have not taken hold, lapsing into their 'previous habits in respect of population'.) (*Ibid.*, 341.) The remainder of the chapter rings the usual variations on the great Malthusian theme: 'due restriction of population [is] the only safeguard of a labouring class'. (*Ibid.*, 351.) And not content with these observations, Mill devotes two more chapters to the subject, disposing of various counterproductive remedies for low wages – minimum wage laws, subsidies, allotments, etc. – before settling on education and colonization as the best means of inducing prudence, the only true solution.
66. V. Stanton, 'A Recent Contribution to Political Economy', *Fortnightly Review* 16 (November, 1874), 666; Taussig, 249; Hollander, vol. 1, 419.
67. Forget, 53, 56.
68. Mill to E. W. Young, 10 November 1867, CW 16, 1327–8.
69. 'Theism', *Three Essays on Religion*, CW 10, 488.
70. H. Spencer, 'His Moral Character', in H. R. Fox Bourne (ed.), *John Stuart Mill: His Life and Works* (Boston: Osgood, 1873), 25–6, 39, 42.
71. See the standard histories of workers and trade unionism, H. Pelling, *A History of British Trade Unionism* (London: Macmillan, 1963), A. E. Musson, *British Trade Unions, 1800–1875* (London: Macmillan, 1972), and E. H. Hunt, *British Labour History, 1815–1914* (London: Weidenfeld and Nicolson, 1981).
72. *Principles*, CW 3, 932–3.
73. *Ibid.*, 931.
74. CW 2, 295–6. So enthralled was he with peasant proprietorship that he could not contain his enthusiasm in one chapter. The sections of Chapter 7, 'Continuation of the Same Subject', praise, respectively, 'the influence of peasant proprietorships in stimulating industry', 'training intelligence', 'promoting forethought and self-control' and 'their effect on population'. (*Ibid.*, 278–96.)
75. CW 3, 768.
76. *Autobiography*, CW 1, 255.
77. C. J. Dewey, 'The Rehabilitation of the Peasant Proprietor in Nineteenth-Century Economic Thought', HOPE 6 (Spring 1974), 22–3. Dewey argues that Mill synthesized Jones's theory and Thornton's

data. In fact, Mill appears to have relied more on Jones's data than his principles. He expresses his appreciation for 'the copious repertory of valuable facts on the landed tenures of different countries' that Jones provides. (CW 2, 248.) But Jones was no advocate of peasant proprietorships (as Dewey acknowledges), and at least half of Mill's references to him take issue with his reservations. Jones's larger objective, of course, was to attack major assumptions of Ricardo and Malthus by appealing to empirical evidence invalidating them.

78. *Principles*, CW 2, 328–9. For a highly critical account of Mill's vacillations see E. D. Steele, *Irish Land and British Politics: Tenant-Right and Nationality, 1865–1870* (Cambridge: Cambridge University Press, 1974), 50–2 and 'John Stuart Mill and the Irish Question: The Principles of Political Economy, 1848–1865', *Historical Journal* 13 (1970), 220–33.
79. The drift of Mill's thinking earlier in the decade has been described by Steele and Kinzer. (Steele, 'John Stuart Mill' and B. Kinzer, 'J. S. Mill and Irish Land: A Reassessment', *The Historical Journal* 27 (1984), 111–27.)
80. *England and Ireland*, CW 6, 527.
81. *Ibid.*
82. *Ibid.*, 512.
83. *Ibid.*
84. *Ibid.*, 514.
85. Hence, the burden of Steele's argument that the departures in *England and Ireland* reflect the lengths to which Mill would go to maintain the empire intact. See L. Zastoupil, 'Moral Government: J. S. Mill on Ireland', *Historical Journal* 26 (1983), 707–17, and B. Kinzer, 'J. S. Mill and Irish Land: A Reassessment', for convincing rejoinders to Steele's charges, and Kinzer's further reservations about Zastoupil's exaggeration of Mill's support for Irish nationalism.
86. Cairnes to Courtney, 9 January 1868, CC, BLPES: 'Fenianism is perfectly explicable without the supposition of any such national sentiment .... Depend upon it, justice in regard to the land is the one and sufficient cure for all discontent in Ireland.'
87. Cairnes to Courtney, 5 March 1868, CC, BLPES; Cairnes to Mill, 21 May 1868, MS HUT 4, Hopkins.
88. Reproduced as Appendix H, CW 3, 1075–86. Among other reservations about peasant proprietorships, Cairnes indicates that there appears to be no direct correlation between well-cultivated farms and long and profitable leases. (*Ibid.*, 1079–80.)
89. 'Leslie on the Land Question', CW 5, 671.
90. *Ibid.*, 672.
91. 'On the Definition of Political Economy', *Essays on Some Unsettled Questions in Political Economy*, CW 4, 324–7; *A System of Logic, Ratiocinative and Inductive*, CW 8, 915–17.
92. 'On the Definition', 321–3.
93. 'Leslie on the Land Question', 673.
94. *Ibid.*, 673.
95. *Ibid.*

96. *Ibid.*, 674.
97. *Ibid.*
98. *Ibid.*, 678.
99. *Ibid.*, 675.
100. *Ibid.*
101. *Ibid.*, 679.
102. D. Martin, *John Stuart Mill and the Land Question* (Hull: University of Hull Publications, 1981), 38–9. He entertained hopes at one time for reclaiming wasteland in Ireland, but in order to convert it into small farms. (*Principles*, CW 2, 330.)
103. 'Leslie on the Land Question', 681.
104. *Ibid.*, 682–3.
105. *Ibid.*, 675.
106. *Ibid.*, 678.
107. 'Maine on Village Communities', CW 30, 213–28.
108. *Ibid.*, 215.
109. *Ibid.*, 215–16.
110. *Ibid.*, 219.
111. *Ibid.*, 221.
112. *Ibid.*
113. *Ibid.*, 222.
114. *Ibid.*
115. Dewey, 'The Rehabilitation of the Peasant Proprietor', 29.
116. J. Robson, 'Textual Introduction', CW 21, lxix.
117. *The Subjection of Women* [1869], CW 21, 263.
118. *Ibid.*, 269.
119. *Ibid.*, 335.
120. *Ibid.*, 336.
121. H. Reeve, 'Review of *Autobiography*', *Edinburgh Review* 139 (January 1874), 123.
122. B. Kinzer, A. Robson and J. Robson, *A Moralist In and Out of Parliament* (Toronto: University of Toronto Press, 1992), 166. For a detailed consideration of Mill's response to the movement within and outside Parliament, see 161–6.
123. Mill to Bridges, 16 November 1867, CW 16, 1328. On the Fenians, see L. O'Broin, *Fenian Fever: An Anglo-American Dilemma* (London: Chatto and Windus, 1971); D. G. Boyce, *Nationalism in Ireland* (Baltimore: Johns Hopkins University Press, 1982), 182–6.
124. Forget suggests only 'that the recantation occurred during the most exciting decade in the history of the trades union movement is not incidental'. (Forget, 'J. S. Mill and the Tory School', 47.) She mentions the Sheffield outrages and the 1867 Royal Commission on Trades Unions, but Mill nowhere in his surviving letters alludes to the former, and, having declined to serve on the latter, has little to say about it. Indeed, it was Reeve's insistence that Mill write on the report of the Royal Commission in addition to Thornton's book that caused him to publish his review in the *Fortnightly* rather than the *Edinburgh*. (Mill to Reeve, 22 March 1869, CW 17, 1582.) Conversely, one might expect that the rise in real wages for the working classes in the 1850s and

1860s would have led Mill and Thornton to question the pessimistic assumptions of the wage fund doctrine. (See A. Reid, *Social Classes and Social Relations in Britain, 1850–1914* (Cambridge: Cambridge University Press, 1995), 24–9, for a summary of recent research on working-class incomes.) This does not appear to have been the case, however.

125. There is little evidence for Forget's belief that Mill practiced something like a division of labour – reserving to himself the task of converting the middle classes and leaving in the hands of others the dissemination of political economy to trades unionists. He was always happy to address working-class audiences, and was willing to subsidize his publisher when the latter had mistakenly advertised a lower price for the People's Edition of the *Principles*: 'I would make any sacrifice rather than consent to fixing the price of the Pol. Ec. higher than the one announced.' (Mill to Longman, 30 April 1865, 1040–1.) See also his extensive correspondence with the self-educated factory worker John Plummer, and, more important, *Chapters On Socialism* (1879), which appears to be intended for a working-class audience.

126. E. Biagini, 'British Trade Unions and Popular Political Economy, 1860–1880', *The Historical Journal* 30 (1987), 811–40.

127. R. D. C. Black, *Economic Thought and the Irish Question, 1817–1870* (Cambridge: Cambridge University Press, 1960), 53.

128. Kinzer *et al.*, *A Moralist*, 183.

129. T. W. Hutchison, *A Review of Economic Doctrines* (Oxford: Clarendon Press, 1953), 13, and 'The Decline and Fall...', 58–64. The observations of J. L. Shadwell, the only pupil of Cairnes's to publish a systematic treatise, were cited earlier. (Chapter 1, note 7.) Writing six years later, in 1883, Henry Sidgwick was even more explicit: 'Some twenty years ago, both the Theory of Political Economy in its main outlines, and the most important practical applications of it, were considered as finally settled by the great majority of educated persons in England. ...In 1871, however, these halcyon days of Political Economy had passed away. Their termination was of course not abrupt; but so far as any date can be fixed for it, I should place it at the appearance of Mill's notice of Mr Thornton's book *On Labour* in the *Fortnightly Review* of March 1869.' (H. Sidgwick, *Principles of Political Economy* (1883), 1.)

130. S. Collini, 'From Dangerous Partisan to National Possession: John Stuart Mill in English Culture, 1873–1933', in *Public Moralists* (Oxford: Oxford University Press, 1991), 311–41.

131. See M. M. Taylor, *Men Against the State* (Oxford: Oxford University Press, 1992).

132. W. L. Courtney, *Life of John Stuart Mill* (London: Scott, 1889), 126.

133. This conclusion is suggested by scholars approaching from opposite perspectives: W. Wolfe, *From Radicalism to Socialism: Men and Ideas in the Formation of Fabian and Socialist Doctrines, 1881–1889* (New Haven: Yale University Press, 1975), 114, 187–9, 204–5; S. Letwin, *The Pursuit of Certainty* (London: Cambridge University Press, 1965), 7–10.

6 THE MILL CIRCLE

1. In 1822, at the age of 16, he had founded the Utilitarian Society; about two years later, he organized the 'Society of Students of Mental Philosophy', a discussion club which met until about 1829 at Grote's home in Threadneedle Street; he was the leading light of the London Debating Club initiated by McCulloch, which met fortnightly at Freemason's Tavern from 1825 to 1829, and brought together Utilitarians, Liberals of different orders and degrees, and eventually a few Tory lawyers and the Coleridgeans Sterling and Maurice. This club succeeded a series of weekly debates in 1825 at the Owenite Co-operative Society between the Socialist members and Utilitarian interlopers. Mill himself, writing of the Utilitarian Society, acknowledged that he 'was for some time a sort of leader and had considerable influence on their mental progress. Any young man of education who fell in my way, and whose opinions were not incompatible with those of the Society, I endeavoured to press into its service.' (*Autobiography*, CW 1, 81, 123–7, 129–35,and J. Robson and J. Stillinger, 'Introduction', xii. The club is not named by Mill in the text.)
2. Mill to Sterling, 15 April 1829, CW 12, 30.
3. *Autobiography*, CW 1, 195.
4. See Bain, *John Stuart Mill: A Criticism, with Personal Reminiscences* [1882] (New York: Kelley, 1969), 39, 93, 166; Packe, 320–1, 349–57; Packe does caution against exaggerating Mill's petulance, 321–4.
5. Examples abound. For particularly egregious instances of the former, see Diary entries for 17 and 19 January 1854 and 8 February 1854 in Hayek, 189–90, 192–3; and of the latter, Mill to Harriet Mill, 29 January 1854, CW 14, 141–2.
6. Cairnes to Nesbitt, ? 9 May 1859, vol. 49, MTC, BLPES; cited by Packe, 411. Only a few days earlier, Mill had suggested to the editor of *Fraser's* that he solicit an article on the gold question from Cairnes, who was deeply gratified by the referral. (Cairnes to Nesbitt, 2 May 1859, Ms 8941 (1), NLI.)
7. L. Stephen, *Life of Henry Fawcett* (3rd edn) (New York: Putnams 1886), 82: 'The philosophic recluse did not come to try our milk punch'.
8. Mill to Fawcett, 5 February 1860, CW 15, 672–3.
9. Mill to Hare, 30 October 1859, CW 15, 642–3; Stephen, 103.
10. Fawcett to Mill, 23 December 1859, Stephen, 102.
11. Mill to Leslie, 18 August 1860, CW 15, 702; See also J. Ingram, 'Biographical Notice of the Author', in T. E. C. Leslie, *Essays in Political Economy* (2nd edn) [1888] (New York: Kelley, 1969), x.
12. Mill to Leslie, 8 May 1869, CW 17, 1599–601. After his deprecatory comments about editors, Mill pointedly makes an exception for Morley, and excuses, with perhaps a flicker of irony, the delayed publication of an article by Leslie in the *Fortnightly*: 'I dare say he is a good deal bothered and he probably thinks that Chauffard's Mittermaier is a subject that can wait better than most.' (*Ibid*., 1600.)

13. W. T. Thornton, 'His Career in the India House', in H. R. Fox Bourne (ed.), *John Stuart Mill: His Life and Works* (Boston: Osgood and Co., 1873), 34–5.
14. *Ibid*., 35.
15. Mill to Thornton, January, 1869, CW 17, 1549.
16. Thornton to Fawcett, October, 1862, vol. 22, item 1011, MTC, BLPES.
17. Mill to Cairnes, 3 October 1864, CW 15, 958.
18. L. Stephen, *The English Utilitarians* (vol. 3) (New York: Putnam's, 1900), 187.
19. J. Morley, *Recollections* (vol. 1) (New York: Macmillan, 1915), 52.
20. Mill to Morley, 4 January 1865, CW 16, 1113.
21. When Mill attempted to publish his review of Thornton's book in the *Edinburgh Review* (with three times the *Fortnightly*'s circulation and without its rebartative Comtist tinge), Reeve, the editor, insisted that Mill also review at the same time the report of the Royal Commission on Trade Unions, and so Mill, who both didn't want to take the additional time nor obscure his recantation, contacted Morley, and was soon taking an almost proprietary interest in the *Fortnightly*. (Mill to Reeve, 16 March 1869 and 22 March 1869, CW 17, 1574–5, 1582. A. Ellegor, 'Readership of the Mid-Victorian Press', *Goteborgs Universitets Arsskrift* 63 (Acta Universitatis Gotoburgensis), 3–38.)
22. '. . . one of Mill's chief friendships in later years was with Thornton, who differed from him in a great many things, but the differences were of the kind to bring into lively exercise Mill's argumentative powers.' (Bain, 174.)
23. The clearest evidence for this is the very extensive correspondence between October 1864 and March 1865 about possible revisions in the sixth edition of the *Principles* (reproduced as Appendix H), CW 3, 1038–95.
24. Appendix H, CW 1, 626. He was a most devoted lieutenant: 'Mill thinks that Sullivan should be answered, so answered he must be, but I am still doubtful as to the way. On this point I will consult Mill further.' (Cairnes to Nesbitt, 14 April 1866, Ms 8941 (15) NLI.)
25. Bain notes clinically that 'the Tender Feeling must in him have been very considerable. He was, throughout, affectionate, genial, kindly.' (Bain, 150.)
26. *Autobiography*, CW 1, 52; see especially 'Rejected Leaves', Appendix G, 611–13.
27. B. Mazlish, *James and John Stuart Mill* (New York: Basic Books, 1975), 157.
28. *Ibid*. 7–8. Briefly, the Oedipus Complex emerges: 'Filial rebellions become more intense, and their fizzling out into submission less common and complete. The psychic price, in anxiety and guilt, became acute, and its prevalence increasingly epidemic.' (*Ibid*., 18.) Why? Following Platt and Weinstein (*The Wish to be Free: Society, Psyche and Value Change* (Berkeley: University of California Press, 1969)), Mazlish argues that 'the Industrial Revolution' encouraged families to instil in boys 'the Achievement Motive' (Mazlish, 21), resulting in a sense of autonomy – and, in consequence, conflict. 'Romanticism' and

'Darwinism' help, the first ushering in 'the Introspective Revolution', the second 'announc[ing] the destruction of the father, that is, of the highest father-figure, God'. (*Ibid.*, 21, 25.) When Mazlish descends from these generalities, he offers detailed and sometimes acute analyses of Mill's relationships, as well as lengthy glosses on seemingly unpromising incidents like the purchase of a coat and the loss of a watch, and, inevitably, interpretations of the only two dreams Mill recorded.

29. *Ibid.*, 203, 229–30, 240.
30. *Ibid.*, 285–7. Mazlish sometimes employs quotation marks, but usually does without. (285–8, 408, 433.)
31. '... the women ... who possessed the highest measure of what are considered feminine qualities, have combined with them more of the highest masculine qualities than I have ever seen in any but one or two men, & those one or two men were also in many respects almost women. I suspect it is the second-rate people of the two sexes that are unlike.' (5 October 1833, CW 12, 184.)
32. Bain, 149. 'It was the opinion of many, that while his estimate of pure sentimental affection was more than enough, his estimate of the sexual passion was too low.' (89–90)
33. Mazlish, 240.
34. *Autobiography*, CW 1, 111.
35. Appendix G, 'Rejected Leaves of the Early Draft of the Autobiography', CW 1, 609, 613.
36. 'What I owe, even intellectually, to her, is, in its detail, almost infinite.' (*Autobiography*, CW 1, 197.); 'Even the merely intellectual needs of my nature suffice to make me hope that I may never outlive the companion who is the profoundest and most far-sighted and clear-sighted thinker I have ever known .... I do not wish that I were so much her equal as not to be her pupil, but I would gladly be more capable than I am of thoroughly appreciating and worthily reproducing her admirable thoughts.' (Diary entry, 8 February 1854, Hayek, 192–3.)
37. *Ibid.*, 195: United with 'her intellectual gifts' was 'a heart which thoroughly identified itself with the feelings of others, and often went to excess in consideration for them'.
38. CW 1, 612.
39. Principally, Sarah Austin. Mazlish, 187–9, 195–6, 308–9.
40. CW 1, 264–5. Helen Taylor, under pressure from Bain, deleted the tribute in the first published version, stipulating that it be added immediately after her death. (Hayek, 313.)
41. Norton to Wright, 13 September 1870, in Norton and Howe, cited by Packe, 497; Thornton, of whom she was very fond, dissented: Helen 'was a companion in all respects worthy of [Mill]'. Thornton to Fawcett, October 1862. (vol. 26, item 1011, MTC, BLPES.) Leslie Stephen, however, expressed the general consensus: 'Everyone who knows them, specially Cairnes, tells me that Miss Taylor's influence over Mill towards the end of his life was greater than could have been supposed; & that she was responsible for his weakest utterances ...'. But then, he asks tellingly, 'who was responsible for Mill's obedience to her?' (Stephen to Norton, 25 December 1874, J. Bicknell (ed.), *Selected Letters*

of *Leslie Stephen*, vol. 1 (Columbus: Ohio State University Press, 1996), 146.)

42. B. and P. Russell, *The Amberley Papers* (vol. 2) (New York: Simon and Schuster, 1966), 311.
43. CW 1, 612: 'I . . . grew up in the absence of love and the presence of fear'.
44. Despite his having been, as James's surrogate, a very exacting tutor (Hayek, 286), John was still regarded with great affection by most of his siblings, until he broke with them over Harriet. (Hayek, 171–5.) James Mill, of course, had actively opposed John's new friendships in the early 1820s. (Bain, 39–40.) And John, for his part, with a quarter of a century head start on his comrades, could hardly help but re-enact the dynamics of the Mill nursery with his new friends. (Mill 'watched with the eye of a grave tutor', Roebuck complained, 'everything I wrote'.) (Roebuck to Falconer, 23 August 1831, cited by W. Thomas, *The Philosophic Radicals* (Oxford: Clarendon Press, 1979), 156.)
45. All of his economist friends, as noted, suffered from disabilities of varying severity. While they were hardly chosen for this reason, the scope they provided for Mill's solicitude may well have endeared them to him all the more. We glimpse him patiently walking beside the Bath chair of the paralysed Cairnes (H. Fawcett, 'Professor Cairnes', *Fortnightly Review* 18 (August 1875), 150.), comforting Thornton (Thornton, 'His Career in India House', 35.), commiserating with the particularly importunate Leslie (Mill to Leslie, 8 March 1870, CW 17, 1706.), etc.
46. Conway, *Autobiography*, 16–17.
47. F. Hirst, *Early Life and Letters of John Morley* (London: Macmillan, 1927), 53. He 'always felt that the chance which led him to write [the *Saturday Review* article] and brought it to Mill's attention was one of the most fortunate events in his life'. (*Ibid*., 52.)
48. Bain remarks that anyone observing Mill's 'plain dinner' would recognize that 'he was exceedingly temperate as regarded the table'. (Bain, 149.)
49. H. Spencer, *An Autobiography* (vol. 2) (New York: Appleton and Co., 1904), 142. Cairnes to Nesbitt, 1 August 1861, MS 8941 (5), NLI.
50. M. Conway, *Autobiography* (vol. 2) (Boston: Houghton, Mifflin, 1904), 16.
51. Leslie, *Essays*, 56.
52. Norton to Wright, 1 May 1869, in S. Norton and M. DeWolfe Howe (eds), *Letters of Charles Eliot Norton* (vol. 1) (Boston: Houghton, Mifflin, 1913), 330.
53. Cairnes to Nesbitt, 1 August 1861, MS 8941 (5), NLI.
54. Collini has distinguished three levels of discipleship, beginning with those who were 'keen student[s] of Mill's double-decker treatises on logic and political economy'. (S. Collini, *Public Moralists* (Oxford: Clarendon Press, 1991), 176.) From his choice of examples, it appears that entrance to the second stage of discipleship involved an active sympathy with Mill's responses to various current events, notably the American Civil War and Governor Eyre's suppression of Jamaican insurrection. Those who entered the inner sanctum additionally subscribed to Mill's 'crotchets': proportional representation, enfranchisement of women,

land reform and co-operation. In fact, the latter really comprise Mill's long-term domestic programme, as opposed to his reaction to crises abroad. And the popularity of specific measures implementing this programme varied as widely as did that of his stands on foreign affairs. Co-operation, for example, no doubt enjoyed much broader support among middle-class readers than did the Eyre prosecution. The 'crotchets' were thus not distinguished so much by their idiosyncrasy or unpopularity as by the fact that they represented long-term social changes: the redistribution of wealth from the aristocracy to the working class, and of power from men to women. This is what the Mill circle signed on for.

55. Cairnes to Nesbitt, 16 October 1859, Ms 8941 (2), NLI. After Cairnes had accepted the appointment, he asked Leslie to send him copies of his examinations. Cairnes found Leslie's questions far too encompassing. (Cairnes to Nesbitt, 17 March 1860, 8941 (3), NLI.)
56. Cairnes to Nesbitt, 4 February 1863, MS 8941 (7), NLI. 'I had received from him ... a letter couched in terms more than usually insolent.' The letter itself complained of a '"studiously offensive" letter' from Cairnes. (Cairnes to Nesbitt, 9 June 1863, MS 8941 (7).)
57. Cairnes to Mill, 26 July 1867, Hopkins. He deeply resented being indebted to someone for whom he had 'no particular admiration or liking'. (Cairnes to Courtney, 4 August 1867, Courtney Collection, BLPES.) 'I could much have wished it had been any other man, but it was impossible to shake him off.' (Cairnes to Nesbitt, 19 August 1867, MS 8941 (17), NLI.)
58. Cairnes to Mill, 2 August 1867, vol. 56A, MTC, BLPES.
59. 'I am quite unable to see the cogency of your inference.' Cairnes to Mill, 7 September 1867, vol. 56A, MTC, BLPES. When he was finally obliged to resign, Cairnes disingenuously assured Mill that if Leslie should succeed him, he would, 'on personal grounds, rejoice'. (Cairnes to Mill, 16 June 1872, vol. 56A, MTC, BPLES.)
60. Leslie to Ingram 19 October 1875 [?] PRO 2808/43/32.
61. Leslie to Mill, 7 February [1871], Hopkins.
62. Leslie to Ingram, 19 October 1875 [?] PRO 2808/43/32.
63. Leslie to Ingram, nd PRO 2808/43/42.
64. Cairnes to Courtney, 19 March 1863, CC, BLPES. Courtney was a rival candidate for the Professorship.
65. Cairnes to Courtney, 3 May 1863; 30 November 1863; 15 October 1864, Courtney Papers, BLPES.
66. Fawcett, 'Professor Cairnes', *Fortnightly Review* ns 54 (August 1875), 151, 149.
67. Cairnes to Courtney, 6 March 1869, CC, BLPES.
68. J. E. Cairnes, *Some Leading Principles of Political Economy* [1874] (New York: Kelley, 1967), 182–5.
69. Cairnes to Mill, 10 September 1870, vol. 56A MTC, BLPES.
70. Cairnes to Mill, 2 May 1872, Hopkins.
71. Hirst, 52.
72. N. de Marchi, 'The Noxious Influence of Authority: A Correction of Jevons' Charge', *Journal of Law and Economics* (April 1973), 179–89.

Checkland's earlier attempt to document Jevons's charges is unconvincing (S. Checkland, 'Economic Opinion in England as Jevons Found It', *Manchester School* 19.2 (May 1951), 143–69), while Coats's survey of the concept of economic authority from Ricardo to Keynes is inconclusive. (A.W. Coats, 'The Role of Authority in the Development of British Economics', *Journal of Law and Economics* 7 (October 1964), 85–106.) In any event, Jevons's charges refer to 'lecturers and examiners', the second and third tiers of intellectual life, and to the susceptibility of readers, as he assured Cairnes and Foxwell. (Jevons to Cairnes, 14 January 1872, R. D. C. Black (ed.), *Papers and Correspondence of W. S. Jevons*, vol. 3 (London: Macmillan, 1981), 245–6; Jevons to Foxwell, 17 November 1879, Black (ed.), vol. 5, 136.)

73. Cairnes to Nesbitt, 11 October 1858, ms 8941 (1) NLI; 'New Theories in Political Economy', *Fortnightly Review* n.s. 11 (January 1872), 71–2.

74. For a sophisticated recent example of the latter, see D. McNally, *Political Economy and the Rise of Capitalism* (Berkeley: University of California Press, 1988). Not surprisingly, however, it is the marginal 'revolution' that has been analysed most frequently by writers questioning the motives of economists: the Marxists and Institutionalists for whom such explanations are especially congenial are also the chief adversaries of the shift in the scope and method of economics that marginalism introduced. Once hailed as prophets without honour, the early marginalists are now reviled as hucksters without principle in several recent works. (P. Mirowski, *More Heat than Light: Economics as Social Physics, Physics as Nature's Economics*) (Cambridge: Cambridge University Press, 1989.) (See also the appraisals in N. de Marchi (ed.), *Non-Natural Social Science: Reflecting on the Enterprise of More Heat than Light* (Durham: Duke University Press, 1993).); J. Maloney, *The Professionalization of Economics, Alfred Marshall and the Dominance of Orthodoxy* (New Brunswick: Transaction, 1991); A. Kadish, *Historians, Economists and Economic History* (London: Routledge, 1989). Among other, less plausible, exogenous explanations for the success of marginalism, see J. Robinson and J. Eatwell, *An Introduction to Modern Economics* (Maidenhead, England: McGraw-Hill, 1973), 34–6; N. Bukharin, *The Economic Theory of the Leisure Class* [1908] (New York: Kelley, 1968); J. Baudrillard, *The Mirror of Production* (St Louis: Telos, 1975); L. Birken, 'From Macroeconomics to Microeconomics: The Marginal Revolution in Cultural Perspective', HOPE 20 (Summer, 1988), 251–64.

75. S. Rashid, 'Richard Whately and Christian Political Economy at Oxford and Dublin', *Journal of the History of Ideas* 38 (1977), 149–52; B. Hilton, *The Age of Atonement: The Influence of Evangelicalism on Social and Economic Thought, 1785–1865* (Oxford: Clarendon Press, 1991); A. M. C. Waterman, *Revolution, Economics and Religion: Christian Political Economy, 1798–1833* (Cambridge: Cambridge University Press, 1991); for some intriguing attempts to generalize about the impact of religion on economic thought, see R. H. Nelson, *Reaching for Heaven on Earth: The Theological Meaning of Economics* (Lanham, MD: Littlefield, Adams, 1991); J. Viner, *The Role of Providence in the*

Social Order (Philadelphia: American Philosophical Society, 1972), E. Kauder, *A History of Marginal Utility Theory* (Princeton: Princeton University Press, 1965), 3–14; H. G. Brennan and A. M C. Waterman, *Economics and Religion: Are They Distinct* (Boston: Kluwer, 1994); and the symposia in *Forum for Social Economics* 25.2, 26.2 (Spring 1996, Spring 1997), 1–26, 1–52. For fuller discussions of the literature in notes 75 and 76, see J. Lipkes, 'Politics, Religion, and the Fate of Classical Political Economy: John Stuart Mill and his Followers, 1860–1875' (Princeton University Ph.D., 1995), 31–46.

76. Theists included individuals across the spectrum of non-Dissenting denominations – Catholics like Mivart and Ward, the Presbyterian Argyll, the High Church Gladstone, the Unitarians Greg and Martineau. What united them was opposition to the agnosticism and materialism of Tindal, Clifford, Huxley, Spencer, *et al.*; their project was to reconcile Christianity and Darwinian evolution. Noteworthy among the vast literature on the topic are E. R. Norman, *Church and Society in England, 1770–1970* (Oxford: Oxford University Press, 1976); P. Hinchliff, *God and History: Aspects of British Theology, 1875–1914* (Oxford: Clarendon Press, 1992); D. W. Wigmore-Beddoes, *Yesterday's Radicals, A Study of the Nineteenth Century* (Cambridge and London: Clarke, 1971); D. Young, *F. D. Maurice and Unitarianism* (Oxford: Clarendon, 1992); F. Turner, *Between Science and Religion* (New Haven: Yale University Press, 1974); J. Moore, *The Post-Darwinian Controversies* (Cambridge: Cambridge University Press, 1979); M. Crowther, *Church Embattled: Religious Controversy in Mid-Victorian England* (Newton Abbot: David and Charles, 1970); R. Helmstadter and B. Lightman (eds), *Victorian Crisis in Faith* (Basingstoke: Macmillan, 1990); surveys by A. D. Gilbert (*Religion and Society in Industrial England, 1740–1914*) (London: Longman, 1976) and H. McLeod (*Religion and Society in England, 1850–1914*) (Basingstoke: Macmillan, 1994); and the anthology edited by G. Parsons (*Religion in Victorian Britain*, vols 1–4) (Manchester: Manchester University Press, 1988).

As a proselytizer of the Religion of Humanity, Mill had much company. On the Comteists, by far the best-known sect, see T. Wright, *The Religion of Humanity: The Impact of Comtean Positivism on Victorian Britain* (Cambridge: Cambridge University Press, 1986); for agnostic theology in Britain, see F. Baumer, *Religion and the Rise of Scepticism* (New York: Harcourt, Brace, 1960), 162–86; B. Willey, *More Nineteenth Century Studies, A Group of Honest Doubters* (Cambridge: Cambridge University Press, 1952); A. O. J. Cockshut, *The Unbelievers: English Agnostic Thought, 1840–1890* (New York: New York University Press, 1966) and B. Lightman, *The Origins of Agnosticism: Victorian Unbelief and the Limits of Knowledge* (Baltimore: Johns Hopkins University Press, 1987), 116–84; for the Secularist movement itself, see F. B. Smith, 'The Atheist Mission', in R. Robson (ed.), *Ideas and Institutions of Victorian Britain* (London, 1967); E. Royle, *Victorian Infidels: The Origins of the British Secularist Movement, 1791–1866* (Manchester: Manchester University Press, 1974) and *Radicals, Secularists and Republicans: Popular Freethought in Britain, 1866–1914* (Manchester:

Manchester University Press, 1980); S. Budd, *Varieties of Unbelief, Atheists and Agnostics in British Society, 1850–1959* (London: Heinemann, 1977) also assesses popular attitudes; see as well the most recent biographies of Besant (Ann Taylor, *Annie Besant* (Oxford: Oxford University Press, 1993) and Bradlaugh (D. Tribe, *President Charles Bradlaugh, MP* (London and Hamden: Archon Books, 1971). Among the best-known works exploring the apotheosis of reason (from a decidedly jaundiced perspective) are, beginning with the Enlightenment, C. Becker, *The Heavenly City of the Eighteenth-Century Philosophers* (New Haven: Yale University Press, 1932); L. Bredvold, *The Brave New World of the Enlightenment* (Ann Arbor: University of Michigan Press, 1961); E. Voegelin, *From Enlightenment to Revolution* (Durham: Duke University Press, 1975); F. Hayek, *The Counter-Revolution of Science* (2nd edn) (Indianapolis: Liberty Press, 1979); F. Manuel, *The New World of Henri St Simon* (South Bend: Notre Dame, 1963); and T. Molner, *Utopia, the Perennial Heresy* (New York: Sheed and Ward, 1967).

77. On the strongly Evangelical backgrounds of the leading Positivists, see Wright, 73, 115, 120.
78. See J. Lipkes, 'Religion and the Reception of Marginalism in Britain', *Forum for Social Economics* 26.2 (Spring 1997).

7 JOHN ELLIOT CAIRNES

1. Cairnes to Nesbitt, 5 January 1860, MS 8941 (3), NLI.
2. A. Weinberg, *John Elliot Cairnes and the American Civil War* (London: Kingswood Press, 1969), 10.
3. *Ibid.*, 11. In a revealing observation, Cairnes, whose feelings toward his father had mellowed by the time the old man died, noted that the presence at his funeral of as many Catholics as Protestants 'very clearly shows my father's illiberal creed was formal merely and never touched his nature, which was especially just and generous'. (Cairnes to Nesbitt, 4 January 1864, MS 8941 (9), NLI.)
4. *Ibid.*
5. *Ibid.*
6. 'John Elliot Cairnes', in L. Stephen and S. Lee (eds), *The Dictionary of National Biography* (vol. 3) (London: Oxford University Press, 1917), 668.
7. *Ibid.*
8. *Ibid.* The admiring Weinberg attributes the directionlessness to 'the drawbacks of a late start as well as . . . uncertainties in his mind'. (Weinberg, 12.) Cairnes was probably supported during this period by his father, who was amassing a considerable fortune. Cairnes was left £4000 and an estate valued at about £800 per annum. His siblings were no less handsomely provided for. (Cairnes to Nesbitt, 4 January 1864, MS 8941 (9), NLI.)
9. Mill to Cairnes, 22 April 1858, CW 15, 554.
10. Mill to Cairnes, 2 March 1859, CW 15, 596.

11. Cairnes to Mill, 8 April 1859, item 1, MTC, BLPES. The letter continues in this vein for several more sentences.
12. Cairnes to Mill, 14 May 1861, item 2, MTC, BLPES.
13. Mill to Cairnes, 19 May 1861, CW 15, 728.
14. Mill to Cairnes, 18 August 1861, CW 15, 738–9.
15. Cairnes to Mill, 25 August 1861, item 4, MTC, BLPES.
16. J. E. Cairnes, *The Slave Power* [1862] (New York: Harper, 1969), v.
17. 'The Slave Power', CW 21, 145; Cairnes protested this 'enormous overestimate ... of my powers and acquirements'. Cairnes to Mill, 8 December 1862, item 8, MTC, BLPES.
18. Mill to Cairnes, 24 June 1862, CW 15, 785.
19. Cairnes to Mill, 21 November 1861, item 5, MTC, BLPES. He concluded with a somewhat facile attempt to reconcile 'intuitionalists' and utilitarians.
20. Cairnes to Mill, 23 May 1869, item 53, MTC, BLPES. It is frustrating watching him grapple unsuccessfully, and at great length, with the problem of how markets are cleared without having recourse to marginalism. He gives up in the end: '... I do not see that a theory of *market* (as distinct from average) prices is of very much moment in a scientific point of view.' See also Cairnes to Mill, 9 November 1866, Hopkins.
21. Cairnes to Mill, 2 May 1872, Hopkins; Cairnes to Mill, 16 June 1872, item 65, MTC, BLPES.
22. 'Appendix H', CW 3, 1047.
23. *Ibid.*, 1052.
24. *Ibid.*, 1058–72; Mill to Cairnes, 1 December 1864, CW 15, 1055–6; 12 December 1864, 1072–3, CW 15; Boylan and Foley cite three changes in Mill's approach to Ireland in the 6th edition of the *Principles* attributable to Cairnes: (1) Mill no longer entertains the possibility of the English agricultural system being established in Ireland; (2) he is less optimistic that the cottier class will disappear; (3) he no longer overrates the Landed Estates Court as an agency for the transfer of land. (T. A. Boylan and T. P. Foley, 'John Elliot Cairnes, John Stuart Mill and Ireland: Some Problems for Political Economy', in A. E. Murphy (ed.), *Economists and the Irish Economy from the Eighteenth Century to the Present Day* (Dublin: Irish Academic Press, 1984), 103–4.)
25. Cairnes to Courtney, 9 January 1868, CC, BLPES; Cairnes dismisses the notion that there is a national feeling for independence behind Fenianism: 'There is nothing I feel more certain of than there is less of this feeling in Ireland than in any country of which I have any knowledge .... Depend on it, justice in regard to the land is the one and sufficient cure for all discontent in Ireland.'
26. *Ibid.*
27. 'Professor Cairnes', *Fortnightly Review* 18 (August 1875), 152.
28. *Ibid.*, 153, 154. Similarly, Courtney observed in his *Times* obituary of his erstwhile mentor that Cairnes 'was the unseen centre of the operations that exposed the character of the University Bill in 1873 and destroyed it .... Its strongest opponents in Parliament and the Press were inspired by his knowledge and counsel.' G. P. Gooch, *Life of Lord Courtney* (London: Macmillan, 1920), 114.

29. Cairnes to Mill, 7 July 1867, item 45, MTC, BLPES.
30. For the definitive discussion of Mill and the Irish University question, see B. L. Kinzer, 'John Stuart Mill and the Irish University Question', *Victorian Studies* 31 (Autumn, 1987), 59–77. Kinzer argues that Mill was initially converted to the cause by Cairnes, after being lukewarm at best. If so, Cairnes's passionate moralism served the younger man well. (See note 44 below.) Nonetheless, Mill, according to Kinzer, was much more attuned to political realities than Cairnes. The MP for Westminster still hoped to help perpetrate a Radical-dominated Liberal party under Gladstone, and thus took care not to offend his leader on this issue, despite his warm feelings for the Queen's Colleges. The 'rapprochement' that Cairnes hailed in his January 1866 letter to Mill was short-lived. (Cairnes to Mill, 9 January 1866, item 32, MTC, BLPES.)
31. Cairnes to Mill, 20 August 1865, item 30, MTC, BLPES.
32. Cairnes to Mill, 7 September 1867, item 48, MTC, BLPES: 'I am quite unable to see the cogency of your inference'. On other issues, he disagreed far more obsequiously: 'I am obliged to confess... I experienced the unusual sensation of being unconvinced by your reasoning. I cannot easily describe my distrust of myself and the discomfort I feel when I find myself in the position of challenging your arguments.' (Cairnes to Mill, 23 May 1869, item 53, MTC, BLPES.) The surprisingly harsh tone of the September letter may have something to do with Cairnes's resentment at Mill's having, in effect, foisted Leslie on him the previous month, while he took sick leave. (Cairnes to Mill, 2 August 1867, item 46, MTC, BLPES; Cairnes to Courtney, 4 August 1867, CL, BLPES.)
33. Cairnes to Courtney, 7 June 1867, CC, BLPES: 'I cannot quite understand the reticence of Mill, Fawcett, and some others'.
34. Cairnes to Courtney, 7 September 1867, CC, BLPES.
35. Cairnes to Mill, 15 February 1868, item 49, MTC, BLPES.
36. *Ibid.*
37. 'What can be better fitted to qualify the virus of bigotry and engender feelings of mutual consideration and respect, what better preparation for the duties of citizenship in a country of mixed religious faith can be imagined, than a system of education which furnishes to the youths of all religious denominations neutral ground on which they may meet and cultivate in common, without reference to the causes which divide them, those pursuits in which they have a common interest?' 'Thoughts on University Reform', *Political Essays* [1873] (New York: Kelley, 1967), 291–2.
38. *Ibid.*, 277–8.
39. 'With the collegiate system would also be lost advantages of a moral and social kind, scarcely, if at all, less important than its more direct and palpable benefits – those manifold helps to the formation of character which arise from bringing young men together at the most impressionable period of life, and placing them under the influence of minds not unsympathetic with theirs, while instructed and mature.' *Ibid.*, 290–1.
40. 'The Present Position of the Irish University Question', *Political Essays*, 340–2. For a clear summary of this complex issue, see Kinzer, 60–71. Other recent discussions include J. Parry, *Democracy and Religion:*

Gladstone and the Liberal Party, 1867–1875 (Cambridge: Cambridge University Press, 1986), 297–306; H. C. G. Matthew, *Gladstone, 1809–1874* (Oxford: Oxford University Press, 1986), 197–201; L. Goldman, 'Introduction: "An Advanced Liberal": Henry Fawcett, 1833–1884', in L. Goldman (ed.), *The Blind Victorian: Henry Fawcett and British Liberalism* (Cambridge: Cambridge University Press, 1989), 23–30.

41. J. E. Cairnes, *The Slave Power* (1st edition) (London: Parker, Son, and Burne, 1862), 290–1. He even hoped that increasing the resources devoted to cotton-growing in India might itself be sufficient to eliminate slavery. (J. E. Cairnes, *Political Economy as a Branch of Liberal Education* (1860), 12–13; cited by Weinberg, 16.)
42. J. S. Mill, 'The Slave Power', CW 21, 162–4.
43. J. E. Cairnes, *The Slave Power* (2nd edition) [1863] (New York: Harper & Row, 1969), 309. The citation is from 'A Few Words on Non-Intervention', which appeared in *Fraser's Magazine* in 1859. 'To suppose that the same international customs, and the same rules of international morality, can obtain between one civilized nation and another, and between civilized nations and barbarians, is a grave error .... In the first place, the rules of ordinary international morality imply reciprocity. But barbarians will not reciprocate. They cannot be depended on for observing any rules.... In the next place, nations which are still barbarous have not got beyond the period during which it is likely to be for their benefit that they should be conquered and held in subjection by foreigners. Independence and nationality, so essential to the due growth and development of a people further advanced in improvement, are generally impediments to theirs.' (Quoted by Cairnes, *The Slave Power* (second edition), 310–11.)
44. That the one need not necessarily imply the other is clear, however, from the career of no less a person than Gladstone. The famous moral crusade he waged during the Midlothian campaign did not portend significant departures in economic policy. Nonetheless, the shift in Liberal foreign and colonial policy is real and significant – and was spearheaded by Mill. A new emphasis placed on civilizing backward people accompanied the interest in moralizing the lower classes at home. (See E. Sullivan, 'Liberalism and Imperialism: J. S. Mill's Defense of the British Empire', *Journal of the History of Ideas* 44 (Oct.–Dec. 1983), 599–617.)
45. 'Our Defences: A National or Standing Army?' *Political Essays*, 199–255.
46. *Ibid.*, 230–1, 246–7.
47. *Ibid.*, 247.
48. 'Thoughts on University Reform', in *Political Essays*, 288–91.
49. 'Our Defences', 199.
50. *Ibid.*, 208–11.
51. *Ibid.*, 230–2.
52. *Ibid.*, 233.
53. *Ibid.*, 228.
54. *Ibid.*, 251. As indicated, Leslie wrote on the same issue four years earlier, and came to similar conclusions. 'The Military System of Europe',

North British Review (December 1867), 404–40; see Leslie's comments on his own shift in position. (Leslie to Chadwick, 17 February 1869/70 (?), Chadwick Papers, Special Collections, University College London.)

55. Stephen, 668.
56. See I. Bradley, *The Call to Seriousness* (New York: Macmillan, 1976), 21.
57. Fawcett's obituary provides the fullest account. (*Fortnightly Review* 18 (August 1875), 149–54); see also the descriptions by Stephen (*DNB*, 668–9), and Weinberg. Cairnes 'can move neither hand, foot nor head & is like a man petrified. Yet he can talk... and is an excellent fellow in every way.' (Stephen to Norton, 15 May 1874, J. Bicknell (ed.), *Selected Letters of Leslie Stephen*, vol. 1 (Columbus: Ohio State University Press, 1996), 136.)
58. The etiology of the disease (*arthritis deformans*) is still unknown, though susceptibility appears to be inherited. Aspirin (first manufactured in 1899) was not available to Cairnes, nor, naturally, were the current therapies cortisone and prednisone. Conversation with Maurice Lipkis, MD, June 1994; conversation, correspondence with Edward Shapiro, MD, July–August 1997.
59. Stephen, 669.
60. Fawcett, 150.
61. *Ibid*., 151.
62. Cairnes to Courtney, 18 May 1863.
63. Cairnes to Mill, 20 May 1867, item 43.
64. Cairnes to Courtney, 7 June 1867.
65. Cairnes was less than pleased with the arrangements. Cairnes to Mill, 26 July 1867, Hopkins. Cairnes to Mill, 2 August 1867, MTC, BLPES; Cairnes to Courtney, 4 August 1867, CC, BLPES.
66. Cairnes to Mill, 9 April 1872, item 63, MTC, BLPES.
67. Cairnes to Mill, 9 November 1868, item 50, MTC, BLPES.
68. Cairnes to Courtney, 21 April 1868, CC, BLPES; similarly, the death is only briefly and elliptically mentioned to Mill. (Cairnes to Mill, 21 May 1868, Hopkins.)
69. However, nearly a year later the death is alluded to, though indirectly, with what appears to be some real bitterness. The occasion is Courtney's apparent neglect of the correspondence: 'I suppose I ought to thank you for the intimation of your continued existence conveyed to me in the superscription on a *Public Opinion* received the other day.... You will be glad to hear that we are in being, and maintain our numbers at the point at which you last heard of us, that is to say (I must not tax your memory too far), Madame et moi et trois petits enfants. Well, no doubt you have been terribly busy...' (Cairnes to Courtney, 6 March 1869, CC, BLPES.) Cairnes undoubtedly felt isolated at some of the spas his sojourns took him to: 'You can hardly imagine what a treat such a letter is to one so completely shut out from all political society as I am. Since we came to Bareges, we have not seen a kindly face; nor made any acquaintance (except the doctor's).' (The substitution of 'political' for 'polite' is revealing.) (Cairnes to Courtney, 4 August 1867, CC, BLPES.)
70. See Cairnes to Courtney, 16 March 1865, 7 June 1867, and 4 August 1867, CC, BLPES; Cairnes to Nesbitt, 22 June 1861, 8941 (5), NLI.

71. Cairnes to Courtney, 16 March 1865, CC, BLPES.
72. Cairnes to Mill, 9 November 1868, item 50, MTC, BLPES.
73. Cairnes to Mill, 2 May 1872, Hopkins.
74. Cairnes to Courtney, 11 July 1867, CC, BLPES.
75. Cairnes to Courtney, 26 May 1863, *Ibid*. Perhaps a similar spasm of guilt at another piece of self-promotion (as he may have subsequently viewed it) was responsible for Cairnes's failure to mention to Jevons an anonymous review of *A Serious Fall in the Price of Gold Ascertained* he published in the *National Review* of October 1863. The failure is 'a source of some mild bewilderment to historians of economic thought'. (T. A. Boylan and T. P. Foley, 'Jevons's Debt to Cairnes: An Unnoticed Review', *The History of Economics Society Bulletin* 7.2 (Winter, 1983), 56–7.) His guilt may have been compounded by a distinct awareness that in hailing Jevons's empirical verifications of his purely theoretical analysis, he was ignoring an important stipulation in his treatise on methodology, *The Character and Logical Method of Political Economy*. See note 111 below.
76. Cairnes to Courtney, 27 August 1867, CC, BLPES.
77. Cairnes to Mill, 25 August 1871, item 60, MTC, BLPES.
78. Fawcett, 153. 'A seat in Parliament has, of course, long been the ideal object of my ambition.' (Cairnes to Nesbitt, 28 May 1866, MS 8941 (15), NLI.)
79. Mill, at any rate, thought so: 'The Slave Power', 145.
80. J. E. Cairnes, 'His Work in Political Economy', in H. Fox Bourne (ed.), *John Stuart Mill: His Life and Works* (Boston: Osgood, 1873), 65.
81. Neither of these two claims for Mill's originality is valid, Cairnes having slighted, respectively, Ricardo and Senior. (D. Ricardo, *On the Principles of Political Economy and Taxation*, in P. Sraffa (ed.), *Works* (vol. 1) (Cambridge: Cambridge University Press, 1966), 100; N. Senior, *An Outline of the Science of Political Economy* [1836] (London: Kelley, 1938), 2–3.)
82. Cairnes, 'His Work in Political Economy', 70.
83. *Ibid*., 71.
84. . . . because actual rent does not generally correspond to Ricardian rent, but is determined by tradition, or, worse, by 'the absolute will of the owners of the soil.' (*Ibid*., 72.)
85. '. . . as a science, it tells us that certain modes of action lead to certain results; but it remains for each man to judge of the value of the results thus brought about.' (*Ibid*.)
86. It is significant that Cairnes should have singled out this proposition, of all the methodological questions Mill addressed. The subject, for both Cairnes and Mill, had been of supreme importance at the outset of their careers as economists, and Cairnes almost habitually reverted to methodological criticisms in disputes with other economists. While Cairnes takes issue with Mill's definition of the scope of political economy – as being concerned exclusively with 'the laws of the mind' – Cairnes's treatise otherwise unreservedly supports and extends Mill's methodological claims. (*The Character and Logical Method of Political Economy* (London: Macmillan, 1875), 30.) He argues, in brief: (1) that, like any

mature science, political economy advances by deduction (*Ibid.*, 71–4.); (2) that its premises are known at the outset, either directly from self-consciousness or from common sense (though he avoids the latter term) (*Ibid.*, 76–7.); (3) that hypotheses substitute for experiment (*Ibid.*, 81.); but (4) that hypotheses cannot be verified (or even falsified): they inevitably depend on 'the absence of disturbing causes' – a situation, unfortunately, never arising. (*Ibid.*, 94.) They express, therefore, only tendencies, and the science is thus insulated from 'realistic' criticism, based on empirical evidence. (*Ibid.*, 99.) In effect, tenets can only be refuted on the grounds of logic (Cairnes's *metier*, luckily). (Notwithstanding his lofty dicta, Cairnes was very glad of Jevons's empirical proof of his own speculations about the movement of the price of gold.) It is of some relevance that, having certified the methodological tools available to the economist, Cairnes at once puts them to two uses: defending the Malthusian doctrine of population (*Ibid.*, 149–81.) and the Ricardian theory of rent. (*Ibid.*, 182–218.) In his methodological work Cairnes is building on Mill, to be sure, but, more to the point, is building a fortification around him, just as Neville Keynes did for Marshall.

87. This small insight 'sufficed to change the entire aspect of human life regarded from the point of view of political economy'. (Cairnes, 'His Work in Political Economy', 69.)
88. *Ibid.*, 30.
89. *Ibid.*, 34.
90. *Ibid.*, 35.
91. *Ibid.*, 26: 'Accept the notion that Demand and Supply are facts of a different order, incapable of comparison and measurement, and you can hardly refuse to acknowledge that they are independent facts which may increase or diminish irrespective of each other. But this is precisely the idea that is at the bottom of most of the prevalent fallacies connected with those terms.'
92. *Ibid.*, 25.
93. *Ibid.*, 103.
94. *Ibid.*, 105.
95. *Ibid.*, 106–9.
96. *Ibid.*, 109–10.
97. *Ibid.*, 110.
98. Cairnes, 'His Work in Political Economy', 47–8. One might expect that Cairnes would object to measuring cost in terms of wages and profits on the matter-of-fact grounds that it necessitates assuming the constant value of money, a rather dubious premise for one who had written much on the gold question. This turns out not to be the case, however.
99. *Ibid.*, 49–57.
100. *Ibid.*, 51.
101. *Ibid.*, 58.
102. *Ibid.*, 74, 80.
103. *Ibid.*, 79.
104. See, for example J. MacDonell, *A Survey of Political Economy* (Edinburgh: Edmonston and Douglas, 1871), 252.

105. J. E. Cairnes, 'Bastiat', *Essays in Political Economy* [1873] (New York: Kelley, 1975), 336–42. Cairnes to Mill, 13 January 1870 and 22 September 1870, MTC, BLPES.
106. *Ibid.*, 61–5.
107. *Ibid.*, 67.
108. *Ibid.*, 71.
109. *Ibid.*, 89–96.
110. *Ibid.*, 93–4.
111. *Ibid.*, 182.
112. *Ibid.*, 183–6.
113. *Ibid.*, 154–6.
114. *Ibid.*, 163.
115. *Ibid.*, 35: 'By all means they must have their rents and interest... but let them take their proper place as drones in the hive, gorging at a feast to which they have contributed nothing.'
116. *Ibid.*, 160.
117. *Ibid.*, 161.
118. *Ibid.*, 157.
119. *Ibid.*, 196–200.
120. *Ibid.*, 197.
121. *Ibid.*, 196.
122. *Ibid.*, 149.
123. *Ibid.*, 322–3.
124. *Ibid.*, 176.
125. *Ibid.*, 178.
126. *Ibid.*, 171–4.
127. *Ibid.*, 174, 173.
128. *Ibid.*, 210.
129. *Ibid.*, 185.
130. *Ibid.*, 268–9.
131. *Ibid.*, 271.
132. *Ibid.*, 272.
133. *Ibid.*, 289. The necessary savings will not be easily made; nonetheless there is a potential fund of 60 million pounds, representing the three-quarters of the workers' share of the annual expenditure on alcoholic drinks that is 'both physically and morally injurious to them'. (*Ibid.*, 288.)
134. *Ibid.*, 292, 293.
135. Ekelund and Olsen claim that Comte had some influence on Cairnes's attitude toward trades unionism and co-operation, and on Cairnes's own use of statistics in *Essays on the Gold Question*. (R. Ekelund and E. Olsen, 'Comte, Mill, and Cairnes: The Positivist-Empiricist Interlude in Late Classical Economics', *Journal of Economic Issues* 7.3 (September 1973), 404–5.) But for the most part, the authors argue, unexceptionally, that Cairnes reacted negatively to Comte's dicta, though the assertion that 'his retreat in defense of essentially abstract, *ceteris paribus* methods profoundly affected the course of economics' is open to question. (*Ibid.*, 406.)

8 HENRY FAWCETT

1. Mill to Fawcett, 26 February 1860, CW 15, 688. Fawcett was blinded by his father in a hunting accident.
2. 'She Prevented Him', two-paragraph note from column in unidentified, undated journal glued to the back endpaper of L. Stephen, *Life of Henry Fawcett* (3rd edition) (New York: Putnam's, 1886) in Newman Library, Virginia Polytechnic Institute and State University, Blacksburg, Virginia. Citing Smalley's *London Letters*, the squib claims Millicent Fawcett, as her husband's secretary, would have had to have attended Cabinet meetings and read confidential papers, something public opinion would not have countenanced. This seems somewhat implausible. Mrs Fawcett was not her husband's secretary. Gladstone's hostility was perhaps more likely responsible.
3. F. W. Soutter, *Recollections of a Labour Pioneer* (London, 1923, 50; cited by L. Goldman, 'Introduction: "An Advanced Liberal": Henry Fawcett, 1833–1884', in L. Goldman (ed.), *The Blind Victorian: Henry Fawcett and British Liberalism* (Cambridge: Cambridge University Press, 1989), 6; Stephen, 56, 67. 'Fawcett's popularity was second only to Mr Gladstone's. But the popularity was not in his case balanced by a corresponding antipathy. You cannot hate a man whom you cannot help trusting .... It was simply impossible to dislike him.' (Stephen, 291–2.)
4. Fawcett has also been fortunate in his biographer and recent critics. Leslie Stephen's *Life* proved to be one of his most popular books, going through four editions within one year. (S. Collini, '"Manly Fellows": Fawcett, Stephen and the Liberal Temper', in Goldman, *The Blind Victorian*, 42.) While this was in part a tribute to his subject, Stephen's fond feelings for his late friend and for the Cambridge milieu in which the friendship flourished helped stimulate the intimate, wry, curmudgeon-with-a-twinkle-in-his-eye tone that makes Stephen's prose so attractive. (Stephen's biography bulks all the larger for the fact that Fawcett's papers have apparently not survived and there remain relatively few letters in other collections.) Fawcett's posthumous good luck continued when, a century after his death in 1884, a conference at Cambridge brought together some of the most distinguished practitioners of Victorian intellectual history. The papers and responses were published five years later.
5. Stephen, 3, 4.
6. *Ibid*., 12.
7. *Ibid*., 38–9.
8. *Ibid*., 31.
9. *Ibid*., 17.
10. *Ibid*., 23.
11. *Ibid*., 37, 38.
12. *Ibid*., 38. Cambridge had also been the nursery for many of Mill's comrades-in-arms in the 1830s: 'the earlier set, of which Charles Austin was the leader...swore by Bentham and used the dyslogistic words

"sentimentalism", "declamation", and "vague generalities" as a kind of Shibboleth'. (*Ibid.*, 23.)

13. Collini, 52–4. He doesn't himself use this term.
14. B. Hilton, in response ('Manliness, Masculinity and the Mid-Victorian Temperament', in Goldman, 60–70) argues for a broader understanding of 'manly', one that encompasses 'manly tears', a manliness the opposites of which are 'beastly' or 'boyish', not 'feminine'. (66, 65)
15. Stephen, 97.
16. *Ibid.*, 98.
17. 'A Popular Exposition of Mr Darwin on the Origin of Species', *Macmillan's Magazine* 3 (December 1860), 81–92.
18. *Ibid.*, 86.
19. *Ibid.*, 87–8. He will be all the more celebrated, Fawcett urges, for having promulgated such simple laws. (83) To miraculously intervene every time a new species is required would be far more inefficient. (82–3)
20. *Ibid.*, 85.
21. *Ibid.*, 88. Nonetheless, it is to Darwin's great credit that he has 'rigorously observed' the method of investigation sanctioned by 'the greatest of logicians'. (84) Darwin, for his part, was flattered to learn that he had received Mill's approbation. (Stephen, 100.)
22. Fawcett, 'A Popular Exposition…', 83–4.
23. *Ibid.*, 92.
24. Stephen, 93–4.
25. *Ibid.*, 103.
26. *Ibid.*, 97.
27. *Ibid.*, 103.
28. *Ibid.*, 47.
29. *Ibid.*, 54–5.
30. *Ibid.*, 105–6.
31. J. Parry, *Democracy and Religion: Gladstone and the Liberal Party, 1867–1875* (Cambridge: Cambridge University Press, 1986), 365. Of the four 'Fawcettites' Parry identifies, only two, Auberon Herbert and Fawcett himself, actually voted against the Bill, Peter Taylor and Lord Edmond Fitzmaurice abstaining. To head a faction consisting of oneself and the arch-individualist Herbert doesn't say a great deal about one's political finesse. Six of the remaining eight British Liberals opposing the bill Parry classifies as 'whig-liberals'. The ten defectors were sufficient to bring down the government, 287–284. See Parry (353–68) for a detailed discussion of the claims of the various constituencies. Goldman rejects Parry's and Matthew's (H. C. G. Matthew, *Gladstone, 1809–1874* (Oxford: Oxford University Press, 1988), 199) defences of Gladstone's case. (Goldman, 27.)
32. Stephen, 284–5.
33. M. G. Fawcett, *What I Remember* (London: Fisher, Unwin, 1925), 92–3.
34. (London: Macmillan, 1875), 44–5.
35. R. Strachey, *Millicent Garrett Fawcett* (London: John Murray, 1931), 88. She is reported to have remarked that 'The three best men I have known were not Christians', the three being her husband, Mill and Sidgwick. Rumours of Fawcett's atheism had long circulated in London. (Strachey,

62.) If the scant information on Fawcett's background reveals no domineering parent of strong Evangelical opinions, Millicent Fawcett's own childhood included such a figure. Her mother's 'narrow and tenacious Evangelicalism', rejected in adolescence, nonetheless led to 'an evangelist's commitment and adherence to morality' on the part of the daughter, according to her most recent biographer. (D. Rubenstein, *A Different World for Women: The Life of Millicent Garrett Fawcett* (Columbus: Ohio State University Press, 1991), 6.) Mrs Garrett, for whom 'prayer and the practice of holiness were ... the true objects of human life', was unflatteringly portrayed in Fawcett's novel *Janet Doncaster*. (Strachey, 3, 56.)

36. Stephen to Thackeray, 24 December 1866, in J. Bicknell, *Selected Letters of Leslie Stephen*, vol. 1 (Columbus: Ohio State University Press, 1996), 38.
37. 'The Effect of an Increased Production of Wealth on Wages', *Fortnightly Review* 15 (January 1874), 77.
38. Stephen, 162.
39. *Ibid.*, 117.
40. *Ibid.*, 170–2.
41. *Manual of Political Economy* (7th edn) (London: Macmillan, 1888), 191.
42. *The Economic Position of the British Labourer* (Cambridge: Cambridge University Press, 1865), 35.
43. *Pauperism: Its Causes and Remedies* (Cambridge: Cambridge University Press, 1871), 163.
44. 'The Effect of an Increased Production ...', 79.
45. *Ibid.*
46. *Manual*, 133–4, 166–7.
47. *The Economic Position*, 29.
48. *Ibid.*, 31.
49. *Ibid.*, 38.
50. *Manual*, 286.
51. 'The Nationalisation of Land', *Fortnightly Review* 12 (December 1872), 628–9.
52. *Manual*, 286–7.
53. 'The Effect of an Increased Production ...', 80.
54. *Manual*, 301.
55. *Pauperism*, 8.
56. *Ibid.*, 9.
57. Stephen, 152.

9 WILLIAM THOMAS THORNTON

1. 'No sportsman who had fired at a squirrel, to hear, a minute after, the crashing of boughs above him and to see a bear come tumbling out of the tree, could be more astonished than Mr Thornton must have been when, promptly on the publication of his work, John Stuart Mill, without a reservation and even without a parley, surrendered.' F. A. Walker, 'The

Wage-Fund Theory', *North American Review*, Jan. 1875, 99, cited by S. Gordon, 'The Wage-Fund Controversy: The Second Round', *History of Political Economy* 5 (Spring 1973), 15.

2. As Taussig may have been the first to note. (*Wages and Capital* (New York: Appleton, 1896), 248.)
3. '[T]he book will be very serviceable in carrying on what may be called the emancipation of pol. economy – its liberation from the kind of doctrines of the old school (now taken up by well to do people) which treat what they call economical laws, demand & supply for instance, as if they were laws of inanimate matter, not amenable to the will of the human beings from whose feelings, interests, & principles of action they proceed.' (Mill to Thornton, 19 October 1867, CW 16.)
4. 'What Determines the Price of Labour or Rate of Wages?', *Fortnightly Review* 7 (old series), 564.
5. Thornton, *On Labour: Its Wrongful Claims and Rightful Dues, Its Actual Present and Probable Future* (second edition) [1870] (Shannon: Irish University Press, 1971), 62.
6. 'History's Scientific Pretensions', in *Old Fashioned Ethics and Common-Sense Metaphysics* (London: Macmillan, 1873), 84–112.
7. 'Huxleyism', in *Ibid.*, 158–98; 'Recent Phases of Scientific Atheism', in *Ibid.*, 199–265.
8. 'Limits of Demonstrable Theism', in *Ibid.*, 268.
9. *On Labour*, 80–2.
10. W. S. Jevons, *The Theory of Political Economy* [1871] (Charlottesville: Ibis, nd), vii, 256–7; see also Cannan, *A History of the Theories of Production and Distribution in English Political Economy from 1776–1848* [1898] (London: Staples, 1953), 186–216.
11. 'The Wages-Fund Theory', *The Fortnightly Review* 26 (September 1879), 401.
12. *History of Economic Analysis* (New York: Oxford University Press, 1954), 671.
13. *Ibid.*, 662–71; M. Blaug, *Economic Theory in Retrospect* (fourth edn) (Cambridge: Cambridge University Press, 1985), 185–7. Other favourable verdicts were cited in Chapter 5.
14. T. Negishi, 'Thornton's Criticism of Equilibrium Theory and Mill', HOPE 18 (1986), 567.
15. M. Donoghue and M. Wright, 'William T. Thornton on the Economics of Trade Unions: The Origins of Efficient Bargaining Theory' (unpublished paper, 1996).
16. P. Mirowski, 'Smooth Operator: How Marshall's Demand and Supply Curves Made Neoclassicism Safe for Public Consumption but Unfit for Science', in R. McWilliams Tullberg (ed.), *Alfred Marshall in Retrospect* (Aldershot: Elgar, 1990); M. White '"That God-Forgotten Thornton": Exorcising Higgling after *On Labour*', in N. de Marchi and M. Morgan (eds), *Higgling: Transactors and Their Markets in the History of Economics* (Durham: Duke University Press, 1994), 149–83.
17. R. Ekelund, 'Mill's Recantation Once Again: A Reply to Professor Negishi', *Oxford Economic Papers* 37, 152–3; R. Ekelund and S. Thommesen, 'Disequilibrium Theory and Thornton's Assault on the Laws of

Supply and Demand', HOPE 21 (1989), 567–92; E. Forget, 'John Stuart Mill, Francis Longe and William Thornton on Demand and Supply', JHET 13 (Fall 1991), 205–21; R. Ekelund, 'W. T. Thornton: Savant, Idiot, or Idiot-Savant?', JHET 19 (Spring 1997), 1–23. I believe Thornton's latter-day critics convincingly demonstrate his lack of theoretical sophistication, and that his attack on the laws of supply and demand was, indeed, something of 'a stab in the dark'. (Ekelund and Thommesen, 558.) 'Similar conclusions', as Forget notes, 'do not necessarily imply similar theoretical structures.' (Forget, 215.)

18. Jevons to Shadwell, 5 December 1872 in R. D. C. Black (ed.), *The Papers and Correspondence of William Stanley Jevons* (vol. 3) (London: Macmillan, 1977), 255.
19. *A System of Political Economy* (London: Trubner, 1877), iii.
20. *Ibid.*, 20; Shadwell argues that wages are ultimately determined by the efficiency of labour. (133–56)
21. 'British Trade Unions and Popular Political Economy, 1860–1880', *The Historical Journal* 30.4 (1987), 822–32.
22. *Ibid.*, 822, 824–6.
23. *On Labour*, 59–61.
24. *Ibid.*, 62.
25. *Ibid.*, 52–3; 72–3.
26. *Ibid.*, 77.
27. *Ibid.*, 79–80.
28. Thus Thornton breaks with classical value theory without anticipating marginalism. Price is determined neither by 'inherent utility or cost of production'. (*Ibid.*, 136.) While something will not be produced if it doesn't satisfy a human desire, and will not continue to be produced if its market valuation is insufficient to cover the cost of production, both utility and cost act only indirectly. The notion of a 'natural price' is a myth – the quantity and quality of the labour required for production varies too greatly. (*Ibid.*, 138.)
29. *Ibid.*, 56–7. In the original version, a 'hundredweight' of herrings is sold for 20 shillings. ('A New Theory of Supply and Demand', *Fortnightly Review* (old series) 6, 423.)
30. Mill, 'Thornton On Labour and Its Claims', 509.
31. *On Labour*, 93.
32. *Ibid.*, 94, 97.
33. *Ibid.*, 100–1. Thornton cannot resist quoting Adam Smith on the tendency of masters to conspire. (*Ibid.*, 102.)
34. *Ibid.*, 108.
35. *Ibid.*, 86.
36. J. S. Mill, 'On the Definition of Political Economy', *Essays on Some Unsettled Questions of Political Economy*, CW 4, 321–39, especially 330–1.
37. The former, with great oversimplicity, to be sure, predicts the likely consequences of excessive additions to or subtractions from the wages fund. If the fund were to be reduced abruptly, the amount saved would presumably be invested in fixed or variable capital, plant or raw materials. But if these were already proportionate to labour, there would now

be a new demand for labour, assuming that machinery doesn't replace labour, and labour's price would correspondingly rise. (H. Fawcett, *A Manual of Political Economy* (7th edn) (London: Macmillan, 1888), 132–3.) If invested in another industry, *its* workers would presumably see their wages rise, and competition would eventually restore equilibrium, as wages in the original industry would ultimately be forced back up. Similarly, if simply appropriated as profits (crudely defined by Mill and Thornton in the debate as income accruing to owners that is spent on personal consumption), once again competition, this time among capitalists, would ratchet up wages, for other entrepreneurs would respond to the incentive of a higher than normal profit rate and contrive to produce whatever good or service was generating that rate. Their rival enterprises would compete with that of the original owner, driving up wages, until the market was saturated. If, conversely, the fund were augmented at the expense of profits, capital would flow out of that industry, seeking a greater rate of return elsewhere, and wages would perforce fall and/or employment shrink.

More compelling, naturally, is the marginalist argument, first stated, in England, by Philip Wicksteed 15 years after Thornton's book, and familiar to readers of any introductory textbook. Under perfect competition, 'the share in the product which falls to any factor, no matter what be the character of that factor or of the service which it renders, is determined by the amount per unit which the concern, as a whole, would find it pay to allow to that factor sooner than have a portion of it withdrawn from co-operation'. (*An Essay on the Co-ordination of the Laws of Distribution* (London: Macmillan, 1894), 10.) While Wicksteed did not derive from marginal productivity (as did J. B. Clark) an endorsement of the prevailing wage rate, the implications for the wage fund theory are clear. The 'fund' is determined by estimates of the prospective demand for the good or service and of the productivity of the final worker hired in any job category – his or her contribution to the anticipated value of that product (itself determined by the urgency of the desire for an additional increment, relative to all other commodities and services, on the part of individual consumers). Given mobility of factors, 'the present distribution [is]...a Distribution according to Service', William Smart concluded. (*The Distribution of Income* (London: Macmillan, 1899), 334–5.) Even without a developed marginal theory of productivity, 'the wages of a working man are ultimately coincident with what he produces', W. S. Jevons announced. (*The Theory of Political Economy*, 259, 261–3.) He objected to the whole idea of treating 'labour as a commodity which is bought up by capitalists'. (256)

38. *On Labour*, 44.
39. *Ibid.*
40. 'What Determines the Price of Labour...', *Fortnightly Review* (old series) 7, 564.
41. *On Labour*, 82.
42. Norgate claims that Thornton's mother was the daughter of a *Greek* merchant. (G. L. Norgate, 'Thornton, William Thomas', L. Stephen and S. Lee (eds), *Dictionary of National Biography* [1917] (London:

Oxford University Press, 1921–2), 790–1.) This is unlikely. Apart from the name not being Greek, Thornton's cousin Edward Zohrab served as Turkish Counsel-General in London, a position a Greek would not have held. (W. T. Thornton, *Zohrab; or a Midsummer's Day Dream; and Other Poems* (London: Longman, 1854), 3.) Thornton himself half-believed he was the descendant of the Persian general who commanded a Turkish army against his own father, as chronicled in Faraudusi's *Shah-Nameh*. (*Ibid*., 44–5.) The next three paragraphs are based primarily on Norgate, obituaries in *The Athenaeum*, n. 2748 (26 June 1880), 822–3, *Illustrated London News* (26 June 1880), 630, and *The Times* (18 June 1880), 9, and the following articles in the *DNB*: C. A. Harris, 'Thornton, Sir Edward', 779; and E. I. Carlyle, 'Thornton, Thomas', 787.

43. *Modern Manicheism, Labour's Utopia, and Other Poems* (London: Parker, 1857), 28.
44. *Old Fashioned Ethics*..., v, vi.
45. W. Thornton, 'His Career in the East India House', in W. Fox Bourne (ed.), *John Stuart Mill: His Life and Works* (Boston: Osgood, 1873), 34.
46. The Dowager Duchess of Argyll (ed.), *George Douglas, eighth Duke of Argyll, Autobiography and Memoirs* (London: Murray, 1906), 274 .
47. 'His Career in the East India House', 35.
48. When Thornton was promoted to First Secretary for Public Works in 1858, he may have made as much as £1200 per annum. (T. Lloyd, 'John Stuart Mill and the East India Company', in M. Laine (ed.), *A Cultivated Mind* (Toronto: University of Toronto Press, 1991), 52; Thornton to Mill, 26 October 1867 and 10 October 1869, Hopkins.) For other accounts of work in the East India House (and its impact on Mill) see A. Harris, 'John Stuart Mill: Servant of the East India Company', *Cambridge Journal of Economics* 30 (May 1964), 185–202; R. Moore, 'John Stuart Mill at East India Company House', *Historical Studies* 20 (October 1983), 498–500; E. Stokes, *The English Utilitarians and India* (Oxford: Oxford University Press, 1959); and L. Zastoupil, *John Stuart Mill and India* (Stanford: Stanford University Press, 1994).
49. 'Recent Phases of Scientific Atheism', *Old Fashioned Ethics*..., 254.
50. *The English Utilitarians* (vol. 3) (New York: Putnam, 1900), 52.
51. *Ibid*., 187. Stephen had offered an earlier cameo in his biography of Fawcett, in which Thornton's 'singular amiability' and his 'calm, slow-working intellect' were also fondly recalled. Thornton persisted in 'cross-examining any acquaintance who had thrown out a remark not perfectly intelligible.... His favourite virtue was candour, and it was not the less genuine because, like other very candid people, he had a certain mild obstinacy which secured him from the risk of conversion, however benevolently he could listen to arguments.... It was characteristic that he was practically quite ignorant of agriculture, although he had written a book of real value... upon peasant proprietorship. Fawcett was a good deal amused by the difficulty of explaining to this most exemplary official, responsible to some extent for the vast public works of India, the system of irrigation of the water-meadows round Salisbury.' (*Life of Henry Fawcett* (New York: Putnam, 1886), 197–8.)

52. F. W. Maitland, *The Life and Letters of Leslie* [1906] (Detroit: Gale, 1968), 189.
53. Stephen to Norton, 2 May 1874, in J. Bicknell, *The Selected Letters of Leslie Stephen* (Columbus: Ohio State University Press, 1996), 136.
54. *John Stuart Mill: A Criticism with Personal Recollections* [1882] (New York: Kelley, 1969), 173–4.
55. *Recollections* (vol. 1) (New York: Macmillan, 1917), 52.
56. Mill to Cairnes, 3 October 1864, CW 15, 958.
57. Mill to Thornton, 16 January 1869, CW 17, 1549.
58. Thornton to Fawcett, nd, October 1862, vol. 26, item 1011, MTC, BLPES.
59. Mill to Thornton, 16 January 1869, CW 17, 1549, italics in original: 'because as she is an architect & master mason all in one, she is carrying on the improvements very slowly, not letting the attention to them interfere too much with her other work'. Taylor also consulted with Thornton on the construction of a 'vibratory', a 30-foot covered walkway for Mill to use in inclement weather. (*Ibid*., 1548.)
60. Mill to Thornton, 28 January 1962, CW 15, 774.
61. Mill to Thornton, 14 June 1862, CW 15, 782.
62. Mill to Thornton, 23 October 1863, CW 15, 892–3.
63. Mill to Thornton, 17 April 1863, CW 15, 853–4, and Mill to Thornton, 19 October 1867, CW 16, 1218–20.
64. Cited in note 42.
65. Thornton's extant correspondence appears to consist of four letters to Mill (three at Hopkins, one at Yale), one to Fawcett (at BLPES), two to Chadwick (at UCL), six to Helen Taylor (at BLPES) and six to Cairnes (at NLI). (I'm indebted to Mark Donahue for calling my attention to the latter.) Two poems in *Zohrab* also suggest the author has a wife and children.
66. Taylor to Thornton, 20 March 1876, vol. 26, item 1012, MTC, BLPES. The lofty Millian sentiments were apparently welcome; her letter, Thornton wrote back, was 'one of the few that have soothed instead of grating upon our feelings. You have not mocked us with hollow commonplaces.' (Thornton to Taylor, 27 March 1876, MTC, BLPES.)
67. Thornton to Mill, 24 September 1872, MS 350, Box 2, Folder 35, Yale.
68. J. E. Hutton, *A History of the Moravian Church* (Second edn) (London: Moravian Publication Office, 1909), 308–16.
69. J. T. Hamilton and K. G. Hamilton, *History of the Moravian Church: The Renewed Unitas Fratrum, 1722–1957* (Bethlehem: Interprovincial Board of Christian Education, Moravian Church in America, 1967), 266; J. T. Hamilton, *A History of the Moravian Church . . . during the Eighteenth and Nineteenth Centuries* (Bethlehem: Times Publishing Co., 1900), 223.
70. J. R. Weinlick and A. H. Frank, *The Moravian Church through the Ages* (Bethlehem: The Moravian Church in America, 1966), 110–11.
71. Hamilton and Hamilton, 393.
72. *Ibid*., 211.
73. Weinlick and Frank, 66, 105; H. A. Snyder, 'Pietism, Moravianism and Methodism As Renewal Movements: A Comparative and Thematic Study' (dissertation, Notre Dame) (Ann Arbor: University MicroFilms,

Inc., 1983), 212. 'What is the sum total of the whole gospel which one must seek in all things and on which all fellowship in the spirit must be based? I call this, in my manner of expressing myself, personal connection with the Savior.' (N. von Zinzendorf, *Einiger seit 1751 von dem Ordinario Fratrum zu London gehltene Predigten* (London and Barby, 1756), 109, quoted by Hamilton and Hamilton, 158.)

74. Hamilton and Hamilton, 155.
75. Snyder, 196–202, 211; Hutton, 81–2. The former recalled the *collegia pietatis* of late-seventeenth-century Germany, and the latter was urged in opposition to what Moravians regarded as a too-great reliance on faith on the part of many Lutherans.
76. Hutton, 301.
77. D. McCorkle, *The Moravian Contribution to American Music* (Winston-Salem: Moravian Music Foundation, 1956).
78. Hutton, 482.
79. Weinlick and Frank, 66.
80. Weinlick, 66; Hutton, 308. In these settlements, as they came to be called, 'the love of Christ would reign supreme'. (Hutton, 310.) Single men and women were housed communally and, of course, separately, in what were called 'choirs'. Their lives were regulated: members dressed uniformly, slept, ate, worked and prayed on schedule, were forbidden to leave even for a day, and obliged to submit major decisions to 'Lot' (whereby a slip of paper withdrawn from a box determined the outcome). (Hutton 313, 406; Hamilton and Hamilton, 39.)
81. He may have been converted by the Moravian leader Peter Boehler; he attended services at the Fetter Lane meeting house, and was active in the Fetter Lane Society. He eventually undertook a pilgrimage to Herrnhut and conversed at length with Zinzendorf. For detailed accounts of Wesley's long flirtation with Moravianism, see Hutton, 283–301 and Snyder, 129–49.
82. 'Sonnet III', 'Stanzas Written in Kensal Green Cemetery', *Zohrab*, 83, 73–8.
83. Moral objections to God – particularly reservations about eternal damnation – were probably more responsible for converting individuals to agnosticism and atheism than ontological doubts. (S. Budd, *Varieties of Unbelief* (London: Heinemann, 1977); E. Royle, *Radicals, Secularists and Republicans* (Manchester: Manchester University Press, 1980).)
84. 'Limits of Demonstrable Theism', in *Old Fashioned Ethics . . .*, 272. The same sentiments were expressed in a sonnet sequence in his earlier collection. (*Zohrab*, 81–94.) Here he credits the doctrine to Zoroaster, once worshipped by his ancestors. (*Ibid.*, 89.)
85. *Ibid.*
86. 'What man . . . /Who, if his son ask for fish, will jeeringly/Give him a serpent, or for bread a stone?/ If ye, being evil, at your children's cry/ Know how to give good gifts, should not much more/ Your heavenly Father, His good things supply/ To them who ask Him?' (*Ibid.*, 17–18.)
87. *Ibid.*, 20.
88. *Ibid.*, 23–4, 24.

89. *Ibid.*, 25, 26.
90. 'Sonnet X', *Zohrab*, 90. Even after death, souls delight in the opportunity to perform 'errands of goodwill' in God's service. ('Stanzas Written in Kensal Green Cemetery', *Zohrab*, 77.)
91. *Ibid.*
92. The first two sonnets in the sequence previously mentioned do attempt to derive God's existence from the laws of nature. (*Ibid.*, 81, 82.)
93. *Ibid.*, 196.
94. 'Recent Phases of Scientific Atheism', in *Old Fashioned Ethics...*, 208–13.
95. *Ibid.*, 217–19, 227. He voices one well-founded reservation about the dearth of the geological record in revealing intermediate forms: he asks if there were possibly not leaps greater than the theory can account for. (*Ibid.*, 223–4.)
96. *Ibid.*, 226.
97. *Ibid.*, 237.
98. *Ibid.*, 235.
99. *Ibid.*, 241–7.
100. *Ibid.*, 254.
101. 'Anti-Utilitarianism', 19.
102. *Ibid.*, 21.
103. *Ibid.*, 260–1n. 'Mr Lewes... maintains that M. Comte created Social Science. Mr Mill considers that he did not create it, but only proved its creation to be possible. With all possible deference, I submit that what he really did was to prove its creation to be impossible.' (*Ibid.*, 260n.)
104. *Ibid.*, 262–4.
105. 'Anti-Utilitarianism', *Old Fashioned Ethics...*, 37. See Mill's references in *Auguste Comte and Positivism*, CW 10, 337, and 'On Liberty', CW 18, 265.
106. 'Anti-Utilitarianism', *Old Fashioned Ethics...* 42. The right specifically at issue for Thornton in *On Labour* is 'the right of the poor to live by labour'. Thornton denies this claim. The rich 'have incurred... [no] obligation of maintaining in the world those whom they were in no degree instrumental in bringing into it'. They would be so obliged in the absence of scarcity, had God created sufficient produce to provide for all human beings. They would also be so obliged, Thornton argues, had 'some communal act or institution' dispossessed some individuals 'of the means of providing for themselves'. (*On Labour*, 115) This stipulation gives Thornton an opportunity to defend private property, which he does on utilitarian grounds: without this institution, the earth would 'have remained untilled, and consequently comparatively unproductive'. (*Ibid.*, 116.) The poor are thus only entitled to a share of what the earth would have produced had it remained unappropriated, an 'infinitesimally small' debt, amply repaid by 'the crumbs which habitually fall from the table of the rich'. (*Ibid.*) 'It was not the rich who placed the poor on earth, and it is not the rich who owe them the means of living here', Thornton concludes. (There is nonetheless an 'obligation... imposed upon them not by in junctions of justice, but by

the force of sympathy and the exhortations of humanity and charity'. (*Ibid.*, 118.)

107. 'Anti-Utilitarianism', *Old Fashioned Ethics*... 15, 42–3.
108. *Ibid.*, 41.
109. *Ibid.*, 40.
110. *Ibid.*, 41.
111. *Ibid.*, 48–9.
112. *Ibid.*, 24–34.
113. *Ibid.*, 26. This is preceded by the familiar conundrum wherein, we are told, one doctor means to kill his patient while a second doctor unintentionally administers an overdose, and we are asked if the two killings are equally immoral. (*Ibid.*, 25.)
114. *Ibid.*, 27–8.
115. *Ibid.*, 38.
116. *Ibid.*, 52–3. He cites Mill's lumpy catalogue of six discrete rights in 'Utilitarianism'.
117. Cairnes, needless to say, was quite contemptuous of Thornton's performance. When 'Anti-Utilitarianism' appeared in the *Fortnightly Review*, Cairnes dismissed it as 'the weakest thing of his, I think, that I have ever read. He might at least have mastered the distinction between "intention" and "motive" before undertaking to refute utilitarianism'. (Cairnes to Mill, 10 September 1870, vol. 56A, MTC, BLPES.) Mill, in response, conceded that 'metaphysical subjects are not among his strong points.... All he says is answered by anticipation in Bentham's Introduction to Morals and Legislation, and in my father's Fragment on Mackintosh'. (Mill to Cairnes, 15 September 1870, CW 17, 1765.) Cairnes, however, did not give up. 'I have exchanged some letters with Thornton on the utilitarian question, but I doubt if I have made any impression. He is going to follow up his last paper with one on "Natural Rights" – God bless the mark!' (Cairnes to Mill, 22 September 1870, vol. 56A, MTC, BLPES.)
118. *Overpopulation and Its Remedy* (London: Longman, Brown, Green, and Longmans, 1846), 3, 44, 268, 290, 307; 114–18. The chief objective of *Overpopulation*, the book that endeared him to Mill, is, quite simply to show (1) that poverty is both a consequence and cause of overpopulation – and, hence, no issue is more critical; and (2) that the resolution of this dilemma depends on the poor postponing marriage. Ultimately, peasant proprietorships provide the most effective incentive to delay matrimony. '[T]he final purpose for which free trade, the allotment system, education, and sundry other expedients, have been so strongly recommended', Thornton concludes, 'is neither more nor less than to diminish the frequency of marriage.' (*Ibid.*, 385.)
119. See W. Grampp, 'Classical Economics and Its Moral Critics', *History of Political Economy* (1971), 359–94; M. Wiener, *English Culture and the Decline of the Industrial Spirit, 1850–1980* (Cambridge: Cambridge University Press, 1981); and B. Collins and K. Robbins (eds), *British Culture and Economic Decline* (London: Weidenfeld and Nicolson, 1990).
120. The 'labourer' is the proverbial 'hewer of wood and drawer of water' and his 'utopia' permits him 'to join the jocund throng, on village

green,/ In course or game athlete [*sic*], or giddy reel', (33) while 'the ploughman, homeward wending wearily' will 'halt to remark the play of light and shade/ In forest glade's perspective greenery,/ Or stoop to cull a herb or mineral,/ Or look up wistful to the western sky.' (35)

121. *Overpopulation*..., 166.
122. *Ibid.*, 185.
123. *Ibid.*, 272–86.
124. *Ibid.*, 297–328.
125. *Ibid.*, 329.

10 THOMAS EDWARD CLIFFE LESLIE

1. [1870] (New York: Kelley, 1968), henceforth abbreviated LS.
2. 'Political Economy and Sociology', in *Essays in Political Economy* [1888] (New York: Kelley, 1969), 198. This posthumous essay collection, edited by J. K. Ingram and C. F. Bastable, replicates a number of essays from Leslie's earlier collection, *Essays in Political and Moral Philosophy* (Dublin: Hodges, Foster & Figgis, 1879). When an essay appearing in both books is cited, reference will be given to the former volume, which is far more accessible. The two anthologies will henceforth be abbreviated PE and PMP. In his letters, though not in print, Leslie is as critical of Cairnes, as documented in Chapter 6. Leslie's letters never give the year, but this can usually be ascertained with some degree of certainty from various references and, for those written to Mill, from Mill's published correspondence. Dating letters in the Ingram collection can be more problematic.
3. Leslie attributes the deductivist strain in Smith to the unhappy reinforcement of Smith's belief in a 'Code of Nature' by his faith in the 'great, benevolent and all-wise Being' assumed by 'natural theology'. ('The Political Economy of Adam Smith', in PE, 26–7.) The 'Code of Nature', in fact the bastard offspring of Greek philosophy and Roman jurisprudence, mistakes legal practices shared by foreigners for 'natural' imperatives. When combined with a belief in a God equally just and benevolent toward all mankind, 'nature' was held to unfailingly exhibit order and harmony. Hence, the beneficent Invisible Hand. (*Ibid.*, 27, 30.)) Mill, on the other hand, was a victim of his early training. James Mill's system was designed 'to crush out all originality and to inspire excessive confidence in the methods adopted' ('John Stuart Mill', in PE, 57.), the methods being associational psychology, utilitarian ethics, representative government, and self-interest and the population principle in economics – 'the keys to every problem in the science of men'. (*Ibid.*, 56–7, 56.) But in addition, Mill's partiality to the 'complete individual liberty which [Ricardian political economy] supposes' also induced him to retain its deductive core. (*Ibid.*, 57.)
4. 'Cairnes' "Leading Principles of Political Economy Newly Expounded"', in PE, 51; see also 'On the Philosophical Method of Political Economy', in PE, 167, 185–6.

5. 'Political Economy and Sociology', in PE, 199.
6. 'The Love of Money', in PE, 3. The argument strikingly anticipates one advanced by several of Bernard Shaw's characters, cf. Kitty Warren in *Mrs Warren's Profession* and Andrew Undershaft in *Major Barbara*.
7. 'Cairnes' "Leading Principles",...' in PE, 51.
8. 'Political Economy and Sociology', in PE, 201.
9. 'On the Philosophical Method...', in PE, 172–3, 173.
10. Leslie appears to forget this nice distinction in his 1879 'The Known and the Unknown in the Economic World', where he associates predictability with very primitive societies. (PE, 222.)
11. 'On the Philosophical Method...', in PE, 179–83, 179.
12. *Ibid.*, 182.
13. 'The Known and the Unknown...', in PE, 231; see also PMP, viii.
14. 'The Known and the Unknown...', in PE, 232, 230.
15. *Ibid.*, 235.
16. *Ibid.*, 224–6.
17. *Ibid.*, 221, 239.
18. *Ibid.*, 239.
19. 'Political Economy and Sociology', in PE, 193; 'The Known and the Unknown...', in PE, 233.
20. *Ibid.*, 233–4. Leslie cites p. 49 of McCulloch's edition of Ricardo's *Works*, presumably the 1846 London edition published by Murray. The quotation, however, appears on page 75, and in P. Sraffa (ed.), *Works and Correspondence of David Ricardo*, vol. 1 (Cambridge: Cambridge University Press, 1966), 133.
21. 'Political Economy and Sociology', in PE, 192–3.
22. 'John Stuart Mill', in PE, 58.
23. 'Political Economy and the Rate of Wages', in LS, 370–1.
24. *Ibid.*, 378.
25. *Ibid.*, 379.
26. *Ibid.*, 362–4.
27. 'Political Economy and the Tenure of Land', in LS, 128; 'The Land System of England, 1867', in LS, 174, 180.
28. PMP, vi.
29. A. W. Coats, 'The Historist Reaction in English Political Economy', *Economica*, n.s. 21 (May 1954), 144; G. Koot, *English Historical Economics* (Cambridge: Cambridge University Press, 1987), 39–53. Maine himself, however, was a student of Sauvigny, so continental influences can't be entirely discounted. The historicist movement in Britain is beyond our scope. J. E. Thorold Rogers, along with Leslie, are usually regarded as precursors rather than the founders of a school. To the extent it was a movement, British historicism flourished (at Oxford, chiefly) from about 1880 to 1900. (Koot's dates are 1870 to 1926.) Its leading lights were William Ashley and William Cunningham. Clearly, the death blows came in 1890, with Marshall's *Principles*, Keynes's *Scope and Method* and the founding of the British (later, Royal) Economic Society and the *Economic Journal*. The establishment of the Cambridge tripos under Marshall's aegis in 1901 was the *coup de grace*. Historicists were marginalized as economic historians. (In addition to Koot, see

important works by J. Maloney, *The Professionalization of Economics* [1985] (New Brunswick: Transaction, 1991) and A. Kadish, *Historians, Economists and Economic History* (London: Routledge, 1989).)
30. 'On the Philosophical Method . . . ', in PE, 189.
31. *Report of the 48th Meeting of the British Association for the Advance of Science* [Dublin, 1878] (London, 1879). Ingram was successively Professor of Oratory, English Literature, and Greek at Trinity, served as college and university librarian, and helped found, or served signally in, a number of institutions, including the National Library of Ireland and the Dublin Statistical Society. He was also the author (anonymously) of the nationalist anthem 'Who fears to speak of Ninety-eight'. (Anon., 'John Kells Ingram', in S. Lee (ed.), *The Dictionary of National Biography*, 2nd Supplement (1901–1911) (London: Oxford University Press, 1912), 339–42.) Especially during the three years that remained to Leslie following the Dublin address, the two men were very close and corresponded frequently.
32. See 'Leonce de Lavergne', in PE, 101–25; 'M. De Laveleye on Primitive Property', in PMP 435–47, and references throughout Leslie's correspondence. Collini suggests that Tocqueville may have been an additional, unacknowledged influence. (S. Collini, 'Particular Polities: Political Economy and the Historical Method', in S. Collini, D. Winch, J. Burrow, *That Noble Science of Politics* (Cambridge: Cambridge University Press, 1983), 264.)
33. In LS, 160–203 and 204–29.
34. 'The Land System . . . ', in LS, 194–201.
35. *Ibid.*, 174.
36. *Ibid.*, 182–9.
37. 'Lord Dufferin on the Tenure of Land', 'Mr Senior on Ireland'.
38. 'Political Economy and the Tenure of Land', in LS, 127.
39. Leslie proclaimed himself a pure pragmatist, like his friend Jevons: 'I have no dogmatic or settled faith about social or state interferences with individual conduct in the economic sphere. The time seems to me not come for a creed on the subject. The German Catheder Socialists made donkeys of themselves by rushing at practical doctrine on the subject, when they really had nothing to say beyond the negative proposition that individual interest was not the only thing to look at.' (Leslie to Ingram, nd, 'Monday' [November ? 1881], 2808/43/51, PRO.)
40. A point noted by Koot, 52. See Koot for the politics of Leslie's historicist successors. If not categorically conservative or socialist, they were nearly all Protectionists.
41. 'The Future of Europe Foretold in History', in PMP, 107.
42. Military service can 'correct peculiar physical, intellectual, and moral defects of individuals, to communicate readiness, sharpness, presence of mind, temper, public spirit, and the power to obey and to command'. 'The Military Systems of Europe in 1867', in PMP, 146–7. As indicated, Leslie hinted to Mill that Cairnes may have plagiarized his argument. (Leslie to Mill, 7 February [1871], Hopkins.) Both economists consulted Chadwick on the subject. (Leslie to Chadwick 31 July [1867], 5 January [1868], and 17 February [1868], Chadwick Papers, UCL.)

43. E. Biagini, *Liberty, Retrenchment and Reform* (Cambridge: Cambridge University Press, 1992), 110–13. Gladstone's 1874 campaign pledge to eliminate the income tax (and substitute taxes on realized property) may have been more of a response to popular radical demands than is sometimes appreciated.
44. Leslie to Mill, 3 January [1871], Hopkins. Gladstone's campaign against the income tax vexed Leslie: 'Gladstone's endeavour to abolish the income tax is one of my reasons for rather wishing his political career would somehow come altogether to a close'. (Leslie to Ingram, 13 December [1880], D2808/43/38, PRO.)
45. Leslie to Ingram, 13 December [1880?], 2808/43/38, PRO.
46. 'Leslie on the Land Question', CW 5, 681.
47. Leslie to Ingram, 'Saturday' [1881?], 2808/43/56, PRO.
48. Leslie to Ingram, nd, but just after 17 March [1879?], 2808/43/55, PRO.
49. Biagini, 86–93; Biagini points out that however unrealistic for urban artisans was the goal of 'returning to the land', it was not an escapist fantasy: 'it was first and foremost normative, for the moral and civic virtues it celebrated, and the kind of relationship between State and society which it implied'. (Biagini, 91.) As noted, Biagini also indicates the extent to which Millite classical political economy, purged of its Whiggishness by the Blackheath Park circle, appealed to and was useful for workers. (*Ibid*., 87; E. Biagini, 'British Trade Unions and Popular Political Economy, 1860–1880', *Historical Journal* 30 (1987), 811–40.)
50. 'Auvergne', in PE, 418.
51. *Ibid*., 421.
52. *Ibid*., 423.
53. In LS, 280–1.
54. 'Westphalia and the Ruhr Basin, 1868–1869', in LS, 253.
55. Most of the information in the following paragraphs comes from the following: J. K. Ingram's 'Biographical Notice of the Author', in PE, ix-xii (a reprint of his *Encyclopedia Britannica* article on his friend); J. M. Rigg, 'Thomas Edward Cliffe Leslie', in L. Stephen and S. Lee (eds), *The Dictionary of National Biography*, vol. 9 [1917] (London: Oxford University Press, 1921–2), 987–8; anon., 'T. E. Cliffe Leslie', *Atheneum*, n. 2823 (February 4, 1882), 158. The contemporary sources estimate that he was born in 1827. T. A. Boylan and T. P. Foley give the date as 21 June 1825. (*Political Economy and Colonial Ireland* (London: Routledge, 1992), 170.) Where the sources differ on other matters, I've relied on Rigg. Ingram gives the following dates: 1842 for the classical scholarship and 1846 for the gold medal, which he claims was in 'Mental and Moral Philosophy'.
56. PE, ix.
57. Lawson, *Five Lectures on Political Economy; delivered before the University of Dublin, in Michaelmas Term, 1843*, cited in R. D. C. Black, 'Trinity College, Dublin, and the Theory of Value, 1832–1863', *Economica*, n.s. xii, n. 47 (August 1945), 144 (emphasis in original); see Black for a full discussion of the anti-Ricardian 'school' at Trinity, and Boylan and Foley for a recent reappraisal of the contributions of Whately and the holders of the Whately Chair.

58. See, of many examples, Leslie to Ingram, 24 May [1880?], D2808/43/25 and Leslie to Ingram, nd, 'Friday' [1881?], D2808/43/64.
59. 'My Belfast chair is wretchedly paid.' (Leslie to Ingram, 19 December [1880?], D2808/43/39, PRO.)
60. Leslie to Mill, 1 November 1871, Hopkins; Leslie to Helen Taylor, 2 June 1873, vol. 5, item 123, MTC, BLPES.
61. Leslie to Ingram, 23 May [1879], D2808/43/24, PRO.
62. Leslie to Ingram, nd, D2808/43/42, PRO.
63. Leslie to Ingram, nd, 'Monday' [November? 1881], D2808/43/51. There were bright spots: Fawcett was outvoted over the Cobden Prize. (Leslie to Ingram, 26 March [1879?], D2808/43/23, PRO.) Nicholson was elected to the Edinburgh chair. ('Nicholson is on my side.') (Leslie to Ingram, 24 November [1880], D2808/43/36, PRO.) Foxwell seemed somewhat sympathetic, 'though his real demigod is Marshall'. (Leslie to Ingram, 20 October [1880], D2808/43/33, PRO.)
64. Leslie to Ingram, nd, 'Saturday' [1879?], D2808/43/60, PRO.
65. Leslie to Mill, 4 March [1870] (vol. 2, item 292, MTC, BLPES), is typical: 'It is provoking that the inflammation from which I suffered so much should just have been upon me at the time I wanted to give my mind and time undisturbed to the work.' His last years were especially agonizing. 'Your letter found me suffering badly and the symptoms continue grave.... I may hold on for a year, but I may not get through tonight.' (Leslie to Ingram, 5 December [1879?], D2808/43/37.) It is possible that he was diabetic: his final letter complains of extreme thirst, without indicating a fever. (Leslie to Jevons, nd [*c.* 17 January 1882], R. D. C. Black (ed.), *Papers and Correspondence of William Stanley Jevons*, vol. 5 (London: Macmillan, 1981), 170.)
66. Leslie to Taylor, 26 January [1875], MTC, BLPES.
67. Their debate over the relative influence of environmental versus hereditary factors was to be re-enacted with much greater acrimony over Mill's accomplishments.
68. Leslie to Mill, 22 January [1871], Hopkins.
69. Leslie to Ingram, 19 December [1880], D2808/43/39, PRO; Leslie to Ingram, nd, 'Saturday' [1881?], D2808/43/43, PRO.
70. Leslie to Mill, 1 November 1871, Hopkins.
71. Conversely, his feelings of persecution at home may have taken their toll on his health.
72. Leslie to Helen Taylor, 20 October and 19 November [1875], vol. 5, items 136, 133, MTC, BLPES. Ingram suggests the loss occurred in 1872 (PE, xi), and this is repeated in the *DNB* and elsewhere. From the sequence of letters to Helen Taylor, as well as references to contemporaneous events, the date would appear to be 1875.
73. The only man, apart from her step-father, for whom she appears to have felt great affection was Leslie's fellow heterodox Millite, the avuncular Thornton. Another disappointed would-be suitor was Theodore Gomperz, a German disciple and translator of Mill. (M. Packe, *The Life of John Stuart Mill* (London: Secker and Warburg, 1954), 429.)
74. Taylor to Leslie, 25 January 1875, vol. 5, item 127, MTC, BLPES.

75. Leslie to Taylor, 26 January [1875], vol. 5, item 128, *Ibid*.
76. *Academy*, April 10.
77. Leslie to Taylor, 11 May 1875, vol. 5, item 130, MTC, BLPES.
78. Leslie to Taylor, 29 May [1875], vol. 5, item 131, *Ibid*.
79. *Ibid*.
80. Leslie to Taylor, 5 June [1875], vol. 5, item 132, *Ibid*.
81. Taylor to Leslie, 6 June 1875, vol. 5, item 133, *Ibid*.
82. Leslie to Taylor, 2 September [1875], vol. 5, item 135, *Ibid*.
83. Leslie to Taylor, 20 October [1875], vol. 5, item 136, *Ibid*.
84. Among them, 'On the Philosophical Method of Political Economy', 'Political Economy and Sociology' and 'The Known and the Unknown in the Economic World'. His sense of the imminence of his death may also have made the essay a more attractive form. His letters contain frequent admonitions about life's shortness. See, for example, Leslie to Ingram, 2 March [1879?], D2808/43/21, PRO: 'Time is so short, and so much that economists abroad as well as at home say is so trite or so nebulous or otherwise so uninstructive and so uninteresting that I grudge them ten minutes of daylight'.
85. PMP, 15. See J. Robson, 'Marriage or Celibacy?: A Victorian Dilemma', in J. Wiener (ed.), *Papers for the Millions: The New Journalism in Britain, 1850s to 1914* (New York: Greenwood, 1988), 185–209, for a diverting account of the popularity of the subject five years later, as revealed by the letters columns of the *Daily Telegraph*. As many as 5000 responses to the question 'Marriage or Celibacy?' were received by the paper during July 1868, of which 270 were printed. (*Ibid*., 188–9.)
86. 'The Celibacy of the Nation', 11.
87. *Ibid*., 14.
88. *Ibid*., 15.
89. *Ibid*., 9.
90. Leslie to Mill, 4 March [1870], vol. 2, item 292, MTC, BLPES.
91. *Ibid*.
92. J. M. Lipkes, 'Historians and the History of Economic Thought: A Response to Lawrence Birken', *History of Political Economy* 25 (1993), 85–113.
93. *The Dictionary of National Biography*, xi, 960. For J. M. Rigg, Charles's as well as Thomas's *DNB* biographer, this treatise remains the non-juror's only work that 'may still be read with interest'.
94. 'Political Economy and Sociology', in PE, 202.
95. *Ibid*.
96. *Ibid*.
97. In PMP, 36–50. The article first appeared in *Macmillan's* in June, 1863, the year Mill's *Utilitarianism* was published, though that essay had itself appeared in *Fraser's* two years earlier, between October and December 1861.
98. *Ibid*., 40. See John Burrow's seminal *Evolution and Society* (Cambridge: Cambridge University Press, 1966).
99. 'Utilitarianism . . .', in PMP, 48.
100. *Ibid*., 45.

101. *Ibid.*, 47.
102. *Ibid.*
103. *Ibid.*
104. *Ibid.*, 49.

11 CONCLUSION

1. Marginalism is not easy to define concisely. Its key insight is captured in the observation by one of Wicksteed's children that 'seconds are never as good as firsts'. (P. Wicksteed, *Commonsense of Political Economy*, vol. 1 (London: Routledge, 1946), 40.) The intensity of demand diminishes with each increment of a desired good or service that we consume. A bowl of chocolate ice cream delights us less with each successive spoonful; even a sunset enraptures us less with each passing moment. It is thus possible to apply the calculus of maxima and minima to market transactions. At the simplest level, if we know A's and B's preferences for apples expressed in oranges (or vice versa) and if we know how many of each fruit each one brings to the apples-and-oranges market to exchange, we can calculate the optimum number of apples and oranges the two ought to walk away with if they are good utility maximizers.

   Broadly speaking, then, the focus of political economy shifts from determining the impact of the distribution of the national income on macro-economic growth to a consideration of the way in which markets are cleared and scarce resources allocated. The demand for additional increments of goods and services becomes the *primum mobile* of economics: Ricardian rent (determined by demand and scarcity) explains the valuation not just of land but of all commodities and services – and of inputs as well as outputs, for the factors of production are rewarded by their marginal contribution to the joint product (and ultimately by consumers' evaluations of that product). Utility replaces cost as the determinant of value and the consumer succeeds the worker as the pivot of economics.
2. M. Schabas surveys responses to Jevons from a somewhat different perspective. (*A World Ruled by Number: William Stanley Jevons and the Rise of Mathematical Economics* (Princeton: Princeton University Press, 1990), 98–118.) And N. de Marchi provides a thorough and convincing explanation of Mill's and Cairnes's lack of interest, emphasizing intellectual commitments. ('Mill and Cairnes and the Emergence of Marginalism in England', *History of Political Economy* 4 (Fall 1972), 344–63; reprinted in Wood, 1, 407–22.) I stress the ideological and moral grounds for the resistance of the orthodox Millites – viz., their distaste for a 'happiness' that does not elevate character, and for consumption in general, and their suspicion of analyses that appeared to deflect opprobrium from landlords. Mathematics, furthermore, was inextricably associated in Mill's mind with intuitionism – 'the great intellectual support of false doctrines and bad institutions'. Its 'chief

strength ... lies in the appeal which it is accustomed to make to the evidence of mathematics'. (*Autobiography*, CW 1, 233.)

3. Mill to Cairnes, 5 December 1871, CW 17, 1862–3.
4. J. E. Cairnes, 'Bastiat', *Essays in Political Economy* [1873] (New York: Kelley, 1965), 343–4. Cairnes deeply regretted that he had not sufficiently emphasized the unfortunate impact of such 'theoretical views on social questions'. (Cairnes to Mill, 22 September 1870, MTC, BLPES.) See also Cairnes to Courtney, 2 September 1869, CC, BLPES.
5. Cairnes to Mill, 13 January 1870, MTC, BLPES.
6. *Some Leading Principles of Political Economy, newly expounded* (London: Macmilllan, [1873] 1884), 17; see also Jevons to Cairnes, 1 July 1874, in R. D. C. Black (ed.), *The Papers and Correspondence of William Stanley Jevons*, vol. 4 (London: Macmillan, 1977), 60–1.
7. *Some Leading Principles*, 20.
8. *Ibid.*, 15.
9. *Ibid.*, 19.
10. Writing to Helen Taylor, Leslie calls Jevons 'as little envious as any man could be. He has always appeared to me modest and amiable, though prejudiced and one-sided on some subjects.' (Leslie to Taylor, 12 December 1874, vol. 5, item 125, MTC, BPLES.) Jevons records them sitting together at the Political Economy Club, where Leslie candidly assessed the effectiveness of a speech he'd just delivered. (Jevons to Harriet Jevons, 5 June 1875, Black (ed.), *Papers and Correspondence*, vol. 4, 116.) Jevons was the recipient of what was probably Leslie's last letter, written in pencil about ten days before he died. 'My dear Jevons, Best thanks for what you have [done]. Please express my thanks to Mr Inglis. Yesterday was my worst for a week: pulse 110. I seem to grow daily weaker. I fear the thirst and want of sleep worse. Ever yours, TECL' (Leslie to Jevons, nd, *Ibid.*, vol. 5, 170.) (Jevons and Inglis Palgrave had organized a petition to Gladstone requesting a Civil List pension for Leslie. The document, with forty signatures, was on Gladstone's desk when Leslie died on 27 January 1882.) (*Ibid.*, 169 note.)
11. 'Marshall's [*sic*] "Economics of Industry"', *Essays in Political Economy* [1888] (New York: Kelley, 1969), 81–2. '[B]elieving that the doctrine of cost of production cannot finally stand', Leslie brashly informed Mill, 'and now rests only on authority not on fact, I should have been delighted had you not reasserted it.' (Leslie to Mill, 2 May 1869, Hopkins.)
12. 'Political Economy and the Tenure of Land', *Land Systems and Industrial Economy of Ireland, England & Continental Countries* [1870] (New York: Kelley, 1968), 128; 'The Land System of England, 1867', *Ibid.*, 174, 180.
13. 'Jevons' "Theory of Political Economy"', *Essays in Political Economy*, 71.
14. *Ibid.*
15. *Ibid.*, 69, 71.
16. *Ibid.*, 70.
17. *Ibid.*, 68.
18. *Ibid.*, 70. Variations in the exchanges of precious metals between adjacent countries may also be subject to mathematical notation. (*Ibid.*, 69.)

19. Leslie to Jevons, 27 July 1879, *Papers...*, vol. 5, 68.
20. Revolutionary economics, on the other hand, did not commit its adherents to reactionary politics, or even to political disengagement. See Chapter 5, note 60.
21. The famous phrase is from the second edition of Jevons's *Theory of Political Economy* (London: Macmillan, 1879), 1.
22. Two observations may be in order:

    a. To characterize Millian political economy as a moral system is not to make any claims about the desirability of its injunctions or their appropriateness in the third quarter of the nineteenth century. Few people today would question the wisdom of voluntarily limiting family size and of saving a portion of one's income. And few economic historians would quarrel with the observation that (1) the striking decline in the birth rate commencing in Britain in the late 1870s, while a response to rising incomes, still further elevated the standard of living for the middle and working classes, and that (2) industrialization was facilitated and sustained by a high rate of savings. That Mill's was a profoundly normative analysis does explain, however, some of its distortions and the tenacity with which they were defended.
    b. Space forbids the consideration of Norton Wise's rich and ambitious explanation of the moral calculus advanced by early nineteenth-century scientific culture generally, and political economy in particular. (M. N. Wise, C. Smith, 'Work and Waste: Political Economy and Natural Philosophy in Nineteenth Century Britain' (Part 2), *History of Science* 27 (1989), 405.)

23. 'Auguste Comte and Positivism', CW 10, 337–8.
24. *Ibid.*, 337.
25. *Principles of Political Economy*, CW 2, 174.
26. *Ibid.*, CW 3, 819–20.
27. *Ibid.*, CW 2, 80. Alternatively, 'a person does good to labourers, not by what he consumes on himself, but solely by what he does not so consume'. (*Ibid.*, 83.)
28. Two examples: Breit claims that 'Mill's proposition can be reformulated into the statement that the demand for labour is greater if the demand of consumers is directed toward more labour-intensive satisfaction'. (W. Breit, 'The Wage Fund Controversy Revisited', *The Canadian Journal of Economics and Political Science* 33 (1966), 515.) This has the merit of being true, but is not, of course, what Mill says. Confronting the fact that Mill's theorem assumes that savings = investment = wage capital, and ignores investments in fixed capital and raw materials, Hollander argues that the reader nonetheless 'is obliged by the very definition of capital to take seriously the requirement for technological capital in the productive sector'. (S. Hollander, *The Economics of John Stuart Mill*, vol. 1 (Oxford: Blackwell, 1985), 374.) Mill's failure to distinguish between different forms of capital permits him to ignore the fact that the production of luxury goods is likely to be more labour-intensive than that of necessities.

For those who choose to take Mill literally, what is perhaps most problematic in his formula, at the most primitive level, is its discounting the role of the entrepreneur in initiating production to satisfy perceived demands. (This is Longe's argument, developed most famously by Schumpeter in *A Refutation of the Wages Fund Theory of Modern Political Economy, as Enunciated by Mr Mill and Mr Fawcett* (1866) and *The Theory of Economic Development* (1912), respectively.) Mill's claim that demand simply alters the 'direction' of labour is misleading. Capital expands and contracts in response to the opportunity for profit, and because human desires are protean and inexhaustible, this opportunity progressively increases with the ability of individuals to apply new technologies to create commodities marginally more attractive to consumers.

29. *Principles*, 72.
30. B. Semmel, *John Stuart Mill and the Pursuit of Virtue* (New Haven: Yale University Press, 1984), 156. See Chapter 4, above.
31. W. Smart, *Second Thoughts of an Economist* (London: Macmillan, 1916), 122–3. See also the most famous of such sermons, Marshall's 'Economic Chivalry', in A. Pigou (ed.), *The Memorials of Alfred Marshall* (London: Macmillan, 1925), 325.
32. *Principles*, 367. To Lord Amberley, Mill averred that his goal was 'to obtain the greatest amount of chastity and happiness for men, women, and children'. (2 February 1870, CW 17, 1693.)
33. *Principles*, CW 2, 352.
34. *Ibid.*, 370.
35. 'Malthus's population principle was quite as much a banner, and a point of union among us, as any opinion specially belonging to Bentham. This great doctrine, originally brought forward as an argument against the indefinite improvability of human affairs, we took up with ardent zeal in the contrary sense, as indicating the sole means of realizing that improvability by securing full employment at high wages to the whole labouring population through a voluntary restriction of the increase of their numbers.' (*Autobiography*, CW 1, 107–9.)
36. 'You must remember that your writings are intended for the public good', Mill reminded Leslie, '& that the editors are not half such good judges of that as you are .... Now having made a real success with your amusing as well as useful articles of travels, the editors ask you for more of the same, & you should give it them, wrapping up good doctrine in this form.' (Mill to Leslie, 8 May 1869, CW 17, 1599–1600.)
37. In addition, holders of the Drummond Chair at Oxford kept alive the anti-Ricardian tradition inaugurated by Whately, notably the iconoclastic Thorold Rogers and Bonamy Price.
38. *Three Essays on Religion*, CW 10, 425–6. Though 'the evidence for it, indeed, if evidence it can be called, is shadowy and insubstantial...', the 'moral tendency of this creed' will produce 'an ennobling effect'. (*Ibid.*, 425.)
39. Mill to Nightingale, 23 September 1860, CW 15, 709. Thornton was also praised, anonymously, in 'Utility of Religion' as a 'cultivated and conscientious man of our day'. (CW 10, 425.)

40. *Autobiography*, CW 1, 43. James Mill had expressed 'surprise that no one had revived it in our own time'. Thornton, for his part, was elated by this recommendation. (Thornton to Taylor (nd), vol. 8, item 49, MTC, BLPES.)
41. *Three Essays on Religion*, CW 10, 485. Notably, its 'inducement to cultivate the improvement of character up to the end of life'.
42. 'Theism', CW 10, 449.
43. *Ibid.*, 450.
44. *Ibid.*, 451.
45. *Ibid.*, 455.
46. *Ibid.*, 482.
47. W. T. Thornton, *On Labour* (2nd edn) [1870] (Shannon: Irish University Press, 1971), 83–4; T. E. C. Leslie, *Essays in Political and Moral Philosophy* (Dublin: Hodges, Foster, & Figges, 1879), vi n., and Leslie to Helen Taylor, 12 December 1874, vol. 5, item 125, MTC, BLPES.
48. While Cairnes's two essay collections (1873), the *Leading Principles* (1874), and the revised version of *The Character and Logical Method of Political Economy* (1875) did not appear until after Mill's death, Cairnes published a number of articles in the late 1860s and early 1870s, and Mill did occasionally respond to articles, cf., J. G. Fitch's 'Educational Endowments' in *Fraser's Magazine* 79 (January 1869). This practice was much encouraged by the *Fortnightly* and the *Contemporary Review*. Henry Fawcett published a new edition of the *Manual* in 1869, and the following year his wife's *Political Economy for Beginners* appeared. This book proved to be 'hugely successful', remaining in print for over fifty years, through ten editions. It went into a second edition in 1872. (D. Rubinstein, *A Different World for Women: The Life of Millicent Garrett Fawcett* (Columbus: Ohio University Press, 1991), 28.)
49. Mill to G. Croom Robertson, 6 November 1871, CW 17, 1850.
50. *Chapters on Socialism*, CW 5, 729–30. Its chief drawback, its encouragement of greed-induced fraud, can be partially offset by wholesalers' co-operatives. (*Ibid.*, 732.)
51. *Ibid.*, 734–6, 738.
52. *Ibid.*, 738–45, 745–6.
53. *Autobiography*, CW 1, 289.
54. 'Theism', *Three Essays on Religion*, CW 10, 487.
55. *Ibid.*, 488.
56. Cited by F. W. Hirst, *Early Life and Letters of John Morley* (vol. 1) (London: Macmillan, 1927), 325.
57. Mill to Amberley, 2 February 1870, CW 17, 1693.
58. *Chapters on Socialism*, CW 5, 729. 'Society . . . is not descending into that abyss [of over-population], but gradually, though slowly, rising out of it, and this improvement is likely to be progressive if bad laws do not interfere.'
59. 'Leslie on the Land Question', [1870], CW 5, 683 *England and Ireland*, CW 6, 524.
60. 'Thornton on Labour', [1869], CW 5, 666. G. Holyoke, *The History of Co-operation in England*, vol. 2, [1879] (New York: AMS, 1971), 143.

61. *Principles*, CW 2, 231.
62. *England and Ireland*, CW 6, 527.
63. *Programme of the Land Tenure Reform Association, with an Explanatory Statement by John Stuart Mill*, CW 5, 691.
64. *Ibid.*, 691–2. Mill is particularly enamoured of the State's conducting such trials – including of its own ability to undertake economic activities. ('Endowments', CW 5, 618–19; Mill to J. B. Kinnear, 22 July 1870, CW 17, 1749.)
65. *Ibid.*, 695.
66. 'The Nationalisation of the Land', *Fortnightly Review* 12 (December 1872), 643.
67. *Ibid.*, 632.
68. *Principles*, CW 3, 937–47.
69. Mill to Thornton, 9 November 1858, CW 15, 574.
70. '[A]nd her approbation', he continued, 'the standard by which, summing up as it does all worthiness, I endeavour to regulate my life.' (*Autobiography*, CW 1, 251.)
71. *Three Essays on Religion*, CW 10, 466–7.
72. 'Stanzas Written in Kensal Green Cemetery', *Zohrab; or a Midsummer's Day Dream; and Other Poems* (London: Longman, 1854), 75–7.
73. H. Mill to J. Mill, 14 and 15 February 1854, Hayek, 195–6.
74. Mill to J. B. Kinnear, 22 July 1870, CW 17, 1749–50.
75. A. Bain, *John Stuart Mill, A Criticism with Personal Recollections* [1882] (New York: Kelley, 1969), 133.
76. Bain, 159. The statement is accurate, of course, in the obvious sense that death would prevent him from doing more work. Packe gives the words as, 'You know that I have done my work'. (M. Packe, *The Life of John Stuart Mill* (New York: Macmillan, 1954), 507.)

Index